Fantasy Kingdom School Of Wizardry
The Prominencius & Primordial
Light from the Darkness

Erick S. Tieman

authorHOUSE®

AuthorHouse™
1663 Liberty Drive
Bloomington, IN 47403
www.authorhouse.com
Phone: 1-800-839-8640

Published by AuthorHouse   9/6/2012

ISBN: 978-1-4772-6689-2 (sc)
ISBN: 978-1-4772-6688-5 (e)

Contents

The 1st Wizardorium Chapter Book For Beginners   1

     Fantasy Kingdom's Prayers   3

     *Light Kingdom Prayers   3

     *Dark Kingdom Prayers   3

     *The Tree Of Knowledge Tarot Card Prayers   4

     *Prayers For Outside My Kingdom   6

     *Fantasy Hierarchy Prayers   7

     *Fantasy Thrones Prayers   8

     *Fantasy Round Table Prayers   9

     *Psychic Continuum Prayers   9

     *Guardian Spirit Messenger Prayers   11

     Plains One Can Visit   11

     *First Heavenly Plain Home Of The Physical Etherics Of Hope And Unicorns.   12

     *Second Heavenly Plain And Home Of Faith And Cherubim.   14

     * Third Heavenly Plain Of Lower Mental And Home Of Love And Elves.   17

     *Forth Heavenly Plain Home Of OM The Universal Spoken Essence Of The Higher Mental And Fearies.   20

     *Fifth Heavenly Plain The Spiritual Home Of Morgan Le Fey.   22

     *Sixth Heavenly Plain Home Of Holy Spirit Intuitional And Merlin.   25

     *Seventh Heavenly Plain The Absolute, Home Of Lepidoptera.   28

     Wizeard Scriptures   35

     *7 Wizardry Prayers Of Peace   63

     *A Knowledge Prayer   64

     A Prayer For Erick   64

     *Arivel's Prayer   64

     *Cupid's Prayer   65

     *Merlin's Prayer   65

*Mernom's Prayer   66

Assessor Of Being Of Light Consciously Knowing Prayers   66

Assessor Of Conscious Being Of Knowing Light Prayers   67

Assessor Of Conscious Being Of Light Prayers   68

Assessor Of Conscious Knowing Of Light Prayers   69

Assessor Of Conscious Light Knowing Prayers   71

Assessor Of Conscious Self Image Prayers   72

Assessor Of Knowing Being Of Conscious Light Prayers   75

Assessor Of Knowing Conscious Being Of Light Prayers   76

Assessor Of Knowing Light Being A Conscious Prayers   77

The Embodiment Of A Buddhist   77

Buddhism Prayers   77

The Embodiment Of A Celtic   79

Celtic Prayers   79

The Embodiment Of A Druid   80

Druid Prayers   80

The Embodiment Of A Humanist   82

Humanistic Prayers   82

The Embodiment Of A Indian   83

Indian Prayers   83

The Embodiment Of A Fantasy Man   84

Mystical Prayers   84

The Embodiment Of The Elemental of Man   86

Nature Prayers   86

The Embodiment Of The Goddess'   87

New Age Wicca   87

New Age Wicca Prayers   87

The Embodiment Of A Psychic   89

Psychic Prayers   89

The Embodiment Of The Seven Spirits Of The Rainbow Rays   91

Rainbow Prayers   91

*Native American Prayers   92

*Mayan Prayers   93

*Egyptian Prayers   94

*Norse Prayers   95

*New Age Shamanism For Selflessness.   96

Erick's Short Cure Book For Self Love   102

Erick's Short Cure Book #2   110

Light From The Darkness 2nd Wizardries Book Primordial For Apprentices

Light From The Darkness 2nd Wizardries Book
   Primordial For Apprentices   115

A Wizards Guide   116

Wizardly Confusciousnemium   116

Confuscious Beginner Prayer & Info. Page   117

Confuscious Beginner Prayers Info. Page For Self Forgiveful Psyche #2   117

Confuscious Beginner Prayers Info. Page For A Self Forgiveful Psyche #3   117

Confuscious Beginner Prayers Info. Page For A Self Forgiveful Psyche #4   118

Confuscious Beginner Prayers Info. Page For A Self Forgiveful Psyche #5   118

Confuscious Beginner Prayers Info. Page For A Self Forgiveful Psyche #6   119

Confuscious Beginner Prayers Info. Page For A Self Forgiveful Psyche #7   119

Cosmic Spirit Names & A Prayer-Spell For Enlightenment   120

Cosmic Spirit Temple Wizardry Prayer/ Evolutionary Elements Are, &
   Questions Are   120

Enchantment For Wizards, Butterfly Occult Round-Table, & Enchantment Spell   121

Experimental Wizards Names   122

How To Create Green Pastures & Wizardlium Magical Words Prayers   123

Healing   124

45 Magical Words   124

How To Create Magical Words   125

Wizardry End's To A Ending Letter Of A Magical Word In Alphabetical Order   126

How To Make A Wizardorium Prayer   127

*How To Schedule Omens   128

*How To Schedule The Use Of Poem/Dream Writing Or Memory
     Poem/Dream Marbles.   134

*How To Schedule A Phrase For An Omen   136

*How To Schedule Omens Through Touch-Sight   138

*How To Reincarnate A Troublesome Ghost Into A Butterfly.   140

*How To Schedule Omens For Psyche Development.   143

*How To Schedule A Message To The Deceased   144

*How To Schedule A Preminision From Omen   145

*How To Schedule To See Dead People   146

*How To Schedule A Past Life Prayer Of Remembrance   146

*The Five Humanism Wizardorium Names   147

*The Humanism Wizadorium Prayistliorium   147

Info. On The 7 Forces Of Magic   148

Mask Of Revelaence   150

Meditation Words   150

Newest Up-To-Date Magical Wizardorium Words   151

Omnious Prayer Of Wizardorius   152

Planetary Temple Names & Their Means   152

Prayer Deity Names Of The Planets   153

Wizard Names Of Quantum Wizardlium   153

*Shaman Healing   154

Shaman Wizardry   154

The 4 Sages   155

*The Different States And Levels Of Being Reborn   156

The Four Sages Wizardry Prayers   156

*The 7'n Archangel Confusions Of Self Prayers   157

*The Seven Spirits Of The Rainbow Rays   157

The Wizardalogic Blessings Plaque Prayer & Info   158

Wish Making   158

Wizardizm Map Of The Brain So Far   159

Wizardologic Blessings Plaque   160

*Wizardorium Omnibelevelance Prayer   161

*Wizardorium Omnibelevelance Prayistliorum   161

Wizidorium Prayer Names   162

Wizardorium Prayistliorum   163

Wizardry Map Of Brain, Body, Spirit, & Center   164

*Wizardry Theory's   164

Wizardry Words   166

*A Wizard's Basic Principles   166

A Wizards Guidance Of Principalities   167

A Wizeards Principalities   167

*A Wizards Wizardorius Of Creation   170

Holius Origin   171

Peace In The Order Of Wizardries Virtues   172

The Virtuous Principalities   173

Wizeardizm Scriptures   175

* Wizardry Card Game   202

Wizards Trinity   205

Wizards Wisdom   205

Solace's Belief   205

*6 Wizardizm Prayer Spells & 3 Expert Wizard Names   206

*7 Wizardizmo's Prayer/Spells Of Peace   206

Fireworks Balloon   208

Firecracker Balloon   208

Wizards Wisdom #2 ~ New Endings For Quote/Prayers   209

A Wizards Wisdom #3 ~ For Quote-Prayer/Spells   209

A Wizards Wisdom #4 ~ For Experienced Quote-Prayer/Spells   210

*New Wizardry Prayer/Spell Words For Experts   211

Merlin's Prayer/Spells   212

Merlin's Astro-Cosmotics Prayer/Spells   212

Making Enlightenment On Top Of Staff   212

About the Author   215

The 1st Wizardorium Chapter Book For Beginners

Fantasy Kingdom's Prayers

*Light Kingdom Prayers

*The Hierarchy - I pray to the hierarchy for self confidence, and in this self confidence wisdom, and in that wisdom kindness, and in this kindness destiny, and in that destiny courage, and in this courage keeness, and in that keeness bravery, and in this bravery vigilance, and in that vigilance hope, and in this hope triumph through the one eternal light so mote it be.

*The Wizard - I pray to Merlin for completion, and in this completion realization, and in that realization accomplishment, and in this accomplishment proper balance, and in that proper balance courage, and in this courage friendship, and in that friendship will power, and in this will power creativity, and in that creativity craft, and in this craft knowledge through the one eternal light so mote it be.

*The Elve's - I pray to the elve Arivel for truth, and in this truth trust, and in that trust passion, and in this passion clarity, and in that clarity communication, and in this communication completion through the one eternal light so mote it be.

*The Huntress - I pray to the huntress for hunting down any spy's against me, watch the lands for invaders, and defend the light kingdom against any intruder with your skilled hands through the one eternal light so mote it be.

*The Druid - I pray to the druid Mernom for helping bring peace to my kingdom, heal the sick, and lead the blind through the one eternal light so mote it be.

*The Armor - I pray to Lepidoptera, Merlin, and Cosmic Master Wizard to have the armor of the iron butterfly for protection through the one eternal light so mote it be.

*The Mask - I pray to Mernom, The Huntress, and Arivel to wear the mask of relevance to give me clarity through the one eternal light so mote it be.

* The Chieftan - I pray to the chieftan for protection, and in this protection clarity, and in that clarity insight, and in this insight inner wisdom, and in that inner wisdom achievement, and in this achievement accomplishment, and in that accomplishment completion through the one eternal light so mote it be.

*Dark Kingdom Prayers

*The Rebellion - I pray to the rebellion to overcome an develop the inner power, and in this inner power sacred wisdom, and in that sacred wisdom awakening, and in this awakening to think positive, ethical, and logical through the one eternal light so mote it be.

*The Sorceress - I pray to Morgan Le Fey for the secret amour, and in this secret amour a celestrial abyssic dream, and in that celestrial abyssic dream the writhing flame, and in this writhing flame I'm resurrected, and in that resurrection empowering darkness, and in this empowering darkness nectar and lemure through the one eternal light so mote it be.

*The Vampires - I pray to the great white bat, my dark command grant me thy, and in this, grant me thy command I will conquer darkness, and in that conquering of darkness I am crowned, and in this crowning of I the moon will radiant from my grace, and in that radiant grace forever more with the flow and ebb of time through the one eternal light so mote it be.

*The Specter - I pray to the ghost for alliance, and in this alliance a writhing flame born unto the darkness, and in that rebirth inspiration, and in this inspiration adornment, and in that adornment adored, and in this adoration worthiness, and in that worthiness, protection, and in this protection devotion through the one eternal light so mote it be.

*The Spy - I pray to the spy to do my bidding and spy on any intruder in my dark kingdom, protect my kingdom from invasion, and secretly attain information and bring this information to me.

*The Satanic Priestess/Witch - I pray to the satanic priestess/ witch for her to cast great magic and power against any enemy that tries to wrong my rights of survival, to become my aid, and to writhe on binding any influence that threatens my life through the one eternal light so mote it be.

*The Tree Of Knowledge Tarot Card Prayers

-Pray these prayers every day to have control of your own fantasy kingdoms.

*Tree Of Knowledge

1. The Magician - I pray to the magician for self confidence, and in this self confidence will power, and in that will power skill, and in this skill initiativeness, and in that initiativeness creativity, and in this creativity originality, and in that originality flexibility, and in this flexibility dexterity, and in that dexterity craft, and in this craft masterfulness, and in that masterfulness capability through the one eternal light so mote it be.

2. The High Priestess - I pray to the high priestess for wisdom, and in this wisdom serenity, and in that serenity serene knowledge, and in this serene knowledge learning, and in that learning common sense, and in this common sense understanding through the one eternal light so mote it be.

3. The Hierophant - I pray to the hierophant for kindness, and in this kindness goodness, and in that goodness good advice, and in this good advice inspiration, and in that inspiration alliance, and in this alliance compassion through the one eternal light so mote it be.

4. The Fortune Wheel - I pray for the fortune wheel to have destiny, and in this destiny fortune, and in that fortune luck through the one eternal light so mote it be.

*Tree Of Fate

1. King - I pray to the king for courage, and in this courage power, and in that power honesty, and in this honesty devotion, and in that devotion responsibility, and in this responsibility experience, and in that experience leadership, and in this leadership intelligence, and in that intelligence success, and in this success aptitude through the one eternal light so mote it be.

2. Queen - I pray to the queen for keenness, and in this keenness understanding, and in that understanding charm, and in this charm love, and in that love worthiness, and in this worthiness warm heartedness, and in that warm heartedness fairness, and in this fairness belovedness, and in that belovedness adored, and in this adornment devotion, and in that devotion admiration, and in this admiration prosperity, and in that prosperity well being, and in this well being security, and in that security abundance, and in this abundance freedom through the one eternal light so mote it be.

3. Knight - I pray to the knight for bravery, and in this bravery skill, and in that skill strength, and in this strength gallantry, and in that gallantry a journey, and in this journey advancement, and in that advancement reliability, and in this reliability patients through the one eternal light so mote it be.

4. Page - I pray to the page for perception, and in this perception vigilance, and in that vigilance agility, and in this agility adeptness, and in that adeptness alertness, and in this alertness loyalty, and in that loyalty friendship, and in this friendship confidence, and in that confidence reflectiveness, and in this reflectiveness concentration through the one eternal light so mote it be.

*Tree Of Rebirth

1. The Star - I pray to the stars for hope, and in this hope satisfaction, and in that satisfaction bright prospects, and in this bright prospects destiny, and in that destiny insight, and in this insight a bright future through the one eternal light so mote it be.

2. The Sun - I pray to the sun for triumph, and in this triumph success, and in that success happiness, and in this happiness accomplishment, and in that accomplishment contentment, and in this contentment warmth, and in that warmth affection, and in this affection sincerity, and in that sincerity friendship, and in this friendship devotion, and in that devotion trust through the one eternal light so mote it be.

3. The World - I pray to the world for completion, and in this completion perfection, and in that perfection success, and in this success assurance, and in that assurance significant influence, and in this significant influence capability, and in that capability fulfillment, and in this fulfillment inner strength through the one eternal light so mote it be.

*Tree Of Life

1. The Empress - I pray to the empress for action, and in this action development, and in that development progress, and in this progress fruitfulness, and in that fruitfulness attainment, and in this attainment accomplishment through the one eternal light so mote it be.

2. The Emperor - I pray to the emperor for realization, and in this realization accomplishment, and in that accomplishment worldly power, and in this worldly power wealth, and in that wealth stability, and in this stability an indomitable spirit, and in that indomitable spirit endurance, and in this endurance leadership through the one eternal light so mote it be.

3. The Lovers - I pray to the lovers for love, and in this love beauty, and in that beauty attraction, and in this attraction perfection, and in that perfection harmony, and in this harmony confidence, and in that confidence trust, and in this trust optimism through the one eternal light so mote it be.

4. Justice - I pray for justice to have fairness, and in this fairness reasonableness, and in that reasonableness proper balance, and in this proper balance harmony, and in that harmony rightness, and in this rightness virtue, and in that virtue honor, and in this honor good intentions, and in that good intentions well meaning actions, and in this well meaning actions advice through the one eternal light so mote it be.

5. Strength - I pray for strength to have courage, and in this courage fortitude, and in that fortitude energy, and in this energy determination, and in that determination resolution, and in this resolution confidence, and in that confidence mind over matter, and in this mind over matter conquest, and in that conquest accomplishment through the one eternal light so mote it be.

6. Temperance - I pray to temperance for patience, and in this patience accommodation, and in that accommodation moderation, and in this moderation reflection, and in that reflection friendship, and in this friendship compatibility, and in that compatibility management, and in this management good influence, and in that good influence consolidation, and in this consolidation ability to compromise, and in that ability to compromise adjustment, and in this adjustment acceptance of reality through the one eternal light so mote it be.

*Prayers For Outside My Kingdom

- Pray these prayers for those outside your kingdom.

*Plant Chrysalis Fearies - I pray to the plant chrysalis fearies born in my kingdom's forest for their wisdom of nature wherein that wisdom I will find the beauty of creation, and in this beauty of creation the powers of healing, and in that power of healing inner strength through the one eternal light so mote it be.

*The Halflings - I pray to the halflings in my village and beyond for their knowledge of inner beauty, inner child, and inner wisdom for in these inner powers the love of the divine spirit, and in this love of the divine spirit the love of all creation through the one eternal light so mote it be.

*The Imps - I pray to the imps in my village and beyond for their insight, and in this insight freedom of thought, and in that freedom of thought imagination, and in this imagination fascination, and in that fascination well being through the one eternal light so mote it be.

*The Pixies - I pray to the pixies that visit my village from the forest for bringing singing, dance, and music to my kingdom for in this entertainment the love of all creation, and in that love of all creation the divine attributes, and in this divine attributes natural love through the one eternal light so mote it be.

*The Mermaids - I pray to the mermaids beyond my kingdom in the sea for protection of my kingdom's sea and to stand for freedom, imagination, and wisdom as we give them thanks for these through the one eternal light so mote it be.

*The Hivest - I pray to the hivest people for those that do hard work like bee's, that which protects our queen, and the collectors of nectar which protects the young and defenseless, their justice their own reward through the one eternal light so mote it be.

*Fantasy Hierarchy Prayers

- This will be your fantasy hierarchy which is comprised of the informant, the oracle, the guide, Merlin, Omen, Solace, and the one. As for the key is held by the guide and the ring held by the one. The guide is the one, and the key is a ring, and the one is the oracle, and the ring is held by the informant, the oracle's name is Omen, and the informant's name is Merlin.

*The Key - I pray for the key to catch and seize the gathering of a harvest reap in comprehending the learning of knowing by persistence, perseverance, and perceiving completion through the one eternal light so mote it be.

*The Informant - I pray for the informant to cause to begin of being apprehended by reason an imagination to take into one's mind and form a conception in which I will conceive through communication through the one eternal light so mote it be.

*The Oracle - I pray for the oracle to remedy the evil consequences of to call to mind again by successfully getting back again the thought returned by the retrieving of clarity through the one eternal light so mote it be.

*The Ring - I pray for the ring to gain possession of a transmition of perceptible signals from two people whom are transmitting to each other by the interception of passion through the one eternal light so mote it be.

*The Guide - I pray for the guide to cause a spread through space and time from one person to another through thought by the transmit of trust through the one eternal light so mote it be.

*The One - I pray for the one to pay attention to the waves coming into the mind by perceptible signals which then assimilate through the senses of the mind to receive truth through the one eternal light so mote it be.

*Merlin - I pray to Merlin for his wisdom, knowledge, and universal divinity through his guidance and teachings of our essential light an higher selves in which you show the basis of our awareness as a collective conscious through the one eternal light so mote it be.

*Omen - I pray to Omen for her ability to see premonitions that will help my kingdom, to see the unseen forces of light, and to quiet our minds through her ever growing wisdom as well to show me the key of being human through the one eternal light so mote it be.

*Solace - I pray to Solace for her ability to compromise and her proper balance of mind to think of others before herself as well her acceptance of others and open minding of logical curtesy, dignity, and virtuosity through the one eternal light so mote it be.

*Fantasy Thrones Prayers

- There are three thrones in my kingdom. The tall chair in the middle and one smaller chair, one on each side of the tall chair. You are also able to apoint on either throne your father, son, and holy ghost.

*The Tall Throne - I pray to (choose to say your choice of ruler either a fantasy character or even yourself during this prayer) as the emperor of my kingdom, I rely on you for courage, inner strength, and power in which in this power truth, and in that truth trust, and in this trust passion, and in that passion clarity, and in this clarity communication, and in that communication completion, and in this completion masterminding through the one eternal light so mote it be.

*The Throne To The Right - I pray to king Lepidoptera the cosmic spirit angel of the rainbow sun to be at one with the great spirit of universal divinity of creation, earth, and wholeness as well to be divine with universal understanding, completion, and the bringer of light when all falls into darkness and sorrow, that which purpose, fulfillment, and triumph comes through the one eternal light so mote it be.

*The Throne To The Left - I pray to queen Lunaris the cosmic spirit angel of the moonlit sun to be at one with the goddess spirit of the divine universal of life, nature, and oneness as well the holder of our memory of universal divinity and bringer of conscious creation, love, and harmony that which truth, beauty, and wisdom comes through the one eternal light so mote it be.

*Fantasy Round Table Prayers

- All conscious self image names below are a name each for a person sitting at the round table inside my kingdom.

Knowing Light Being A Conscious - I pray to knowing light being a conscious for truth , and in this essence of truth love, and in that love all reality extending, and in this reality integrity of thought, and in that integrity of thought the true principle of freedom through the one eternal light so mote it be.

Conscious Knowing Of Light - I pray to conscious knowing of light for trust, and in this trust inner knowing, and in that inner knowing all levels of reality, and in this reality everything understandable, and in that understanding perfection through the one eternal light so mote it be.

Conscious Light Knowing - I pray to conscious light knowing for passion, and in this passion the core presence of our creating light, and in that creation realization, and in this realization limitless being of light, and in that limitlessness the force of light through the one eternal light so mote it be.

Conscious Being Of Light - I pray to conscious being of light for clarity, and in this clarity the simplest form, and in that simplest form acknowledgment, and in this acknowledgment our physical self part of the greater whole, and in the greater wholeness power through the one eternal light so mote it be.

Knowing Conscious Being Of Light - I pray to knowing conscious being of light for communication, and in this communication our essential an higher self, and in that state of higher self the unseen forces of light, and in this unseen force of light completion through the one eternal light so mote it be.

Knowing Being Of Conscious Light - I pray to knowing being of conscious light for completion, and in this completion a form of knowing, and in that form of knowing a conclusion, and in this conclusion multiple levels of a journey, and in those journey's a new experience through the one eternal light so mote it be.

Conscious Being Of Knowing Light - I pray to conscious being of knowing light for masterminding, and in this masterminding an act of creating a collective conscious, and in that conscious collective the focusing of manifesting an outcome, and in this manifestation being guided by the unseen forces of light through the one eternal light so mote it be.

*Psychic Continuum Prayers

- These prayers are for the creation of your own psychic continuum.

*The Garden - I pray to the garden for inside this garden beauty, and in this beauty butterfly's, and in that garden flowers, and in this garden abundance, and in that abundance natural law, and in this natural law the love of creation, and in that love of creation the love of it through the one eternal light so mote it be.

*The Hill - I pray to the hill for on top of this hill the other side seen, and on this hill is perseverance, and in that perseverance persistence, and in this persistence perception of completion, and in that perception of completion the reaching of the other side through the one eternal light so mote it be.

*The Watchers - I pray to the watchers for their guidance, and in this guidance fascination, and in that fascination fantasy, and in this fantasy wonder, and in that wonder brilliance, and in this brilliancy accomplishment through the one eternal light so mote it be.

*The Fruit - I pray to the fruit for virility, and in this virility youthfulness, and in that youthfulness playfulness, and in this playfulness young at heart, and in that youthful heart well being through the one eternal light so mote it be.

*The Tree - I pray to the tree for it's inner knowledge, and in this inner knowledge inner strength, and in that inner strength endurance, and in this endurance stability, and in that stability proper balance, and in this proper balance beauty through the one eternal light so mote it be.

*The Crown - I pray to the crown for wisdom, and in this wisdom acceptance, and in that acceptance leadership, and in this leadership bravery, and in that bravery freedom, and in this freedom acknowledgement through the one eternal light so mote it be.

*The Bridge - I pray to the norse god heimdall whom guards the sacred rainbow bridge, I pray for your incredible insight, and in this incredible insight the love of all creation, and in that love of all creation splendor through the one eternal light so mote it be.

*The Path - I pray to Merlin for his incredible insight, and in this incredible insight incredible endurance, and in that incredible endurance incredible wisdom, and in this incredible wisdom the finding of knowledge on my path through the one eternal light so mote it be.

*The Sun Disk - I pray to the celtic sun god Belenus the keeper of the sun disk, I pray for vigilance, and in this vigilance completion, and in that completion accomplishment, and in this accomplishment procreation, and in that procreation endurance, and in this endurance the light through the one eternal light so mote it be.

*The Bell - I pray to the bell for an awakening, and in this awakening adornment, and in that adornment love, and in this love procreation, and in that procreation accomplishment, and in this accomplishment completion through the one eternal light so mote it be.

*The Way - I pray to the way for finding my path on this spiritual journey, and in that spiritual journey the celebration of life, and in this celebration of life a true quest, and in that true quest the love of it, and in this love of it the true path through the one eternal light so mote it be.

*Guardian Spirit Messenger Prayers

- Guardian spirit messenger names are based on elemental psychic physics. The process is simple that what usualy happens is a person intercepts another's thought pattern by electrical appliances turning on such as what this process goes along with what's called 'the tree of knowledge effect.' In which the same process happens when you eat.

*The Heater - I pray for the heater for when it is turned on to tell me logic of the eternal divine spirit, to grant me your blessings for the love of all creation for having compassion and encouragement so that with your inspiration I will receive the gift of clairvoyance on truthful communication and self empowerment through the one eternal light so mote it be.

*The Refrigerator - I pray for the refrigerator for when it turns on to grant me it's spoken essence of truth in that your guiding light in finding wisdom through a selfless journey of inner strength and to find balance of my compassion to awakening and enlightenment through the one eternal light so mote it be.

*The Vaccum - I pray for the vaccum for when I turn it on it will tell me of my own divinity through inspiration in that everything that happens is divine, natural, and beautiful in the eternal sense of deep inner knowledge I will find spiritual growth from your prosperity through the one eternal light so mote it be.

*The Microwave - I pray for the microwave for when I turn it on to tell me of grace with the flow and ebb about strength of mind, heart, and spirit an to bless me to gain spiritual wisdom with the time we spend together, you are the spirit of kindly hym for protection and companionship through the one eternal light so mote it be.

*The Television - I pray for the television for when I turn it on to not lie to me and show me the freedom of imagination through your psychic power I will achieve wisdom to dare new thoughts so that I will be with the union of my eternal self through the one eternal light so mote it be.

*The Air Conditioner - I pray for the air conditioner for when it turns on as the guardian of the powers of invocation to bring solace into my life by it's ever knowing intuition I will gain confidence for spiritual, emotional, and elemental fulfillment through the one eternal light so mote it be.

Plains One Can Visit

Feel free to memorize any plain and home of whomever you choose to journey there spiritualy and seek wisdom. Merely do wizardry prayer for I'n whole realm and it should help belief of what creature or other it is in your fantasy psyche.

*First Heavenly Plain Home Of The Physical Etherics Of Hope And Unicorns.

*The remembrance of a unicorn the cosmic spirit angel of the rainbow sun and guardian of the powers of invocation I pray to you for your gentleness of bringing solace into my life by helping me brake down the challenges that stop me from receiving your eternal knowledge an wisdom so that I will be guided by your warm heart in merging with universal understanding through the one eternal light so mote it be.

*The remembrance of a unicorn the cosmic spirit angel of the rainbow sun I pray to you for your angelic knowledge in helping me achieve clarity of thought through your inspiration of independence affectionately guiding an assisting me in realizing the various levels of truth as well you whom instills wisdom to the human heart I ask for your teachings in achieving a spiritual awakening of finding balance to my angelic clairvoyance so that through your encouragement of harmony I will develop the inner power of unconditional love through the one eternal light so mote it be.

*The remembrance of a unicorn the cosmic spirit angel of the rainbow sun, great spirit I pray to you for the creation of all, the rising sun and moon, ancient keeper of the way of life and all that I see, guide me today as I need your strength and wisdom to make my hands honor the things you've made as I go on my journey, make my ears listen to your voice and make me understand so that I may come toward all that I must face, may you always walk in beauty through the one eternal light so mote it be.

*The remembrance of a unicorn the cosmic spirit angel of the rainbow sun and understanding I pray to you for your guidance in helping me find spiritual enlightenment through understanding an the acceptance from your eternal love in caring for others as well for myself self love an the love for others through the one eternal light so mote it be.

*The remembrance of a unicorn the cosmic spirit angel of the rainbow sun and honesty I pray to you for your teachings and guidance on inspiring me about honesty and independence through your eternal self so that I will have my spirit filled with hope and a promise in the belief of the ideals of youthfulness through the one eternal light so mote it be.

*The remembrance of a unicorn the cosmic spirit angel of the rainbow sun, nature, and grounding I pray to you for your teachings and guidance on keeping my natural law fruitful through your sacred wisdom of earth so that I will harvest my dreams I have worked hard for through the one eternal light so mote it be.

*The remembrance of a unicorn the cosmic spirit angel of the rainbow sun I pray to you for your teachings and guidance through your wisdom of spiritual growth in helping me achieve prosperity with your gentleness and purity of heart so that I will have strength of mind and the development of my own personal power through the one eternal light so mote it be.

*The remembrance of a unicorn the cosmic spirit angel of the rainbow sun I pray to you for your teachings and guidance of grace with the flow and ebb, evermore the hand of nature keeping me, and the strong spirit of a unicorn bathing me in the eternal shining light through the one eternal light so mote it be.

*The remembrance of a unicorn the cosmic spirit angel of the rainbow sun and eternal spirit of light I pray to you grant us protection and in that protection the love of the divine spirit, and in that love of the divine spirit awareness, and in that awareness knowledge, and in that knowledge that righteous of things, and in that righteous of things the love of it, and in that love of it goodness, beauty, and truth, and in that goodness, beauty, and truth the love of all creation through the one eternal light so mote it be.

*The remembrance of a unicorn the cosmic spirit angel of the rainbow sun and a lord of cosmic universal merging I pray to you for your physical etherics of mankind's universal, being the sacred being of hope, and the absolutions of life in that I ask for your teachings and guidance through your quest of truth on becoming who we are meant to be in that learning from the union of my eternal self I will have clarity of thought and serenity of heart so that I will be bringing forth all producing things through the one eternal light so mote it be.

*The remembrance of a unicorn the cosmic spirit angel of the rainbow sun, universal merging, and the first sense I pray to you for your teachings and guidance in helping me succeed with prosperity through your sacred wisdom and understanding of merging universal so that I will be inspired through independence to rely on my own intuition through your encouragement of passion about truthful communication through the one eternal light so mote it be.

*The remembrance of a unicorn the cosmic spirit angel of the rainbow sun, hope, assessor of who?, and the phrase 'I am' I pray to you for your teachings and guidance in helping me receive omens for the phrase 'I am' so that I will be assisted with myself realizing the various levels of truth within truth itself of who and having an open heart to allow this truth as omens to come to me in the phrase 'I am' as well through your unconditional forgiveness the inspiration of my gift of clairvoyance and in this clairvoyance the encouragement of truthful communication through the one eternal light so mote it be.

*The remembrance of a unicorn the cosmic spirit angel of the rainbow sun and earths great lord I pray to you for your teachings and guidance through your independence of well being an knowledge, of red ray and earth, eternal goodness, the root of who I am, hope omniparient of physical etheric, sensuality of knowledge passionate through the one eternal light so mote it be.

*The remembrance of a unicorn the cosmic spirit angel of the rainbow sun and a lord of cosmic angelic omniparient I pray to you for your teachings and guidance in your reflection of the beauty of life I will be inspired toward awareness and enlightenment so that I will be more open minded about discovering the light within and bless me with deep inner wisdom so I will find the encouragement of finding my life's purpose through adventure and liveliness through the one eternal light so mote it be.

*The remembrance of a unicorn the cosmic spirit angel of the rainbow sun, hope, and a lord of cosmic solace I pray to you for your teachings an guidance in helping me achieve my desires at heart an through your knowledge of spiritual hope I will balance my heart from selfish desire ridding selfish questions to become the humanist I am meant to be as well for you to influence passion, romance, an love in my heart through the one eternal light so mote it be.

*The remembrance of a unicorn the cosmic spirit angel of the rainbow sun and healing I pray to you for your guidance in granting me the ability of sensuality an through your sacred wisdom of finding greater passion as I will prosper from your knowledge whom instills truth an compassion within my heart as well the encouragement of receiving companionship where I ask to achieve spiritual fulfillment with another person in that which your blessings are eternal through the one eternal light so mote it be.

*The remembrance of a unicorn the cosmic spirit angel of the rainbow sun I pray to you for helping me communicate with unicorns by bringing their presence to me so that my heart will open to receive their guidance in teaching me to not be alienated as well to rekindle my hearts fire on wanting knowledge for understanding the messages from higher realms through the one eternal light so mote it be.

*The remembrance of a unicorn the cosmic spirit angel of the rainbow sun and merging universal I pray to you for your understanding in teaching me the hidden truths behind all things an grant me unconditional forgiveness in that I will learn from your vast knowledge an wisdom to be guided by your light an learn of knowledge from your wisdom about love which will help me overcome any resentment an jealousy through the one eternal light so mote it be.

*The remembrance of a unicorn the cosmic spirit angel of the rainbow sun and enlightenment I pray to you in that you will help the universal consciousness of unicorns toward more enlightenment so unicorns feel like the miracle that they are in that they will teach more of us to discover the light within ourselves an freedom of thought through the one eternal light so mote it be.

*The remembrance of a unicorn the cosmic spirit angel of the rainbow sun I pray to you for your teachings an guidance on receiving help in finding more insight an through your eternal wisdom an love I ask to gain prosperity an with your blessings, healing, an eloquence I will accept my gifts as well from your nobility an your example of free will have the self determination of finding my true self through the one eternal light so mote it be.

*Second Heavenly Plain And Home Of Faith And Cherubim.

*Cherubim cosmic spirit angel of the rainbow sun an liberation I pray to you for your guidance in helping me overcome my spiritual struggle by showing me how to make my goals an desires happen through your ever knowing intuition an help me rely upon it to inspire me from receiving your eternal wisdom on being in harmony with the universe through the one eternal light so mote it be.

*Cherubim cosmic spirit angel of the rainbow sun I pray to you for your help in overcoming the challenge of having an open heart so that I will receive your compassion an encouragement on having the inner guidance I need for my visions an your inspiration for my gift of clairvoyance that encourages truthful communication an self empowerment of it which is my desire for spiritual development in my heart an the pure thoughts to inspire me that I must first find self love to love another through the one eternal light so mote it be.

*Cherubim cosmic spirit angel of the rainbow sun I pray to you, keepers of the west, I give thanks to you as you guide me today as I do what I know to be right, make me truthful an honest at all times, so that I may show great respect for my fellow beings an to the ancestors of all people, I pray for your help in keeping me balanced an teaching me the ways of mother earth an of the creator through the one eternal light so mote it be.

*Cherubim cosmic spirit angel of the rainbow sun, Know, an harmony I pray to you for your guidance on leading me on a journey to help me be surrounded by the people I love while showing me self love through harmony an the acceptance of this love so that I will show this love to the ones I love through the one eternal light so mote it be.

*Cherubim cosmic spirit angel of the rainbow sun an prosperity I pray to you for your teachings and guidance on inspiring willingness in me to achieve my goals and dreams through your open heart so that I will prosper from the dreams I have worked hard for through the one eternal light so mote it be.

*Cherubim cosmic spirit angel the rainbow sun an of freedom and truth I pray to you for your teachings and guidance to find the freedom in revealing my eternal self through your inner truth about life so that I will communicate easily with all of nature and the heavens through the one eternal light so mote it be.

*Cherubim cosmic spirit angel of the rainbow sun I pray to you for your teachings and guidance through your understanding of powerful new beginnings in helping me achieve spiritual enlightenment with your power of being, a guardian entity, so that I will bring the dark side of myself into submission and gain spiritual wisdom through the one eternal light so mote it be.

*Cherubim the cosmic spirit angel of the rainbow sun and the eternal flame I pray to you for your teachings and guidance of your hands aiding me, my souls healer to shield me from sin and snare, keep I this day with you and even I will be, on rough course faring and the days the rising sun blesses me through the one eternal light so mote it be.

*Cherubim cosmic spirit angel of the rainbow sun and Eternal divine spirit I pray to you grant us your blessings and in that blessings strength, and in that strength peace of mind, and in that peace of mind to come to the love of all creation, and in that love of all creation the love of it, and in that love of it selfless love for another, and in that selfless love the eternal light of self love, through the one eternal light so mote it be.

*Cherubim cosmic spirit angel of the rainbow sun | pray to you for your manifestation of OMism and the absolutions universe as | ask for your teachings and guidance on growing with the virtues of the human heart to transform my consciousness from it's limited self to my eternal self through your seperation of illusion from awareness so that myself is capable of enduring all things through the one eternal light so mote it be.

*Cherubim cosmic spirit angel of the rainbow sun | pray to you for your teachings and guidance in helping me get in touch with my deepest inner wisdom so that | will have best use of my psychic ability and the encouragement through awareness to get in touch with my deepest feelings in that | will grow with these virtues in the human heart through the one eternal light so mote it be.

*Cherubim cosmic spirit angel of the rainbow sun and the phrase 'I feel' | pray to you for your teachings and guidance in helping me receive omens for the phrase 'I feel' so that | will be assisted with myself realizing the various levels of truth within truth itself of what and having an open heart to allow this truth as omens to come to me in the phrase 'I feel' as well through your unconditional forgiveness the inspiration of my gift of clairvoyance and in this clairvoyance the encouragement of truthful communication through the one eternal light so mote it be. *Cherubim cosmic spirit angel of the rainbow sun, majesty and greatness | pray to you for your teachings and guidance through your hope in truthful clairvoyance, of orange ray and water, Mer of healing with eternal awareness, clairvoyance of what | feel, faith is omnipatient, astral of endurance in intuition and ambitious through the one eternal light so mote it be.

*Cherubim cosmic spirit angel of the rainbow sun and lord of cosmic angelic omnipatient | pray to you for your teachings and guidance of governing the wheel of the sun to help me be inspired to be balanced in a loving relationship which generates kindness and love and to open my heart an mind so that | will express the harmony in the reflection of my heart so that | will attune with my eternal self for spiritual fulfillment through the one eternal light so mote it be.

*Cherubim cosmic spirit angel of the rainbow sun and the lord of cosmic belief | pray to you for your teachings an guidance through your eternal wisdom of friendship, companionship, an of relationships so that | will prosper an allow your love to fill my heart as well to harvest the dreams | have worked hard for through the one eternal light so mote it be.

*Cherubim cosmic spirit angel of the rainbow sun an virility | pray to you for your guidance on granting me the ability to have the inner strength of overcoming self indulgence as well the stability of emotional control an through your inspiration of endurance receiving the gift of impressing others | ask to achieve a promise to dare new thoughts in that which your blessings are eternal through the one eternal light so mote it be.

*Cherubim cosmic spirit angel of the rainbow sun and light | pray to you for your guidance on helping me to overcome my nightmares as well with your blessed light an warmth of heart to teach me on having a healthier clairvoyance, intuition, an imagination so that | will be in your light through the one eternal light so mote it be.

*Cherubim cosmic spirit angel of the rainbow sun and passion I pray to you for your eternal loving kindness in teaching me how to overcome the challenge of helping the ones I care about as well with your guiding light I will confide within myself about your wisdom an listen as I confide within you as well through the one eternal light so mote it be.

*Cherubim cosmic spirit angel of the rainbow sun and awakening I pray to you in that you will help the consciousness of me toward showing yourselves the purification an self revelation that you are so you will understand that you are more of a genius then what you seem an so that you will teach more of us the battle between the flesh an the spirit as well light an illusion for world peace through the one eternal light so mote it be.

*Cherubim cosmic spirit angel of the rainbow sun I pray to you asking for your teachings an guidance to help me brake down the challenges to find inspiration an with your eternal blessings to guide me as well I will self heal an with your growing compassion find myself closer to you an divination through the one eternal light so mote it be.

* Third Heavenly Plain Of Lower Mental And Home Of Love And Elves.

*I pray to elves, the cosmic spirit angels of the rainbow sun for helping me overcome the challenge of taking risks an enlighten me to have the courage to understand an hear others feelings as well guiding me on my desire of finding inner peace an the expression of my true self with your ever knowing ethical decisions through the one eternal light so mote it be.

*I pray to elves, the cosmic spirit angels of the rainbow sun for your guidance in leading me on a journey through selfless love an to teach me how to find the inner strength of expressing myself better an through your self love of forgiveness an kindness I will find balance in my compassion for mankind as well to encourage me to awakening an enlightenment so that I will express my true self an have the courage to hear an understand other people's feelings to awaken my memory of eternal love through the one eternal light so mote it be.

*I pray to elves, the cosmic spirit angels of the rainbow sun keepers of the north, guide me today as I give thanks for all my gifts you've shown me as your help in every day of life, give me strength to overcome when needed an watch over those who dwellith without clothing, food, and medicine, hear me; I need your wisdom in seeking pure thoughts an with good intentions through the one eternal light so mote it be.

*I pray to elves, the cosmic spirit angels of the rainbow sun so that you may redeem me from evil as well lead me back to Know so that I will be cleansed in the eternal light an liberated so that I will receive the desire to stay young at heart as well to finish my goals with your blessings an unconditional love to guide me an make amends with unity in my heart so I will receive harmony of mind an enthusiasm for my spiritual well being through the one eternal light so mote it be.

*I pray to elves, the cosmic spirit angels of the rainbow sun an compassion for your teachings and guidance on inspiring my inner strength and compassion through your unconditional forgiveness an harmony so that I will be more open through self love an the love of others through the one eternal light so mote it be.

* I pray to elves, the cosmic spirit angels of the rainbow sun and love for your teachings and guidance in bringing nature into my heart through your beauty of love in nature so that I will achieve purity of body, mind, and spirit through the one eternal light so mote it be.

*I pray to elves, the cosmic spirit angels of the rainbow sun for your teachings and guidance through your companionship of protection in helping me achieve this while on my journeys and at home so that I will find my true purpose in life and reconnect with ancient knowledge through the one eternal light so mote it be.

*I pray to elves, the cosmic spirit angels of the rainbow sun and divine light for your teachings and guidance of my love to Know make warmer, the love of you would I feel, come I with the spirit of kindly hym, come into my heart and your love surrounding me, hither in mine ever living soul through the one eternal light so mote it be.

*I pray to elves, the cosmic spirit angel of the rainbow sun for you to grant us your spoken essence of truth, and in that essence of truth the ridding of selfish questions, and in that ridding of selfish questions the instilment of my heart with hope, and in that instilment of hope your guiding light, and in that guiding light the finding of wisdom, and in that wisdom unity, through the one eternal light so mote it be.

*I pray to elves, the cosmic spirit angels of the rainbow sun for your manifestation of knowism, being the third question to our third sense, and the absolutions of the galaxy as I ask for your teachings and guidance on knowing that everything that happens is fate and natural timing of Know's divine plan in that through your synchronized balance in the next steps of my life's purpose I will be encouraged and blessed through Know's divine inner wisdom so that by natural law I am present everywhere simultaneously through the one eternal light so mote it be.

*I pray to elves, the cosmic spirit angel of the rainbow sun for your teachings and guidance in helping me achieve my hearts desires so that I will discover the light within as well to open up space in my consciousness for my visions to manifest into reality through the one eternal light so mote it be.

*I pray to elves, the cosmic spirit angels of the rainbow sun for your teachings and guidance in helping me receive omens for the phrase 'I realize' so that I will be assisted with myself realizing the various levels of truth within truth itself of when and having an open heart to allow this truth as omens to come to me in the phrase 'I realize' as well through your unconditional forgiveness the inspiration of my gift of clairvoyance and in this clairvoyance the encouragement of truthful communication through the one eternal light so mote it be.

*I pray to elves, the cosmic spirit angels of the rainbow sun for your teachings and guidance through your faith of respect in communication of yellow ray and fire, a elvish harper in the firmament, eternal honor, healing when I realize love is omnipresent, lower mental of concentration, healing creative through the one eternal light so mote it be.

*I pray to elves, the cosmic spirit angels of the rainbow sun for your teachings and guidance in that you will grant wisdom in interpreting my visions and dreams so that through your encouragement to think positively and remain optimistic, I will be of nobility and affection so that I will be awakened with the feelings of complete inner peace through the one eternal light so mote it be.

*I pray to elves, the cosmic spirit angels of the rainbow sun for your guidance on my journey through life in that I will find forgiveness an from your teachings I will discover the light within so that my visions will manifest in reality an I ask through your beautiful heart to become enlightened as well of awareness through the one eternal light so mote it be.

*I pray to elves, the cosmic spirit angels of the rainbow sun for your guidance on granting me the ability of spiritual aspirations an through your good logic an high intellect the gift of more free will an to see an choose creative alternatives as well I ask to achieve the enlightenment of virtuosity in that which your blessings are eternal through the one eternal light so mote it be.

*I pray to elves, the cosmic spirit angels of the rainbow sun for your guidance in receiving healthier communication as well with your eternal wisdom on achieving to be creative an with your acceptance of me through your warm heart to have the desire to be creative an help make passage of this creativity through the one eternal light so mote it be.

*I pray to elves, the cosmic spirit angels of the rainbow sun for your guidance in helping me overcome the challenges to enjoy the freedom of variety in my life an through your ever wisdom the courage to understand other people's feelings an to express my true self from your guiding light so that I will not be limited or restricted in any way through the one eternal light so mote it be.

*I pray to elves, the cosmic spirit angels of the rainbow sun in that you will help my subconscious toward retrieving insights from my deepest desires an show me the beauty of creation that I am an help me understand that I am eternal whether I like it or not so that you will watch over an protect those who are scared, alone, or have been mistreated through the one eternal light so mote it be.

*I pray to elves, the cosmic spirit angels of the rainbow sun asking for your teachings an guidance to aid me in braking down the challenges so that I will learn as with your eternal compassion the way of wisdom an your eternal blessings to guide me on my journey through life through the one eternal light so mote it be.

*Forth Heavenly Plain Home Of OM The Universal Spoken Essence Of The Higher Mental And Fearies.

*I pray to the fearies, cosmic spirit angels of the rainbow sun for your guidance in gaining confidence for spiritual, emotional, an physical fulfillment as well to love an be loved by your ever growing nourishment that I am thankful for your wisdom an acceptance of me as my acceptance of bringing you into my heart through the one eternal light so mote it be.

*I pray to the fearies, cosmic spirit angels of the rainbow sun for your teachings an guidance in helping me spark the memory of my own divinity through your inspiration of being in a balanced loving relationship an to open my heart, mind, an spirit to find self love and selfless love of another so that everything that happens is divine, natural, an beautiful in the eternal sense in which I will attune with my eternal self an express the harmony of Know through your spiritual fulfillment through the one eternal light so mote it be.

*I pray to the fearies, cosmic spirit angels of the rainbow sun, keeper of the east, help light my way in times of darkness as I give thanks for the reasons of life itself, land of the rising sun, encourage my spirit with hopes as promises and guidance to those without these, teach me the way of the creator, the great spirit my father, the fireblood in us and grandfather sun for we'd be animals, not men without his comfort an of warmth through the one eternal light so mote it be.

*I pray to the fearies, cosmic spirit angels of the rainbow sun so that I will kindle the desire to be easy going as well generous in that through your eternal wisdom help me be peace loving an that through your wisdom which generates kindness an love I will find myself balanced with loving kindness an in a loving relationship between us an the ones I love through the one eternal light so mote it be.

*I pray to the fearies, cosmic spirit angels of the rainbow sun for your teachings and guidance on passion an love through your sacred wisdom an warm heart so that I will be spiritualy liberated through my struggles of freedom from the heart an to show this love to others through the one eternal light so mote it be.

*I pray to the fearies, cosmic spirit angels of the rainbow sun for your teachings and guidance in having stability in mind and longevity of heart through your inner knowledge so that I will be protected and have inner strength through the one eternal light so mote it be.

*I pray to the fearies, cosmic spirit angels of the rainbow sun for your teachings and guidance through your knowledge in working against any evil in helping me achieve ridding the evil that hurts my heart so that I will become a warrior like you as an enemy of all evil and gain spiritual knowledge from it through the one eternal light so mote it be.

*I pray to the fearies, cosmic spirit angels of the rainbow sun for your teachings and guidance, of my eyes not tempted and Know with me in each ray of light, Know with me protecting every day and night, the lord with me directing I, the lords eternal divine love through the one eternal light so mote it be.

*I pray to the fearies, cosmic spirit angels of the rainbow sun, grant us your teachings, and in that teachings guidance, and in that guidance the communication of true feelings, and in that communication of true feelings the remembrance of my spiritual destiny, and in that spiritual destiny the truth of all life, and in that truth of all life courage, and in that courage the inspiration and gift of love, through the one eternal light so mote it be.

*I pray to the fearies, cosmic spirit angels of the rainbow sun for your manifestation of Godism, being the forth question to our forth sense, and the absolutions of the cosmos as I ask for your teachings and guidance in leading me on a journey through selfless love in that I will be encouraged to awakening and enlightenment as well to awaken the memory of eternal love through my divinity so that I will have unlimited power of self through the one eternal light so mote it be.

*I pray to the fearies, cosmic spirit angels of the rainbow sun for your teachings and guidance in helping me by granting wisdom in interpreting my dreams and visions so that through your fostering of love, justice, truth, and joy I will be liberated in your encouragement of awakening and enlightenment through the one eternal light so mote it be.

*I pray to the fearies, cosmic spirit angels of the rainbow sun for your teachings and guidance in helping me receive omens for the phrase 'I understand' so that I will be assisted with myself realizing the various levels of truth within truth itself of where and having an open heart to allow this truth as omens to come to me in the phrase 'I understand' as well through your unconditional forgiveness the inspiration of my gift of clairvoyance and in this clairvoyance the encouragement of truthful communication through the one eternal light so mote it be.

*I pray to the fearies, cosmic spirit angels of the rainbow sun for your teachings and guidance through your warm heart of kindness and love, green ray and air, a thunder bird of love in eternal beauty, independence where I understand, OM the omnipotent of higher mental, independence through love, open hearted through the one eternal light so mote it be.

*I pray to the fearies, cosmic spirit angels of the rainbow sun for your teachings and guidance in that I ask through your encouragement to watch over and protect me as well to purify and cleanse my spirit of the surrounding negative energy so that the essence and power of faith will instill calmness in conflicts within and fill my mind, heart, and spirit with tranquility and contentment in that you will help retrieve insights from my subconscious mind so that I will find acceptance in my personal power through the one eternal light so mote it be.

*I pray to the fearies, cosmic spirit angels of the rainbow sun for your guidance in encouraging newness an exploration within my heart an to dare new thoughts to inspire my spirit with hope as well the courage to find truth in my desires an I ask to fill my spirit with hope, grace, an love so that I will find unity with your blessings through the one eternal light so mote it be.

*I pray to the fearies, cosmic spirit angels of the rainbow sun for your guidance on granting me the ability of better vitality an through your generous heart the gift of independence an lightheartedness where I ask to achieve prosperity in that which your blessings are eternal through the one eternal light so mote it be.

*I pray to the fearies, cosmic spirit angels of the rainbow sun for your guidance in teaching me how to heal others through love as well to guide me with your light in helping me understand to have an open heart so that I will show this love to others an accept this love into my heart through the one eternal light so mote it be.

*I pray to the fearies, cosmic spirit angels of the rainbow sun to strengthen my spirit so I will overcome the challenge of being the natural healer that I am as well my desire to achieve this goal as I pray to you for your truth, patience, an love of the human heart through the one eternal light so mote it be.

*I pray to the fearies, cosmic spirit angels of the rainbow sun in that you will help my vision of the world toward enlightenment an find the beauty of visions in Know's heart so he will understand that he is amazing an with a good heart himself or an herself and I ask of you to project the beauty of the visions in Know's heart to all mankind's consciousness for eternal because there is to much suffering in the world through the one eternal light so mote it be.

*I pray to the fearies, cosmic spirit angels of the rainbow sun asking for your teachings an guidance in helping me find the way of love as well to find love an with your warm heart I will find a spiritual awakening in myself an rid what has blocked me from receiving your love directly in that which I will find understanding of the remembrance of my spiritual destiny an I ask from your eternal wisdom to expand my awareness so that I will receive your blessings

through the one eternal light so mote it be.

*Fifth Heavenly Plain The Spiritual Home Of Morgan Le Fey.

*I pray to Morgan Le Fey the cosmic spirit angel of the rainbow sun for your guidance by helping me to understand as well to communicate with the ones that I love effectively from your ever growing vast knowledge aiding me to think in a logical manner an increasing my ability to understand in an orderly way through the one eternal light so mote it be.

*I pray to Morgan Le Fey the cosmic spirit angel of the rainbow sun for your wisdom of achieving in helping me attain my hearts desire on finding my path so that you will inspire me towards awareness an enlightenment an teach me about my consciousness to discover the light within as well through your blessings and deep inner knowledge the encouragement in my quest for truth so that you will reveal Know's divine plan for me an the next steps of my life's purpose through the one eternal light so mote it be.

*I pray to Morgan Le Fey the cosmic spirit angel of the rainbow sun, keeper of the south, land we face always, help light my way in times of darkness, make my spirit strong with the great lord, sun and great spirit, watcher over all mother earth, make nature fruitful and grant us fulfillment for when we harvest our dreams we and my people have worked hard for, affectionately guide my people with compassion and inner strength through the one eternal light so mote it be.

*I pray to Morgan Le Fey the cosmic spirit angel of the rainbow sun to help teach me how to listen an see inwardly so that I will become more sociable an with your wisdom which is eternal I will please others as well be taught the way through your guiding light through the one eternal light so mote it be.

*I pray to Morgan Le Fey the cosmic spirit angel of the rainbow sun for your teachings an guidance on inspiring me to be balanced in a loving relationship through your natural divine beauty of the eternal sense so that I will become open of mind and heart through the one eternal light so mote it be.

*I pray to Morgan Le Fey the cosmic spirit angel of the rainbow sun for your teachings and guidance of teaching mankind and I to have love of animals through your protection of them and earth so that I will show this love more to my companions of wild natures animals and earth itself through the one eternal light so mote it be.

*I pray to Morgan Le Fey the cosmic spirit angel of the rainbow sun for your teachings and guidance through your creativity in helping me achieve to be a seeker of knowledge with your love of arts and ancient secrets so that I will become the same, a seeker of ancient secret knowledge and love of the arts through the one eternal light so mote it be.

*I pray to Morgan Le Fey the cosmic spirit angel of the rainbow sun for your teachings and guidance, of the holy spirit with me strengthening, yet may you yourself Know of life be at my side, you to me as a star and guide from life to death and rebirth again through the one eternal light so mote it be.

*I pray to Morgan Le Fey the cosmic spirit angel of the rainbow sun, grant us honesty, and in that honesty the inspiration of independence, and in that inspiration of independence a promise of hope, and in that hope wisdom to the human heart, and in that wisdom unconditional forgiveness, and in that unconditional forgiveness compassion, and in that compassion truthful communication, through the one eternal light so mote it be.

*I pray to Morgan Le Fey the cosmic spirit angel of the rainbow sun for your creation of omega manism and being the absolutions of illuminiti as I ask for your teachings and guidance through your selfless love, inner strength, and being the fifth question to our fifth sense in that I will express my communication as an individual spoken essence of the universe through the one eternal light so mote it be.

*I pray to Morgan Le Fey the cosmic spirit angel of the rainbow sun for your teachings and guidance in inspiring my gift of clairvoyance and encourage truthful communication through your heavenly voice comes unconditional forgiveness to open my heart so that I will receive this inspiration of my gifts from your eternal love through the one eternal light so mote it be.

*I pray to Morgan Le Fey the cosmic spirit angel of the rainbow sun for your teachings and guidance in helping me receive omens for the phrase 'I will' so that I will be assisted with myself realizing the various levels of truth within truth itself of how and having an open heart to allow this truth as omens to come to me in the phrase 'I will' as well through your unconditional forgiveness the inspiration of my gift of clairvoyance and in this clairvoyance the encouragement of truthful communication through the one eternal light so mote it be.

*I pray to Morgan Le Fey the cosmic spirit angel of the rainbow sun for your teachings and guidance through your humanistic responsibility and will of blue ray, a gargoyle with divine light protecting, eternal blessings from OM, how I will with Know find OM, spiritual individuality of courage idealistic through the one eternal light so mote it be.

*I pray to Morgan Le Fey the cosmic spirit angel of the rainbow sun for your teachings and guidance through your heavenly voice the communication of true feelings in helping me find remembrance of my spiritual destiny of the truth in all life between this world and the heavens to encourage who I am meant to be through your gift of love the courage of your inspiration an inner strength so that I will walk in the light of the eternal spirit through the one eternal light so mote it be.

*I pray to Morgan Le Fey the cosmic spirit angel of the rainbow sun for your teachings in helping me learn as well with your guiding light to overcome the challenge of finding wisdom an to maintain an optimistic outlook on life an tranquility of finding inner peace with calmness in the conflicts within my heart through the one eternal light so mote it be.

*I pray to Morgan Le Fey the cosmic spirit angel of the rainbow sun for your guidance on granting me the ability of devotion to Know as through your love the will to express my true self an to become a seeker of wisdom where I ask to achieve the knowledge which comes forth from your wisdom of the heart in that which your blessings are eternal through the one eternal light so mote it be.

*I pray to Morgan Le Fey the cosmic spirit angel of the rainbow sun for your guidance in showing me my gift that Know has given me by helping me understand that we are not separate from Know with your wisdom an love guiding me in finding my personal power an the understanding with it of receiving your enlightenment through the one eternal light so mote it be.

*I pray to Morgan Le Fey the cosmic spirit angel of the rainbow sun for your guidance in bringing remembrance to my spiritual destiny so that I will achieve new ideas an with your eternal wisdom to show me how to brake down the challenges for me to express myself through your love an peace of heart as well help me recognize my true feelings an communicate these to the ones I love through the one eternal light so mote it be.

*I pray to Morgan Le Fey the cosmic spirit angel of the rainbow sun to fill my fathers spirit with hope, trust, an love in that he will have fulfillment for his dreams he has worked hard for as well having success and prosperity through your guiding light so that his heart will be filled with compassion an inner strength through the one eternal light so mote it be.

*I pray to Morgan Le Fey the cosmic spirit angel of the rainbow sun for your teachings an guidance as with your divine essence to show me the way of happiness the inspiration of having fulfillment in love an ask of you to find the truths in my desires so that I will learn from the inner truth as with your wisdom of the human heart to develop the inner power to find harmony through self love an the courage to express my true self through the one eternal light so mote it be.

*Sixth Heavenly Plain Home Of Holy Spirit Intuitional And Merlin.

*I pray to Merlin the cosmic spirit angel of the rainbow sun for your guidance in encouraging me into the acceptance of others an to gain respect for myself to help me serve others with that same respect as well with your acceptance to appreciate the beauty of love, to be sociable, an harmonious within absolution through the one eternal light so mote it be.

*I pray to Merlin the cosmic spirit angel of the rainbow sun for your love in the human heart in helping me find the compassion of communication as well I ask for your forgiveness so that I will grow with the virtue of forgiveness in encouraging me to heal friendships by getting in touch with my deepest feelings so that my divinity to this world will transform my consciousness from the limited self to the eternal self through the one eternal light so mote it be.

*I pray to Merlin the cosmic spirit angel of the rainbow sun, keeper of the heavenly night, this my offering of praise, humble my prayer, honesty my reverence of my love for you, purity my thoughts of truthfulness, compassion my kindness, clarity my vision, guide me today to awaken my spirit and give me your knowledge so I will learn the lessons you've hidden, through the one eternal light so mote it be.

*I pray to Merlin the cosmic spirit angel of the rainbow sun so that I will find inner peace from your loving heart as I know not to be lazy an am willing to learn from your acceptance of me that of guiding me with your affection, purity, an divine beauty you will teach me to be intuitive an warmhearted from your contentment so that I will find tranquility of mind, heart, an spirit through the one eternal light so mote it be.

*I pray to Merlin the cosmic spirit angel of the rainbow sun for your teachings and guidance on helping me to become healed from a broken heart through your peaceful essence and divine plan of me I will mend my spirit and become who I am meant to be through the one eternal light so mote it be.

*I pray to Merlin the cosmic spirit angel of the rainbow sun for your teachings and guidance of inspiring peace in the order of my virtues through your knowledge of the stars so that I will be encouraged from your deep inner wisdom whose great grace blesses me with liveliness in achieving my hearts desires through the one eternal light so mote it be.

*I pray to Merlin the cosmic spirit angel of the rainbow sun for your teachings and guidance through your freedom of imagination in helping me achieve wisdom with your psychic power so that I will be enriched in life of mind, heart, and spirit through the one eternal light so mote it be.

*I pray to Merlin the cosmic spirit angel of the rainbow sun for your teachings and guidance through your encouragement of harmony, bless my inner power to overcome, open my heart and instill wisdom in it so I will heal through the one eternal light so mote it be.

*I pray to Merlin the cosmic spirit angel of the rainbow sun grant us the gift of an open heart, and in that open heartedness the integrity of liberation, and in that integrity of liberation awakening and enlightenment, and in that awakening and enlightenment the expression of my true self, and in that expression of my true self the courage to hear and understand other people's feelings, and in that understanding the memory of eternal love, and in that eternal love divine logical dignity, through the one eternal light so mote it be.

*I pray to Merlin the cosmic spirit angel of the rainbow sun for your knowledge of atomism, being the sixth question to my sixth sense, and the absolutions of munipuli in that I ask for your teachings and guidance through your unconditional forgiveness of having an open mind and heart so that my spirit will be cleansed in the eternal light and to understand myself receiving total knowledge through the one eternal light so mote it be.

*I pray to Merlin the cosmic spirit angel of the rainbow sun for your teachings and guidance in rekindling the artistic fires in my mortal heart and through your gift of prophecy to inspire my clairvoyant and psychic abilities so that I will learn from my sixth sense through the one eternal light so mote it be.

*I pray to Merlin the cosmic spirit angel of the rainbow sun for your teachings and guidance in helping me receive omens for the phrase 'I think' so that I will be assisted with myself realizing the various levels of truth within truth itself of why and having an open heart to allow this truth as omens to come to me in the phrase 'I think' as well through your unconditional forgiveness the inspiration of my gift of clairvoyance and in this clairvoyance the encouragement of truthful communication through the one eternal light so mote it be.

*I pray to Merlin the cosmic spirit angel of the rainbow sun for your teachings and guidance through your clairvoyance of honesty and procreation of indigo ray an light, a griffin as the rising sun are thee eternal light, know of why I think of the holy spirit omniscient, intuitionaly of spirituality whose passion intuitive through the one eternal light so mote it be.

*I pray to Merlin the cosmic spirit angel of the rainbow sun for your teachings and guidance in that I ask for your blessings to watch over those in sickness and in pain, turmoil and distress, to bless them from freedom of pain, peace of mind, inner strength and endurance, to watch over and protect those whose path leads into darkness and sorrow through the one eternal light so mote it be.

*I pray to Merlin the cosmic spirit angel of the rainbow sun to help me find understanding an prosper from it as well to find the way of merging with universal through your vast knowledge an wisdom which generates kindness an love so that with your guidance to inspire compassion, integrity, an inner strength I will overcome my struggles through the one eternal light so mote it be.

*I pray to Merlin the cosmic spirit angel of the rainbow sun for your guidance on granting me the ability of finding serenity within mind, heart, an spirit as through your knowledge I will find the power to be healed as well to heal the ones I love an I ask to achieve this in that which your blessings are eternal through the one eternal light so mote it be.

*I pray to Merlin the cosmic spirit angel of the rainbow sun for your guidance in achieving serenity of heart an to brake down the challenge to have clarity of thought so that with your love an wisdom I will have my heart rekindled of desire once more as well with your guiding strength to release my mind an bring tranquility through the one eternal light so mote it be.

*I pray to Merlin the cosmic spirit angel of the rainbow sun for helping me become more nurturing an caring as well showing me the gifts that I have by your encouraging truthful communication so that I will show the love within my heart to the ones that I love so that I will grow closer to them through the one eternal light so mote it be.

*I pray to Merlin the cosmic spirit angel of the rainbow sun to fill my son's or an daughters heart with playfulness an lightheartedness so that my son's or an daughters heart will be filled with inner strength, compassion, an encouragement on his or an her journey through life an to watch over an protect him or an her through the one eternal light so mote it be.

*I pray to Merlin the cosmic spirit angel of the rainbow sun for your teachings an guidance asking for understanding to receive the desire to stay young at heart an through your eternal love, passion, an wisdom I wish to learn of your knowledge an free will of finding pleasure an sociability through the one eternal light so mote it be.

*Seventh Heavenly Plain The Absolute, Home Of Lepidoptera.

*I pray to the remembrance of Lepidoptera the cosmic spirit angel of the rainbow sun for helping me brake down the challenges that restrain me from receiving your eternal love an thinking before acting as well guiding me with your light in inspiring me with physical comfort, practicality, an patience through the one eternal light so mote it be.

*I pray to the remembrance of Lepidoptera the cosmic spirit angel of the rainbow sun for your communication with the heavenly realm which links us to all living things in helping me through your love an guidance to bring remembrance to my spiritual destiny an to overcome my broken heart so that I will find my true feelings for another with seduction an a relationship spiritualy and physicly which will expand my awareness through your hopes an dreams of others so that I will find the encouragement to heal an use my gifts to become who I am meant to be through the one eternal light so mote it be.

*I pray to the remembrance of Lepidoptera the cosmic spirit angel of the rainbow sun for your guidance needed, a guest of love, nourisher of land, for the earth is my mother and the great spirit my father, without you no one would exist, show me the way so there is no more loneliness, so that each of us and days together will be good and long upon the earth, make me remain close to the great spirit an treat those thereon the earth and all that dwell with respect, through the one eternal light so mote it be.

*I pray to the remembrance of Lepidoptera the cosmic spirit angel of the rainbow sun so that with your eternal light of truth will guide me in encouraging these truths in me an finding the truth in my desires so I will learn to be less nervous when I want to succeed in achieving at passion, romance, an love through the one eternal light so mote it be.

*I pray to the remembrance of Lepidoptera the cosmic spirit angel of the rainbow sun for your teachings and guidance on inspiring me to achieve oneness with nature and all life through your luminous encouragement of expanding my awareness to get in touch with my feelings so that I will communicate easily with earth, nature, and the heavenly realm through the one eternal light so mote it be.

*I pray to the remembrance of Lepidoptera the cosmic spirit angel of the rainbow sun for your teachings and guidance in encouraging me to get in touch with my deep inner wisdom through your psyche ability so that I will be blessed in the eternal light and to grow with the virtues of love in my heart and to expand my awareness with true feelings in the quest for truth through the one eternal light so mote it be.

*I pray to the remembrance of Lepidoptera the cosmic spirit angel of the rainbow sun for your teachings and guidance through your love of procreation in helping me achieve sexual companionship with your wisdom of life, unity, and sexuality so that I will practice the rainbows laws of harmony in having more respect for relationships, companionships, and friendships at heart through the one eternal light so mote it be.

*I pray to the remembrance of Lepidoptera the cosmic spirit angel of the rainbow sun for your teachings and guidance on leading me on my journey through selfless love, self love, and love for another to encourage me to awakening and enlightenment, to express my true self to another, bless me so that I will awaken my memory of eternal love, romance, and passion through the one eternal light so mote it be.

*I pray to the remembrance of Lepidoptera the cosmic spirit angel of the rainbow sun, grant us the memory of our divinity, and in that memory of our divinity nourishment of spiritual fulfillment, and in that nourishment of spiritual fulfillment beauty in the eternal sense, and in that beauty in the eternal sense balance in a loving relationship, and in that balance of a loving relationship the achievement of my hearts desires, and in that achievement of my hearts desires the revealing of the next steps of our life's purpose, and in that revealing of purpose growing virtues, through the one eternal light so mote it be.

*I pray to the remembrance of Lepidoptera the cosmic spirit angel of the rainbow sun for your wisdom of universalism, being the missing link to our seventh sense, and the absolutions of sublimini in that I ask for your teachings an guidance on truthful communication through your encouragement of inspiring my gift of clairvoyance to be open so that my halo is capable of transmitting and receiving in all directions through the one eternal light so mote it be.

*I pray to the remembrance of Lepidoptera the cosmic spirit angel of the rainbow sun for bringing remembrance to my spiritual destiny through your true feelings in the quest for truth in helping me overcome the way between awareness and illusion so that I learn from my seventh clairvoic sense in that I ask for your teachings and guidance to expand the beauty of the visions in my heart through the one eternal light so mote it be.

*I pray to the remembrance of Lepidoptera the cosmic spirit angel of the rainbow sun for your teachings and guidance in helping me receive omens for the phrase 'I know' so that I will be assisted with myself realizing the various levels of truth within truth itself of which and having an open heart to allow this truth as omens to come to me in the phrase 'I know' as well through your unconditional forgiveness the inspiration of my gift of clairvoyance and in this clairvoyance the encouragement of truthful communication through the one eternal light so mote it be.

*I pray to the remembrance of Lepidoptera the cosmic spirit angel of the rainbow sun for your teachings and guidance through your psyche of the great spirit universal and violet ray of thought, a unicorn of shining light are the eternal spirit of Know, which I know Lepidoptera omnidirectionaly, the absolute of awareness whose forgiveness mystical through the one eternal light so mote it be.

*I pray to the remembrance of Lepidoptera the cosmic spirit angel of the rainbow sun for your teachings and guidance to encourage my heart with courage an hope so that i will find the truth in my desires to rid selfish questions and bond with unity in that through your guiding light to find the wisdom of having inner peace and in that inner peace a good heart and good will toward mankind through the one eternal light so mote it be.

*I pray to the remembrance of Lepidoptera the cosmic spirit angel of the rainbow sun to help me overcome an succeed as well to wrap a deep feeling of harmony around all mankind an I so that with your eternal wisdom, friendship, an loving kindness I will have courageable spiritual intuition an from your sacred knowledge an heart I will find enlightenment through self love an from this love of others as well contentment an selfless love of another through the one eternal light so mote it be.

*I pray to the remembrance of Lepidoptera the cosmic spirit angel of the rainbow sun for your guidance on granting me the ability of feeling oneness with all life an through your wisdom of finding purpose I ask to achieve better awareness in that which your blessings are eternal through the one eternal light so mote it be.

*I pray to the remembrance of Lepidoptera the cosmic spirit angel of the rainbow sun for your guidance in teaching me to be with understanding of earth an nature an to help me brake down the challenge of me understanding how to merge with universal enlightenment so that my desire of being at one with nature an the wilderness is true within my heart an with your knowledge to guide my heart an with your love to help me receive the courage of feeling at peace with earth through the one eternal light so mote it be.

*I pray to the remembrance of Lepidoptera the cosmic spirit angel of the rainbow sun so that my guardian angel an guiding light is blessed more everyday to influence my family an I toward a higher good an my family an I are blessed because of it in strengthening an encouraging my family an I as a constant friend an guide at my side through the one eternal light so mote it be.

*I pray to the remembrance of Lepidoptera the cosmic spirit angel of the rainbow sun asking for your teachings an guidance in helping me be with fertility an the understanding that I must first love myself in order to love another as with this love prosperity an abundance will come from an through your blessed eternal knowledge of passion an love I will achieve the understanding in the magic of sex through my inner power through the one eternal light so mote it be.

*Wizardly Throne Prayers

- There are three thrones in my kingdom. The tall chair in the middle and one smaller chair, one on each side of the tall chair. You are also able to apoint on either throne your father, son, and holy ghost.

*The Tall Throne - Prestothilogy i praise to (choose to say your choice of ruler either a fantasy character or even yourself during this prayer) as the emperor of my kingdom, I rely on you for courage, inner strength, and power in which in this power truth, and in that truth trust, and in this trust passion, and in that passion clarity, and in this clarity communication, and in that communication completion, and in this completion masterminding through the one eternal light mysteriorum change-o abracadabra.

*The Throne To The Right - Prestothilogy i praise to king Lepidoptera the cosmic spirit angel of the rainbow sun to be at one with the great spirit of universal divinity of creation, earth, and wholeness as well to be divine with universal understanding, completion, and the bringer of light when all falls into darkness and sorrow, that which purpose, fulfillment, and triumph comes through the one eternal light abracadabra be amen.

*The Throne To The Left - Prestothilogy i praise to queen Lunaris the cosmic spirit angel of the moonlit sun to be at one with the goddess spirit of the divine universal of life, nature, and oneness as well the holder of our memory of universal divinity and bringer of conscious creation, love, and harmony that which truth, beauty, and wisdom comes through the one eternal light abracadabra change-o blessed be amen.

*Wizardry Round Table Prayers

- All conscious self image names below are a name each for a person sitting at the round table inside my kingdom.

*Knowing Light Being A Conscious - Alakazam i praise to knowing light being a conscious for truth , and in this essence of truth love, and in that love all reality extending, and in this reality integrity of thought, and in that integrity of thought the true principle of freedom through the one eternal light blessed art be amen.

*Conscious Knowing Of Light - Abadazad i praise to conscious knowing of light for trust, and in this trust inner knowing, and in that inner knowing all levels of reality, and in this reality everything understandable, and in that understanding perfection through the one eternal light blessed art be amen.

*Conscious Light Knowing - Hocus Pocus i praise to conscious light knowing for passion, and in this passion the core presence of our creating light, and in that creation realization, and in this realization limitless being of light, and in that limitlessness the force of light through the one eternal light blessed art be amen.

*Conscious Being Of Light - Sucliblu i praise to conscious being of light for clarity, and in this clarity the simplest form, and in that simplest form acknowledgment, and in this acknowledgment our physical self part of the greater whole, and in the greater wholeness power through the one eternal light blessed art be amen.

*Knowing Conscious Being Of Light - Change-o i praise to knowing conscious being of light for communication, and in this communication our essential an higher self, and in that state of higher self the unseen forces of light, and in this unseen force of light completion through the one eternal light blessed art be amen.

*Knowing Being Of Conscious Light - Presto i praise to knowing being of conscious light for completion, and in this completion a form of knowing, and in that form of knowing a conclusion, and in this conclusion multiple levels of a journey, and in those journey's a new experience through the one eternal light blessed art be amen.

*Conscious Being Of Knowing Light - Abracadabra i praise to conscious being of knowing light for masterminding, and in this masterminding an act of creating a collective conscious, and in that conscious collective the focusing of manifesting an outcome, and in this manifestation being guided by the unseen forces of light through the one eternal light blessed art be amen.

*Wizardly Kingdom Prayers

*The Hierarchy - Prestophoricalthilogy i praise to the hierarchy for self confidence, and in this self confidence wisdom, and in that wisdom kindness, and in this kindness destiny, and in that destiny courage, and in this courage keeness, and in that keeness bravery, and in this bravery vigilance, and in that vigilance hope, and in this hope triumph art change-o blessed art be zenith through the one eternal light in the lords name so mote it be.

*The Wizard - Prestophoricalthilogy i praise to Merlin for completion, and in this completion realization, and in that realization accomplishment, and in this accomplishment proper balance, and in that proper balance courage, and in this courage friendship, and in that friendship will power, and in this will power creativity, and in that creativity craft, and in this craft knowledge art change-o blessed art be magus through the one eternal light in the lords name so mote it be.

*The Elve's - Prestophoricalthilogy i praise to the elve Arivel for truth, and in this truth trust, and in that trust passion, and in this passion clarity, and in that clarity communication, and in this communication completion art change-o blessed art be wizards through the one eternal light in the lords name so mote it be.

*The Huntress - Prestophoricalthilogy i praise to the huntress for hunting down any spy's against me, watch the lands for invaders, and defend the light kingdom against any intruder with your skilled hands art change-o blessed art be mysteriorum through the one eternal light in the lords name so mote it be.

*The Druid - Prestophoricalthilogy i praise to the druid Mernom for helping bring peace to my kingdom, heal the sick, and lead the blind art change-o blessed art be divinorium through the one eternal light in the lords name so mote it be.

*The Armor - Prestophoricalthilogy i praise to Lepidoptera, Merlin, and Knowledge to have the armor of the iron butterfly for protection art change-o blessed art be merry(siorum) through the one eternal light in the lords name so mote it be.

*The Mask - Prestophoricalthilogy i praise to Mernom, The Huntress, and Arivel to wear the mask of reveleance to give me clarity art change-o blessed art be abracadabliorum through the one eternal light in the lords name so mote it be.

* The Chieftan - Prestophoricalthilogy i praise to the chieftan for protection, and in this protection clarity, and in that clarity insight, and in this insight inner wisdom, and in that inner wisdom achievement, and in this achievement accomplishment, and in that accomplishment completion art change-o blessed art be ilusiun through the one eternal light in the lords name so mote it be.

*Wizardly Prayers For Outside Your Fantasy Kingdom

- Pray these prayers for those outside your kingdom.

*Plant Chrysalis Fearies - Prestophoricalthiology i pray to mysteriousliorum of plant chrysalis fearies born in my kingdom's forest for their wisdom of nature wherein that wisdom I will find the beauty of creation, and in this beauty of creation the empowerment of healing, and in that empowerment of healing inner strength through the one eternal light blessed art be.

*The Halflings - Prestophoricalthiology i pray to diviniorum the halflings in my village and beyond for their knowledge of inner beauty, inner child, and inner wisdom for in these inner empowerments the love of the divine spirit, and in this love of the divine spirit the love of all creation through the one eternal light blessed art be.

*The Imps - Prestophoricalthiology i pray to blessedartheest the imps in my village and beyond for their insight, and in this insight freedom of thought, and in that freedom of thought imagination, and in this imagination fascination, and in that fascination well being through the one eternal light blessed art be.

*The Pixies - Prestophoricalthiology i pray to artblessedyee the pixies that visit my village from the forest for bringing singing, dance, and music to my kingdom for in this entertainment the love of all creation, and in that love of all creation the divine attributes, and in this divine attributes natural love through the one eternal light blessed art be.

*The Mermaids - Prestophoricalthiology i pray to artblessedbe the mermaids beyond my kingdom in the sea for protection of my kingdom's sea and to stand for freedom, imagination, and wisdom as we give them thanks for these through the one eternal light blessed art be.

*The Hivest - Prestophoricalthiology i pray to the wrighthe that the hivest people for those that do hard work like bee's, that which protects our queen, and the collectors of nectar which protects the young and defenseless, their justice their own reward may they have comfort through the one eternal light blessed art be.

*Wizardly Psyche Continuum Prayers

- These prayers are for the creation of your own psychic continuum.

*The Garden - Prestophoricalthiology i pray to the garden for inside this garden beauty, and in this beauty butterfly's, and in that garden flowers, and in this garden abundance, and in that abundance natural law, and in this natural law the love of creation, and in that love of creation the love of it through the one eternal light diviniorum artblessedyee.

*The Hill - Prestophoricalthiology i pray to the hill for on top of this hill the other side seen, and on this hill is perseverance, and in that perseverance persistence, and in this persistence perception of completion, and in that perception of completion the reaching of the other side through the one eternal light diviniorum artblessedyee.

*The Watchers - Prestophoricalthiology i pray to the watchers for their guidance, and in this guidance fascination, and in that fascination fantasy, and in this fantasy wonder, and in that wonder brilliance, and in this brilliancy accomplishment through the one eternal light diviniorum artblessedyee.

*The Fruit - Prestophoricalthiology i pray to the fruit for virility, and in this virility youthfulness, and in that youthfulness playfulness, and in this playfulness young at heart, and in that youthful heart well being through the one eternal light diviniorum artblessedyee.

*The Tree - Prestophoricalthiology i pray to the tree for it's inner knowledge, and in this inner knowledge inner strength, and in that inner strength endurance, and in this endurance stability, and in that stability proper balance, and in this proper balance beauty through the one eternal light diviniorum artblessedyee.

*The Crown - Prestophoricalthiology i pray to the crown for wisdom, and in this wisdom acceptance, and in that acceptance leadership, and in this leadership bravery, and in that bravery freedom, and in this freedom acknowledgement through the one eternal light diviniorum artblessedyee.

*The Bridge - Prestophoricalthiology i pray to the norse god heimdall whom guards the sacred rainbow bridge, I pray for your incredible insight, and in this incredible insight the love of all creation, and in that love of all creation splendor through the one eternal light diviniorum artblessedyee.

*The Path - Prestophoricalthiology i pray to Merlin for his incredible insight, and in this incredible insight incredible endurance, and in that incredible endurance incredible wisdom, and in this incredible wisdom the finding of knowledge on my path through the one eternal light diviniorum artblessedyee.

*The Sun Disk - Prestophoricalthiology i pray to the celtic sun god Belenus the keeper of the sun disk, I pray for vigilance, and in this vigilance completion, and in that completion accomplishment, and in this accomplishment procreation, and in that procreation endurance, and in this endurance the light through the one eternal light diviniorum artblessedyee.

*The Bell - Prestophoricalthiology i pray to the bell for an awakening, and in this awakening adornment, and in that adornment love, and in this love procreation, and in that procreation accomplishment, and in this accomplishment completion through the one eternal light diviniorum artblessedyee.

*The Way - Prestophoricalthiology i pray to the way for finding my path on this spiritual journey, and in that spiritual journey the celebration of life, and in this celebration of life a true quest, and in that true quest the love of it, and in this love of it the true path through the one eternal light diviniorum artblessedyee.

Wizeard Scriptures

...Fore with a monster finds solace a simple meaning that a beast feels more then angels could art bare in love... <u>Quote by: E.J.J.</u>

For thouest archuet before any lovist is before solstice, that art thy only knowledge to give with only beautiful the heart could too.

Love thine art for art thouest lives - for and thine of fain in poetry made of love yet still, ...not a question an still a maiden not as thy art she liveth my queen yet us of nether still felt a forever life...together holding hands.

For thou art before love is before a wizards love, thou art love thou art for art made of love. Thou made of art for art thou made of before creation thou made of the heart - art.

For thou before art is life, hast thou before forever life art loves.

Thou before a garden for thou art loved of creation not for grant.

Withou art with seed bearing fruit is before knowledge of the fruit - a garden beloved.

For thou art love be then art cherished by virtuous before wizards - a world of gardens before the heart.

For thou art self forgiving - a turning world of understanding.

For art before entirety hope an peace in entirety of creation withou life.

For art self forgiving is a divinorium yet a selfless humanly self known.

For art a cherishable entirety virtuious is 'the cosmic spirit wizard'.

For art a selfless peacefulness is a divination - thou art a humanly self.

For thou art before lore's is a humanly loved flower of art an knowledge.

For thou art greater the aloneness the lesser the life-quest to conquer with love yet if self forgiving - I art gifted to Heaven then so doeth art they o withou.

For art before dreams is celebration withowling the liveth. For art selfless wolves made more worth then men - have died more in vain then men.

For thou art nurtured more truthful - truer then held in love to judge not.

For art withou before a heart of truth is not yet burdened - not the love of a wizard art merely knows.

For art a wizard merely knows held in love that art nurtured to judge not.

For art is creation an creation unto life is us looked upon of not suffering but of love.

For art made of the heart art wisdom.

For art before love is before wizards - for art love thou art.

Thou art for art made of love - for art love thou art.

For art with solace given a child - the love of solace.

Love thou art for before love - 'thou art for art and thou made of.'

For thou art before love is our creation ever to learn not of sorrow's but of love.

For art a wizard abandoned then forewith who that has seen beauty undone by woe.

Not of creation yet for thou art acceptance then of rest in solstice is still those at sorrow's gates forgaven.

Judge not yet ye be lesser judged then saught not to learn from life a question yet art given who that has seen rest in solace?

For art before hope is then not broken but of silence to suffer is then not to live a question?

For art before harmony wizards to beast yet monsters of men lived more true a question?

Art which wizardries's could bare in love weighs already the love in a humanly heart - yet not a man that lived unto them?

Art beast as monsters even of men that've lived true - died then not to live with what they've learned?

And thou made of love, thou made of art for art thou made of.

For art wizardries's bare in love that they lived not burdened - though burdened a man then art beast as monsters even.

Art wizardries's that could bare in love though yet to feel a just heart taken and not broken - solace to beast?

For art burden not then the monster then at first how a monster?

Though to judge a monster that burdens is not to just the self to bare not acceptance that those haven't felt to lived true - then to worry not?

For art compassionate not of hate yet - but before solace thou yet only to hold those lost not compassionate is forgaven.

For art a world of madness brought not loved take upon themselves a angels tears that taught the lost - brought also seen in compassion is righteous, though unto themselves is madness forgaven?

For art forgotten lest merely-some knows madness - a heart forgotten not still in their hearts a heart forgaven to learn.

For thou art love thou art for art thou made of.

Thou made of art for art thou made not of acceptance?

For art thou true that's accepted yet lest thou yet feel sorrow that is true not also lost then not unto the forgotten?

For art withou a butterfly cherished not to die though a heart spritualy touched - art a wizards a world heavenly.

For art a cherished world we'ar 'art thou' in the heavens oceans above.

For art acceptance of another's understanding a smile to the heart yet 'art not' trespassers of another's understanding.

Heart-felt is a smile as a face upon the monsters in our own hearts - we take advantage of our own heart-felt truths.

For art not to destroy the self yet look up upon your own advantage of understanding.

For art not a monster of heart but of acceptance of heart-felt truth.

Love art wisdom for thou art loved, for art thou art for art thou for the hearts wisdom.

Art alone spent the time with hands dieing that though art loved in might that thou be lost not in sorrow spent alone - yet of love in memories like others.

Though art even in love we're lost but for thou art lost not without thine as flowers even miss us - a heart treasured withou a humanly loved heart.

For art remembrance of not sorrow yet of not sorrows nor the suffering of lives lived as each heart made not alone that bares virtue.

Thou art lived as like the blessing of the heart yet are treasured withou.

Art valley's in us for art like a blooming flower of love's remembrance.

For art sages of us we live as the heart not in fear - mayeth of us be not ghosts but then of gardens.

Art to nurture our hands as the chosen free for art thou learn free,

to nurture our hands unburdened then a truer nature of our hands with hope unburdened.

For art hate is bequieling yet wisdom bares not knowledge in hate so art thou then the love of wisdom then art bequieling?

For thou art made beautiful with feelings alone, not thou a heart made - yet not art in pain.

For art not alone with a cold sea of flowers but with arms to be held by not the unlost then the lost themselves to become truer not alone then dreams thou hast yet thou fall an we are not alone then?

For thou art yet a turning world itself - art a world yet turning round.

For art creation of life withou the sun art, not blind - grown to learn then.

Art not in sorrow of tears in fain, bring not tears of fain as a self gift yet the heart lov'ed peaceful.

A heart lost art unknown - felt the heart believe, not art confuscious.

Art a divinorium before creation a humanly self unto the greater of hearts - art more peaceful then men.

Heart-gifted before love is divine in giftedness to bloom as art understanding is.

Not art another's understanding yet truer self understanding.

Wizardries's art love of smiles not in naïve or jadedness, art live with wizardries's tears not in vain.

Love art worlds made of, what worlds are made of - art another's love.

Yet art she or he bequieling in love - is but dreams to live for one another ye ought' though not a failure, only a seeker that history repeats itself like others.

Though alone a maker of art - a failure maker, not art in vain in aloneness yet if alone then ought' ye alone not alone.

Ye art of dreams in history that repeats itself - yet a seed of truth a flowers bloom.

Ye art alone not a failure art in love a giving fall not bequieled yet art human.

Art unto which the heart touched in beauty yet not untrue but of forgiveness a man then not in beauty?

Forgiveness though is the heart spiritualy touched ought' not confused - as the heart is belief.

Acceptance, that've ought' art.

For thou art even forgotten being loved yet unto that've ought' taught the lost, ye of a world unto self forgaven a world of madness brought also not loved - art merely not 'I'm forgotten' but me of a world also brought not loved unto the lost.

Art monsters of men art beast as monsters even - so art thou even a man with meaning of life suffer to judge not another simple meaning.

For art thou truer held in love are those still not abandoned ye ought' passed lost then hope in the love of wizards.

Ought' ye that've withou we'ar lov'ed art unto thouest a liv'ed divinorium.---- art love.

Aught' thee with being held in love then art held not alone abandoned yet ye ought' burden then not or then burdens.

Ye ought' flowers of fall art lov'ed oath'ed in rain, still'n ye art bloomed in love so art their petals aren't for grant found by love with the liv'ed.

Of solace art wizardries's sing found by love - they walk with flowers so they're petals aren't for grant to themselves falling in love.

So art we aren't grant to ourself's then us found by love - a heart founded from love.

Ought' ye that've withowling liv'ed we'ar art archuet ye divinorium lov'ed aught' thouest withou lovist thine.

As a heart is found by love, to have it not grant to it's petals again - love is lost cause love was found.

Art a humanly loved heart a guardian of loves remembrance.

Made not alone wit hatted then a bequile ought' ye though a virteous man then suffering of the heart made not alone - ye aught' love again?

Ye known art changes the heart made not alone then remembrance the heart had taken, so art to not compaseth our hearts being unwound with love again - then not the eyes of madness upon virtues then a flowers bloom we'ar near truer dreams to come.

Art thou meant alive to dream ought' alive - they that see virtue is in another's eyes a silloete which love comes.

Ye through which love comes - of voices from a garden, then not a garden showered on from the tears of wizards, a silloete garden.

Though falling like a petal of a flower from a silloette garden then truer in hope, yet truer a struggle in their hearts in love more then death.

Art not the spirit in wilt of a lifetime the speed of pain - ye for each a lifetime of simple gestures then wisdom for art made of the heart then.

Ye ought' a sea of flowers in gestures, for the love of wisdom art felt the heart believe - then felt knowledge of the heart not in hate.

For thou art to bless beauty in life - a heart, ye aught' beauty in life with love and harmony, a heart believes with time then.

Art a heart forgaven to bless beauty in life then us treasured unburdened yet not blind.

A heart unburdened but bequieled burdened yet not blind then not in fear of ye treasured by sages of another's love is yet an unknown fear.

Fighting away someone's fears, being afraid, being sorry dieing knowing to hold the others hand destroys only a garden of paper flowers.

Be self forgiving from never talking against yourself in your head, be not then the influence jaded or naïve - as art the causes of happiness to know to forgive.

As belov'ed solace thy hearts kingdom still yet of love, rest, or death. ….

as belov'ed thy heart loved, ought' love thy heart for art thy heart a belov'ed, love thy heart - for art belov'ed the heart.

'Art not' when not ourself's ye even ought' lost-felt art love not crave then we not blame ourselves then aught' yet us found in our hearts.

For withou art before love as the lonliest emotion is before solace's mystical eve's still, and art merry with goddesses of song.

For thou art before love is before wizards in thou art love before thee eternal divinity.

Art love, made of love my heart being in mysteriorum of art made - creation.

Art love, yet of art are we made of love - art love.

We've become a mystery of the naked an belov'ed before truer unity is before thee eternal law of mysterious - art love.

Eerily art such love then made of love thou art haven's art magic.

Love creeply thy heart for the heart art eerily love of two even hearts art us then we the heart.

Love art encouragement then also not crave not to self yet a elden merry heart to love the heart is divine.

Creepily when life is loved most is loved most when we're not real monsters then but of monsters we're not then - art love.

Ourselves gifted 'loving of life' art heart a merry may of worlds and thy one.

For the heart worships the gifts of the self gift of love - then not so we'd be living ever after yet a heart will treasure an isle on an on.

Of not art solace falling in the wind like a petal then ye art withou not each petal from the heart art not wilt yet art solace falling in the wind unto a flower then each petal that fall a flower.

Not tears that fall either a simple gesture for art in love then lost.

Ye not tears that fall either a simple meaning that thine and thouest truer a struggle thou's spirit not wilt in their hearts more then death their hearts love more then death, for art then a eon the speed of pain in love.

A sleeping dream ought' drempt that ye fore withou eternal light above us neither in darkness, thee a kingdom of light blessed therewith truer art of not struggles in men is heaven.

Art where dreams fall in love - whence dreams fell in love, art virtues still seen upon a world not lost of dreams.

Together made not forgotten art where dreams fall in love is an artist truer near a sea of dreams.

For a petal from a flower lost one simple meaning in a silloette.

Art not simple the self then not simple themselves - even then after a struggle then a leader twice a leader unfair.

We are love then truer even after even after our way to grow then is not in fear if learning to grow then.

For art everything not the same as 1 even 2 the same as natural life formed the difference alone.

A heart not of war a leader gifted - though ye ought' a heart not of war thou a leader unknown gifted a healer twice a healer then.

Take grant not a healer twice a healer art not a monster for ought' twice a healer not a monster a leader then gifted in the heart of not war.

Aught' a selfless self though held made truer art those selfless of love held then made truer a selfless self.

Ought' made fore with our likeness as with pollin feel so in love of a flower.

Art given centuries of creation withou self forgivence yet ye the likeness as like of rain falling, a flower blooming, & mist falling upward in spirit.

For art sea's of pollin fall to land withou the sun art & standing life not burdened by their own, though ought' sea's of pollin fall to land thouwith the sun to bare it's rays giving light.

Wizards - a sea of love vast in light, a simple vast of creation in fury which created increments & sacraments for art the creation of pollination.

Bring unto a heaven a more sacred balance for mankind to live and it was.

Butterfly's are admist vast & saught that take not grant creation and merely quest an seek amongst solace's flowers in entirety then.

For art many bliss of wizardries's that grant creation in life embraced an withou not sorrow's embraced because of the butterfly - a virtueous made creature.

Flowers were now life flowers giving grant to creation of pollination's entirety.

The learning of a heart in a wizard had hav'en so art her a bliss true of being an a wizardries's of gardens.

To love thy heart for solace's heart art belov'ed.

Solace art inspiration to find the love in a heart - let acceptance reign ought' the balance of beauty then.

A wizards art garden of hearts is heart-felt truth - that've lov'ed with oath'ed belovedness, ye art wizards a divinorium.

Wizards thy art beloved theest a heed withou ye ought' archuet that've usly wrighthe still, we are oath'ed arc ye.

Wizards art a self humanist gifted heart that've unknown lov'ed beautiful, theest thy heart beateth of wrighthe a belov'ed usly - art thy heart beateth of wrighthe arc theest a belov'ed usly, ye ought' Solace withou art.

Wizards as a self gift wit howling usly, yet ought' with Solace withou art a self gift withowling the heed of blind flock.

Wizards art the love a garden beloved art merely-some knows arc anothers heart grown to learn then is.

Solace with well-wisdom has destiny, ye aught' a world then of wisdom from the heart then art virtue a better guidance then.

A wizard, a blessed righteous with guidance and wisdom - art self reliance taught to the hearts of all with well-wisdom.

Wizards in non-resentment has stable inner strength - pro-creativeness art a blessing in wisdom of self courage, peaceful courage.

A wizard forgives himself with the love of self-forgineness, ye aught' theest unknown - ye arc the heralds sing in glory for us.

Wizardry oath'ed with the tears of nature yet belov'ed arc the heralds in wrighthe for withiest - as the heed are lov'ist to the wit howling of men.

Solace knowledge of the heart with love is eternal, ye ought' the heralds of evil destroyed by the reaction of love that givith - harboring not as like a inner child vast with wisdom in spiritedness.

Art emotions as feelings even vast with love & liberation - so art wisdom blessed by the reaction of love that've withou oath'ed archuet by thy art wrighthe in thy lov'ed.

Mysteriorum art withiest ought'ed in wrighthe that a lovist a divinorium thy arc - Withou beloved usly wrighthe not wit-howling unto the lost.

Art a wizards garden thou art a humanly loved self before the cherished virtue of flowers.

Free-spiritedness ought' guidance yet wisdom of the heart to understand is wisdom blessed.

Love in acceptance is beauty - beauty then the guidance & wisdom.

Headstrong compassion for inner wisdom is friendship, ye aught' wisdom as headstrong compassion then seen not of ignorandi.

Compassion is friendship not lost as truer a world nurtured before all hearts is headstrong, ye ought' beloved oathed in the arc of theest free.

Art ye ought' a heart grown to learn then thou art merely-some knows - yet ye art a self of divinity, ye ought' love again.

A heart not art in confuscious is humanly, ye a unique understanding of acceptance in the way of understanding, art human.

Usly art withiest archuet that've a divinorium that ye thouest art thy theest, yet of art heralding heed in wrighthe before the eeb.

Wit-hatted aught' art yet art not, withouest then a mere theest oath'ed with usly wit-hatted - a lonesome divination.

Love art wisdom, for art love thou art - before the hearts wisdom, for art withiest heed love.

Ye thouest withhowling archuet art, art thy lovist that've divinorium thouest art heed heralds, as heralds arc beloved we'ar art ought' thouest

With thinest wrighthing self forgivence with eeb - usly thy heralds a heralds wit-hatted or self forgaven with self love.

Art livith a divinorium harmonious is righteous through the eeb of faith's encouragement - art the heart a fantasy story then, or wisdom to encouragement.

Greater remembrances - accomplishments.

A memorable person a alli, ye aught' a greater memorable that've haven a broken heart unmutable - art a divinorium to the peace of remembrance.

A isle of eebs wit-hatted heeds wrighthing usly heralding withiest arc theest oath'ed as thy art beloved we'ar that've lovist archuet thouest

Ye a divination withowling withou lov'ed saught ought.'

Cherishable before creation a virtue among wizards before knowledge thou made of the heart- art.

Attaining hope is precious as hopelessly the need to rather not pass-away - attaining spiritual guidance is desirable so may free the hopeless not into the lost.

Spiritual destiny with prosperity is abundant, ye ought' self love to endure first before the love of wizardry.

Whom we're meant to be is cosmic wisdom, the beauty in goodness, beauty, and truth - also beauty whom we're meant to be.

A heart broken, a many of efforts to get understanding, then ought' feel self forgiven unto others - be a heart then not broken in vain.

For thouest art beloved to have divine inspiration, ye aught' through the one eternal light that is cosmic with inner strengh - strength & celebrative compassion.

Free-spirited are the unhurt or an the lost, as yourself's trust is the emotions to feel for more-so lov'ed memories.

Art not abandoned in memories, art not truth of 'art not' before tresspassers - a willing in interpret must be put forth of endearment.

Encourage in forgiveness is the same respect of the one eternal light.

Communication is compassion, encouraging to heal the deepest wounds found in virtue of compassion.

The limited self to the eternal self, eternal self through the one eternal light is ecouragement to heal forgivence.

Humble thou art love - purity my thoughts of truthfulness, compassion my kindness.

Appreciate the beauty of love then beauty may you teach me, whom I am meant to be - peace in the order of the virtues.

Knowledge of the stars inspire peace, as in inspiring peace in the order of my virtues - a rainbow sun.

Knowledge of the stars are teachings to the peaceful whom yet divine a plan for me.

Acceptance is from what your learned willingly as though from a broken heart - art virtuous meant to be.

Guiding my courage to desire the understanding to hear others feelings, art inner strength ought' inner strength of balance.

Love of forgiveiness is memorable of eternal love given so art the understanding of peoples encouragement with selfless love - an awakening to enlightenment.

So that thou's true self has conquored feelings that compassion is truer enlightenment.

Ye, a ethical inner peace guide me to over come good intensions to seek ye's inner wisdom.

To stay yound at heart is compassion through your unconditional forgiveness for spiritual well-being.

Compassion for inspiriing inner strength in unconditional forgiveness.

May redeem me, as a eternal light of spirit angels - cosmic spirit harmony.

Guidance on inspiring my inner strength a unconsciounal forgiveness.

May redeem me from help in every day life over those who dwellith like me - a desire young at heart to finish libiration.

Purpose in life is the spirit of kindly hym. . . though the love would surround me I hither with mine of love in nature.

Being helped in achievment as well to open desirable teachings.

The ridding of selfish questions with guiding light is that everything happens with fate.

Firmament, eternal honor, & hope are the trinity of great wisdom - so that through your encouragement optimism.

Unconditional forgiveness is the inspiration ought' by clairvoyance in the encouragement of truthful communication.

Faith of respect - is unconditional forgivence unto a soul.

Good logic & high initiative is good for creative aspirations.

Art livieth a healthier communication that is passage of creativity in usly -

this creativity is the one eternal.

Fostering love, justice, & truth is the bequieling of madness if not felt-love of the heart - the heart conquors more then the beguiling if faithful.

Encouragment to awakening an enlightenment is courage fallowed by inspiration.

And awakening the memory of eternal love haven a limitless of self forgivence to another.

Various levels of truth, guidance in helping usly receive inspiration - truthful communication then.

Encouragement of truthful communication is indipendent comunication.

That've archuet generous thought's of truth art a divinorium of peace.

Art matterable concepts of trust then theest arc usly wittings of a hatter.

Withhowling a way through sensations of passion a divinorium wit-howling.

Thy a cause of imaginative clarity haven a hither beloved arc.

Ought' withiest reasonable ideas of communication then thou'ed oath'ed in woe that've we'ar beloved.

Lov'ed peaceful notions of completion for art purposeful as ye aught' are

then.

Haven an optimistic reverence of prayer is a hither of divinities still'n of woe withou.

Born of noble birth art sylphs ye though undines art free born and man & woman born again in self as usly thy self born.

Art ye spiritual in revelations of the self that've experience usly aware of natures relativity arc beloved of aspiring courage aught' hithered experienced of the aware.

Haven confidence of knowledge selfishly art human ye ought' though to conquor sacred value knowledge selfless a question.

Of universal contemplation withouest usly we'ar wrighthing esential free choice theest a individual raising in confidence to make usly equal in quality.

Art thou determination of confidence in experiencing the aware in universal contimplation is ye ascending for providial passion & individuality.

Convincing the heart in us is seeing intuitively that which art the capacity to percieve completion.

Withowling thy prosperities happiness is devotional in the essential withou considering aught' ye oath'ed devotional form of hithering in the act of revealing the act of self healing.

Contentment withou a form of concentration thriving then ought' ye invokust of divine care to self as haven understanding theest.

Apprehending happiness ought' that've a arc thiest heed a comprehended alliance thouest giving strength imbetween to become mutual ye aught' then a state trustworthy to hither.

A regard to loving aspirations ye lov'ed of adornment ye though art archuet a haven theest heed to self a compassionate certainty a question.

Theest hither a state of being certain haven kindly hym... aught' rediscover the liking to fondness ye art that've woe unto the intangible universe is then theest a divinorium oath'ed of kindness braught a question.

Expressing privilage to aspect divine encouragement that've ye purposeful we'ar theest arched usly a question.

Woe the supremely good for art hither aspirations dynamic irresistible towards continualy learning uplifted a question.

Fasination is the feeltness of belief hither promises to the self hearted individual so art withiest ye ingenious a question.

Withowling development of concentration thy abundency forseen abundantly development encouragement of thy abundency fruitful a question.

Self fulfillment is likely for the encouragement causing beloved joy withou & withiest a possessive glory unto they're hearts learning.

Oath'ed unto theest a arc possessing glory art yet that've not wit-hatted but only beloved contentment.

Joy & the expression of it art still'n ye a beloved oath'ed with heralds in wrighthe not bequiling usly art virtuous though and thou'ed compassionate.

Sentimental consideration of the human heart is the love of the humanly heart not in heed of the wit-hatted.

Art a generosity of art inspiring then helpful in resemblance of approval then unto the one divine light may nature then assertive confidence in usly.

Art a cosmic spirit of the angel sun as assertive of nature of confidence mayeth attain well-strong desire in resemblance of quality as ye art approval of skilled inthusiasm for withou teachings & guidance.

Devotion to love is affectionate & warmhearted to have a strong affectionate warm-hearted devotion towards natures magic.

Nature ought' assertive confidence thy is well with the best resemblemance & quality through the one eternal light.

Helpin us imply trustworthiness art usly fairness of adherence to the rainbow sun.

Art better integrity & wholesomeness outh'ed thy integrity through idealism in the one eternal light ye ought' standered ideals.

Warm-heartedness a vivid effect of curious givings impressioned by deep influence unselfishly.

Art for affection for another hither tenderness warm hearted means which hither harmonious tender love a question.

Art impression by a deeply influence ye proper a haven that've spiritual.

Art a deeply influence of warm heartedness arc spiritual abundence be for art thine or thouest we'ar independent each.

Understanding truth convincing then the act and result of art seeing intuity.

Art a spiritual like mystical awareness is aught' by belov'ed art compassionate.

Withouest of awareness an wise ould' rediscover hidden knowledge.

An art an interest in discovering art in knowledge then exciding & desired.

*Ye cosmic spirit of the rainbow sun lovist compassion aught' spiritual strength wherein haven thouest & withiest is harmony usly compassionate.

Theest essence of compassion that've which all is the flow through the eeb & beloved ever withowling simple limitless passion hithering the trust of light withouest love which continualy arched withou trust of light.

Woe greater the principle of trust still'n wherein passion art a simpleness of form ould' extend & connect a beings presence theest of the simplest heed of forces.

For art platonic love being a divinorium in reality is a principle of limitless energy manifesting usly not wit-hatted in theest a passionate reality of truth in who we are.

Theest trust comes an awakening of the essence & presence of truth art thou our creater the simpleness wrighting in form.

Completion which'ed extends passionate energy in art withouest simplest forms with heed then theest the heralds a isle.

Natural exchange of truth hither conclusions in the essence of love itself.

Simplest completion of knowledge woe's passion as a greater sence of wisdom & heed.

A passionate self-healing in our greater of self art hither ourselves greater a self of truth.

A greater self of truth - a one eternal light.

The noumenon belief arc extraordinary as archuet the supernatural force of powers in natural forces.

Theest inspiration of natural forces art conceptual impressions to judge tentatively before then the eeb that've we'ar nature to produce the unbelief as art being human.

We are with'of a heart bettering our world free-spirited to overcome oath'ed through guidance.

That've we'ar beloved - art thy ougth'ed wherein theest & arc withouest heralding usly in wrighthe of heed wit-hatted withiest ought' aught' lov'ed withou withhowling divinoriums that've ye thouest archuet a lovist an eeb of an isle thou'ed which'ed ould' hither a haven still'n of woe gotten.

Of the heart the love of a wizards wisdom for love art thou as thou made of, thou made of art for art thou loved.

We'ar virtuous made creatures not art in pain then a humanly loved self, a world of heavenly art a heart then found by love. A world of gardens before the heart treasured then a humanly loved heart.

Art made of mysterious, art love - made of love my heart art creation.

Art livith life a journey man that've loveth be, peace unto us in spirit.

Of thy loveth be for withou art before solace herself arc the heralds of solumness, still yet belov'ed our own hearts kingdom of still song, dance, & feast.

As thy heart art liveth so yet a being of art the life that death has no dominion.

As the blessed for art made of life a truer heart yet not blind yet not a fool before the gift of self love.

Ought' yet of art are we made of, is that've wizards before thee eternal law of mysteriorum that haven usly, art love.

*Thouwith self confidence led to wisdom that've liveth hope in triumph.

Which'ed keeness of wisdom leads to a belov'ed destiny hast wisdom the encouragement towards destiny.

Withou vigilence & proper balance - hope, triumph, & bravery.

Which'ed hope arched in bravery a vigilent accomplishment.

Lest hope that passion is clarity thence completion of knowledge mysteriorum arched within hope is belov'ed.

Courage thouest in friendship hast eternal ye thou art which'ed an empowered withowling bless'ed.

A light kingdom of peace leads the blind thouwith a blind man hast know peace to this kingdom that've lov'ed thence art to heal the sick a question.

Hither art with skilled hands withence clarity of insight oath'ed wearing a mask of revelaence thence insightful.

A wizards inner empowerment is thouest a celestial dream writhin in flame of the soul, lest liveth through the flow & eeb with hope.

Aught' self confidence in the willing empowerment which'ed hope in the serence knowledge of learning thence ought' be good inspiration towards self reliance.

Relianc'ed knowledge with dexterity of craft art which'ed masterfulness thence art ye a belov'ed capability to be controlled from self reliance.

Hope that serenity is thence wisdom for art sence & understanding fallow.

Compassion, goodness, & destiny art that've keeness in fairness towards the self thence ought' that we'ar a understanding charmed one.

Mysteriourum within courage & fairness art a understanding charm ye ought' thouwith worthiness to fairness in devotion.

Adornment & devotion art prosperous thence lest prosperous be for art thence devotion towards one's abundence bless'ed.

Liveth destiny in galentry is a journeyman's friendship in loyalty.

Confidence reflected in friendship art serence in reflectiveness of consitration thencewith art that've belov'ed reflectiveness of one's own heart.

Bright prospects in reflectiveness in friendship art thouwith lov'ed through the one eternal light.

The stars for hope art destiny's insight may mysteriourm reflect in agility towards a satisfied reliability of self as a wizard or wizardrie's.

Through fullfillment inner strength serene significant influence through the one eternal light.

Development of fruitfulness thencewith contentment of warm-hearted aspirations arched thence capability of fullfillment.

Significant affection is the ensurance towards success with inner strength fullfillement.

Evelopement in fruitfulness serene action we'ar development which'ed

Communication belov'ed is assurance in serenity & friendship.

Reasonable trust withou confidence is virtuous honor in self reliance ye though hencewith confidence trust.

Relianc'ed reasonableness is proper balance forwith a wizard thy trust brings the proper balance of harmony to feel complete.

Haven beauty in the attraction of trust-felt balance thence unto reasonable proper balance theest advice thence righteous virtue.

Haven belov'ed mysteriorum good influence within considerastion of the heralds beloved with your compromise withou ajustment acceptance.

Determination in hope of natures magic art the beauty of creation the empowering of healing the self art love the divine spirit of hope then.

Freedom of fascination which'ed a imps insight thence art mysteriorum

beyond insight.

Freedom of the imaginasion thy are heed towards the completion of one's self ye thencewith lest belov'ed

The mayest empowerment of the loving spirit withiest inner wisdom is lovist divine.

*Divine the truth of all life for the cosmic spirit angelus's of the rainbow sun for art thouest & thinest divine with the eternal's - lunaris moon and rainbow sun.

A diviniorum awakening in the eternal's love art arc the encouragement of memory in the eternal's love.

Thouest & Thinest awaken the memory of eternal love aught' theest & usly compassionate in the absolutions of divinity between lunaris moon and rainbow sun alike.

Encouragement to awakening is a heralds of truth in life's truth & nature's magic.

Relianc'ed of a journey-man could be a spiritual destiny of truth in all life & natures magic - ye ought' thinest & thouest haven manifestation of guidance, proper balance, & visionary wisdom then & nor-so teachings which'ed art unknown - still a humanly wizard & wizardrie's.

Fostering love, truth, & joy withence divinity granted by wisdom from lunaris moon and rainbow sun art divine in encouragement to usly.

Allowing truth to overcome ye ought' trust to thunder birds also art spiritual angelus's that've understanding various levels of truth.

A higher mental independence through a warm-heart art art thinest & thouest guidance be.

Cleansing of negativity heralds in usly retrieving insights towards diviniorum, trust in loving-kindness a greater self of truth, & unity withence the self.

A strengthened spirit through the one eternal light art healing in truth, patience, and love in usly with hope in truer unity in self relianc'ed.

Serence relianc'ed in theest & withiest art with hencewith understanding is usly & thy of understanding in healing the humanly heart - art relianc'ed through the one eternal light.

Truthful communication of the one eternal light if fain with clairvoyance then art hencewith clairvoyance in the inspiration in the gift of self love that've harmonized truth.

Nor-so unconditional forgiveness is truthful communication through humanistic responsibility & humanistic quality's in usly equal to the divine.

A spiritual destiny in the truth of all life is truthful communication towards the divine light & the eternal's in blessings.

A Dininiorum of light is pollinessence towards a individual with peaceful courage.

Remembrance of my spiritual destiny is a self gift of love divine in protecting usly art's individuality for spiritual destiny of truth.

The self gift of love, courage, & individuality art the ability of finding wisdom unburdened.

Express my true self within thence-with the devotion of wisdom that've falows art of wrighthe in fulfillement, firmament, and wisdom thencewithence thinest & thouest lov'ed peace & hearts forged in truth's in empowerment for divine happyness & inspiration.

Whitch'ed thouwith withowling through the eeb & flow art that've belov'ed ought' saught already the arched withence mysteriousliorum aught' still lov'ed & withiest an withouest art a diviniorum henceforth mayest find compassion in the deepest of acceptance.

Nor-so the witt-hatted ask for self forgiveness so art oath'ed bequieling in their encouragement for self forgiveness.

Finding compassion for communication art the deepest feeling for encouraging in forgiveness ye art the heralds mayest transfer our limited self to the eternal's self's because of virtue - which'ed theest and usly encouragement to heal.

Granting the gift of an open heart thinest & thouest therewith art nor-so the empowerment to overcome with relianc'ed towards usly the self hope.

*Lest encourageful our abilities in rekindling the artistic fires in our mortal hearts - thy usly our self giftedness belov'ed withence our self gift.

A spirit cleansed in the light of understanding a self gift - allow this truth to become clairvoyant & relianc'ed.

Arched in unconditional forgiveness hence with encouragement hencewith clairvoyance in encouragement we'ar withence usly in theest in belov'ed learning.

Through our self gift within truth lyes a belov'ed heralds in heed towards our mortal heart's self gift of trust - to relianc'ed truthful communication.

Which'ed the expression of our true self is rebianc'ed to instill wisdom withou serence in mysteriourum to be healed.

Hencewith open-heartedness thence is integrity towards liberation towards harmony in understanding our truer self in courage - peaceful courage then.

Thinnest & thouest arc an awakening thence the rainbow sun grant us the self gift of an open heart which'ed our inner-empowerment to overcome understanding to awakening.

That've instilled wisdom to heal art a truth in inspiration that our spirits are absolute.

Serence through mind, heart, and spirit shows the gifts of truthful communication in showing the love within our hearts gift.

Inner strength, compassion, & encouragement as a journeyman through life that've the one eternal light watch over us, protecting.

Ould' blessings in obella art rebianc'ed withen the one eternal that've art serence tranquility for the rainbow sun - art rebianc'ed in lightheartedness.

Hencewith clarity a heart in love of the spirit through a wizards or wizardries knowledge - art guiding strength we find the empowerment to be healed through the one eternal.

Livith in the gift of caring art rebianc'ed art theest an eternal love, a gift.

Thencewith divine spiritual awareness - the love of the divine spirit.

In the awareness the knowledge of the righteous of things & in that belov'ed and in that belov'ed goodness the love of it.

Beauty, goodness, & truth is the becoming of who we are in the love of creation.

Withowling ourselve's our physical eithics of universal - arched with the cosmic spirit wizard art that've learning our eternal self mysteriorum of life, mysteriorum in life of producing all forthcoming things ye thouest a spirit angel - art hast meant to be in learning a quest of truth.

Liveth the cosmic spirit universal of thouest prayers withence clarity of thought mysteriorum.

Henceforth through your quest of truth a universal merging serence with the one eternal light art that've life liveth a quest in who we are.

Archuet, the truth of the love of all creation art belov'ed which'ed the cosmic spirit angelus arched in our quest for truth hencewith merging with the absolutions of ourselves.

Art understanding withence universal merging lest the unconditional forgiveness withence who we are in indipendence.

A well-being of knowledge we'ar inspired & bless'ed hencewith wisdom towards encouragement.

To love more then death is eternal life ye art though the loneliest emotion is suicide by nature.

Bless'ed us with deep inner wisdom forwith the love in our hearts to find our life's purpose encourageful.

The rainbow sun, hope, & cosmic solace art with spiritual hope arched ye for art usly us having guidance & relianc'ed influence that instils truth & compassion forwith our hearts to prosper.

Withence companionship rekindling our hearts fire grants hidden truths.

Thouest wisdom that'of which'ed vast knowledge blessed knowledge.

Art holy the cosmic spirit rainbow sun an lunaris moon as wisdom for saught an found from love is they.

The the lordess an lord art wisdom of the heart found from love then thouest the cosmic spirit rainbow sun an lunaris moon saught love for thou art.

Thou an thine art theest of the cosmic spirit rainbow sun an lunaris moon unto us from the heed found from love ye that've ought' saught they in thou an thine art loved unto the lov'ed aught' found from love again.

To this world the cosmic spirit sun an lunaris moon art both the one eternal light unto a divination - it's petals aren't for grant then when shined upon.

Founded art they the cosmic spirit rainbow sun & lunaris moon with usly as thou & thine art not for grant lov'ed unto the lost ought' found from love again thouest & thinest artist art in the heavens that've theest both ye aught' and found from love again through us which'ed & of wisdom an found from they.

Withiest & withiest a diviniorum ought' thee world from the cosmic spirit rainbow sun & lunaris moon which'ed aught' lov'ed in our hearts with both as the one eternal that've love in our hearts art lov'ed to be founded by them both.

Lest ye that've rehanc'ed thencewith the lord with'ed a isle & ebb of theest both that've we'ar belov'ed unto thence.

For thou art the rainbow sun art lunaris moon, that've thee cosmic spirit wizard theest - the three as art the cosmic spirit light of divinity, the cosmic spirit light wizeard, & the cosmic spirit light wizard of divinity - art divinity, creation, and wholeness.

Love self forgivence as not anger to self is to become then blessed with beauty in life, art not against the self - be not naïve or jaded for sacraments as to know only the causes of happiness alone.

To not destroy your own advantage ye upon your own understanding is

Your advantage. We're virtuous made creatures with a relationship with belief. As to look up upon our own advantage of understanding , arc the harolds of heart giftedness of the cosmic rainbow sun then thou art.

Thou art warmheartedness arc spiritual abundance be.

Withouest usly we'ar theest an individual to make usly equal in equality.

The heart art made of thou, ye art we made from love.

My heart mysterious before love - as the heart is creation.

Ye art lov'ed withou that've a divinorium we'ar ought' love.

Felt-love truth as a garden of us belov'ed in merely art.

We are each a made creature again virtious in love yet we'ar those not art in pain by the cosmic spirit.

A relationship with the heart is belief. To be heavenly art most cherished as aught' a dininorium most peaceful to men.

Art thouest peaceful - thou art compassionate found from love as the love in memories.

Feltness of the heart believing art confuscious though a relationship with the heart is belief.

A world of gardens before the heart - ye of a flowers bloom virtious is the cherished like a treasured isle.

A flower is the humanly loved heart, before love is before the heart in love.

Ye before ought' the heart then made with love withou before a hearts wisdom - for art love then thou art.

Love, maiden of solace as a heart before wisdom before the heart made of love, wisdom thou art then.

Acceptance, that've ought' art.

Forgiveness, that've ought' art.

Spiritualy Touched that've ought' art.

Understanding that've ought' art.

Love the heart for it is art in wisdom as belief is the heart before the mind yet belief is made with the hearts wisdom and before the heart is also made of freedoms from the mind ye a unique understanding of acceptance in the way of understanding, art human.

To live before hope are they that've not broken for seen in the rest of solcace, though rest in solstice still at sorrows gates forgaven.

Abandoned with Solace may creation ever to learn.

The heart art wisdom yet nurtured to judge not seen in beauty.

Love thou art before judgement & before love all forgotten in mist.

Forwith who that has that could bare harmony that've acceptance reign in the rest of solace.

Unto life is usly burdened yet upon suffering thou art solace art made of love.

Wizards to beast forgaven for art before hope not abandoned being with solace a wizard not abandoned - for art love thou art.

Braught not loved yet a heart forgiven yet only art thou made of acceptance.

But of acceptance a heart+felt truth is but of acceptance of the heart.

A heart treasured not alone are not sorrows nor the suffering of lives lived in compassion.

Dequiling art the chosen free for non haven's -belief like a blooming flower baring virtue that's lost withou a humanly loved heart.

Not in fear that wisdom bares not knowledge yet wisdom bares not hate of the heart nor the suffering of lives lived.

Giftedness to bloom art immaculate that love is divine yet a peaceful without naive or jadedness.

*7 Wizardry Prayers Of Peace

1. I pray to my 'Wisdom Star Of Wizardry' to thank you for myself receiving universal enlightenment so I felt like a true warrior as with guiding me on my spiritual birthright direction as through your cosmic wisdom I may find myself at peace, blessed be the love, the light, & beauty in goodness, beauty, an truth blessed art be.

2. I pray to my 'Excellent Wisdom Star Wizard' to thank you for myself receiving blessed love every day to me in my world as from your help which platonic omnibelevelance I may know more of harmonious abundentcy as with through your wisdom inspiration comes, peace be with you, blessed be friendliness.

3. I pray to my 'Excellent Spirit Wisdom Wizard Of Joy' to thank you for myself receiving to stay focused on optimistic virtueism as with through your wisdom the righteous way of helping me relinquish my darker memories as with myself in this humble prayer thanking your loving kindness in guiding me, blessed be natural decisions freely made in luck & peace be with you.

4. I pray to my 'Cosmic Spirit Wizardress Of Galactic Wisdom' to thank you for myself receiving my senses opened to the possibilities of love around my world as with through your wisdom I may find the balance of my loving kindness in sharing as with caring in that I become more free+spirited, through the love of the divine eternal, peace be with you, blessed be.

5. I pray to my 'Virtuous Wisdom Star' to thank you for myself receiving more my senses opened to the beauty of my world as with myself to learn more in becoming one with nature as with it's giving energy as through your wisdom I've seen inwardly to the beauty of earth, with simple answers in friendliness, peace be with you, blessed be.

6. I pray to my 'Wizardress Of Emotional Bonding' to thank you for putting me on a more righteous path for myself's virility & youthfulness as with through your wisdom 'ever growing love' as that peace be with you my wizardress star, blessed be.

7. I pray to my 'Cosmic Saint Angelus Of The Light' to thank you for me receiving more platonic love in friendship as through your wisdom may I be in wonder an wonderful with intensions, peace be with you.

*A Knowledge Prayer

I pray to 'Master my Knowledge' the cosmic spirit angel of the rainbow sun for the universal spoken essence of the higher mental and the all knowing seeing eye of conscious self image for the spiritual temporal whole of the spoken essence of the universe and physical reality by ubiquitously present everywhere simultaneously, to bring the ovious to the eye an mind of me having total knowledge without alike or equal so I will be capable of enduring all things by bringing forth all producing things as one not doubted yet genuine by the noticeable courageously resolute of the capability in transmitting and receiving from my halo in all directions as well I'm not influenced or changed but only a mindful worth of remembering a unique violation of good taste through the one eternal light blessed be.

A Prayer For Erick

I pray to 'A Cosmic Wizard' for you to teach Erick Sven Tieman to realize the beauty of creation that he is and make him understand that he is eternal whether he likes it or not and that his wisdom is mystical so that he realizes the purification and self revelation that he is and for him to understand that he is more of a genius then what he seems in that through your sacred knowledge Erick Sven Tieman should feel like the miracle that he is through the one eternal light blessed be, so mote it be.

*Quote From Erick - 'Art liveth life, loveth be, and peace unto you with Hallowmas spirit as beloved thy heart loved, love thy heart of all hallows eve for art thy heart - for art beloved the heart and for thine or an thou art before love of Hallowmas is before winter solace for thouest art before Solace is before thee eternal law of mysteriorum - art love.'

*Arivel's Prayer

I pray to Arivel the cosmic spirit angel of the rainbow sun for the universal spoken essence of the higher mental and the all knowing seeing eye of conscious self image for the reason and understanding of a perceptible real through the full awareness in the significance of the worth to admire highly and connotes sufficient implification of implying a deep love in high estimation of excellence and an excess of considering worth in the capability of realization of the substantial real to make me noble and the promote of self actualization that influences going beyond the extent of the exceptional usual as well to set me free from obligation for a necessary reasoned judgment for the act of concluding to the state of being intellectualy enlightened by spiritual luminous with the quality of something of the power to be in the state of fascination through the one eternal light blessed be.

*Cupid's Prayer

I pray to Cupid the cosmic spirit angel of the rainbow sun for compassion and in this compassion spiritual strength wherein harmony is the essence of compassion from which all is the flow through the ebb an evermore the simple, limitless, and passion in which comes the trust of light with love which continually is greater as the principle of trust wherein passion of it's simpleness of form that extends and connects a being's presence from the simpless of forces, for platonic love being a reality and the limitless energy of a principle in manifesting a passionate reality of truth in who we are, from trust comes an awakening of the essence and presence of truth, our creator the simpleness of form - the completion which extends passionate energy in the simplest of forms wherein natural exchange of truth comes is a conclusion in the essence of love itself at our simplest completion of knowledge, passion our greater sense of wisdom, ourselves the greater self of truth through the one eternal light so mote it be.

*Merlin's Prayer

I pray to Merlin the cosmic spirit angel of the rainbow sun for the universal spoken essence of the higher mental and the all knowing seeing eye of conscious self image to concentrate on accumulating the mass force of focus in directing it toward the center of an objective for an imagination of a preeminent value with realms transcending phenomena by the perceptible real of the essential nature of reality with an ardent eagerness of interest through a wistful persistent of a urgent longing to feel a compassionate ending with to overpower with the light of confounding brilliancy to crush a burden from an abuse of power that weighed me emotionaly down in the years of repressing natural self by helping me from a seemingly magical transforming power of influence of being moved deeply in ecstatic admiration of influence to rise above through the beyond by triumphing over the negative aspects and I will be capable of being aware through the attainment of understanding by notions through the senses for a zealous support of eagerness expressed by a warmth of feeling of the quality an state of being distinguished by alertness through unusual mental keeness through the belief of the real to be unreal of having an infinite duration of continuation without intermission in a seemingly endlessness wherein the point of concentration with proper directed attention for the conceptual impression of a known imagined experience that creates an illusive general concept to my conscious knowing by the reason and understanding of a perceptible real of a perceptible feltness of being spiritualy touched by a realization of the mind from the capability of being appraised by the substantial real to be fully aware of the significance to grasp the worth and admire highly to connote sufficient understanding of implying a deep love in high estimation of excellence of the significant enough to be worth considering to make noble of going beyond the extent of the exceptional usual by the state of being intellectually enlightened by spiritual luminous for the quality of something with the power of being the state of fascination through the one eternal light blessed be.

*Mernom's Prayer

I pray to Mernom the cosmic spirit angel of the rainbow sun for the universal spoken essence of the higher mental and the all knowing seeing eye of conscious self image for a distinguished noumenon by belief in the extraordinary of a supernatural source of power of natural forces to inspire with the conceptual impression of known imagined experience that which will create an illusive general concept to my conscious knowing for having an infinite concentration of duration in continuation without intermission with proper directed attention to judge tentatively the approximate significance of determination and the nature to produce the unbelievable while focusing sensibly for an appreciable ponderable notion that will help me wistfully transcend phenomena by a perceptible enchanting brilliancy through the one eternal light blessed be.

Assessor Of Being Of Light Consciously Knowing Prayers

I pray to Master Merlin the wizard assessor of being of light consciously knowing and the cosmic spirit angel of the rainbow sun for your teachings and guidance for me to be praised excessively from my motives of interest that will encourage and gratify me with the assurance that something is right and portray favorably on through the one eternal light so mote it be.

I pray to Master Merlin the wizard assessor of being of light consciously knowing and the cosmic spirit angel of the rainbow sun for your teachings and guidance for me to express gratitude by reason of a pleasing contentment and appreciative benefits to have a fascinating illusory of an exiting personality through the one eternal light so mote it be.

I pray to Master Merlin the wizard assessor of being of light consciously knowing and the cosmic spirit angel of the rainbow sun for your teachings and guidance for the quality and fact of being with generous means by a characterized noble and forbearing spiritual abundantcy with a feeling of well being through the one eternal light so mote it be.

I pray to Master Merlin the wizard assessor of being of light consciously knowing and the cosmic spirit angel of the rainbow sun for your teachings and guidance for me having a deeply felt honesty marked by genuiness of a token of what is to come by having the qualities which inspire hope through the one eternal light so mote it be.

I pray to Master Merlin the wizard assessor of being of light consciously knowing and the cosmic spirit angel of the rainbow sun for your teachings and guidance for a valuably productive state of mind and outlook on life and to be the quality and state of holy means by the suggesting the blessed state of the heavenly divine through the one eternal light so mote it be.

I pray to Master Merlin the wizard assessor of being of light consciously knowing and the cosmic spirit angel of the rainbow sun for your teachings and guidance for me to be marked by elevated principles and feelings of optimism and high mindedness by a devotion to an ideal conception of a likeness to something with importance through the one eternal light so mote it be.

I pray to Master Merlin assessor of being of light consciously knowing and the cosmic spirit angel of the rainbow sun for your teachings and guidance for me to be marked by especial aptitude for rediscovering originality, resourcefulness, and cleverness of conception as well to be influenced by divinely supernatural inspiration through the one eternal light so mote it be.

Assessor Of Conscious Being Of Knowing Light Prayers

I pray to Know Microcosmic Universal Knowledge assessor of conscious being of knowing light as the cosmic spirit angel of the rainbow sun for your teachings and guidance so that I will harvest the dreams and goals I have worked hard for through the fulfillment of oneself through the possibilities of my character and personality as well through your love and peace in the quest for truth, true feelings, awareness, and expansion of these virtues through the possessing of vitality through accomplishment I will accumulate the mass force of focus in directing it toward the center of an objective to separate awareness from illusion as well to prosper from your vast knowledge and luminously encourage my hopes and dreams through the one eternal light so mote it be.

I pray to Know Microcosmic Universal Knowledge assessor of conscious being of knowing light as the cosmic spirit angel of the rainbow sun for your teachings and guidance to offer love on my journey of bringing remembrance to my spiritual destiny in the quest for truth by the wistful persistent of a urgent longing to feel a compassionate ending as well through your wisdom of peace and love, true feelings of communication I will have the possessing of vitality through accomplishment to inspire my inner strength, endurance, and virility in which through your loving kindness I will find the preeminent value of imagination with realms transcending phenomena by the perceptible real of the essential nature of reality through the one eternal light so mote it be.

I pray to Know Microcosmic Universal Knowledge assessor of conscious being of knowing light as the cosmic spirit angel of the rainbow sun for your teachings and guidance for the encouragement of becoming who I am meant to be through creativity, grace, love, and joy I will find the fulfillment of oneself through the possibilities of my character and personality I will be the possessing of vitality through accomplishment of understanding, clarity of thought, and serenity of heart to bring tranquility of mind, heart, and spirit as well through your beauty and wisdom the acceptance of my personal power and gifts through the one eternal light so mote it be.

I pray to Know Microcosmic Universal Knowledge assessor of conscious being of knowing light as the cosmic spirit angel of the rainbow sun for your teachings and guidance for the creation of all life on inspiring me to be just and fair so that I will have the fulfillment of oneself through the possibilities of my character and personality I will achieve balance through your wisdom I will accumulate the mass force of focus in directing it toward the center of an objective wherein harmony of mind and I as a spiritual being of light will be liberated by the possessing of vitality through accomplishment through the one eternal light so mote it be.

I pray to Know Microcosmic Universal Knowledge assessor of conscious being of knowing light as the cosmic spirit angel of the rainbow sun for your teachings and guidance for inspiring feelings of thankfulness and gratitude through your warm hearted wisdom I will have a preeminent value of imagination with realms transcending phenomena by the perceptible real of the essential nature of reality to fill my heart with serenity and love of life by the overpowering with the light of confounding brilliancy of a wistful persistent of a urgent longing to feel a compassionate ending through the one eternal light so mote it be.

I pray to Know Microcosmic Universal Knowledge assessor of conscious being of knowing light as the cosmic spirit angel of the rainbow sun for your teachings and guidance for your wisdom in helping me achieve purity of body and mind from your cleansing energy of love I will achieve the possessing of vitality through accomplishment from the fulfillment of oneself through the possibilities of my character and personality I will find a new preeminent value of imagination with realms transcending phenomena by the perceptible real of the essential nature of reality of your divine balance and feelings of truth with insight through the one eternal light so mote it be.

I pray to Know Microcosmic Universal Knowledge assessor of conscious being of knowing light as the cosmic spirit angel of the rainbow sun for your teachings and guidance for courage so that I will have the ability to see and choose creative alternatives by accumulating the mass force of focus in directing it toward the center of an objective I will find the possessing of vitality through accomplishment and the fulfillment of oneself through the possibilities of my character and personality's sense of beauty to fill my mind with contentment through the one eternal light so mote it be.

Assessor Of Conscious Being Of Light Prayers

I pray to Master Arivel the elve assessor of conscious being of light as the cosmic spirit angel of the rainbow sun for your teachings and guidance for me to gain the result of success for a favorable and desired outcome by the attainment of succeeding by the capability of being comprehended by intelligible apprehensibility to have the capability of being understood through the one eternal light so mote it be.

I pray to Master Arivel the elve assessor of conscious being of light as the cosmic spirit angel of the rainbow sun for your teachings and guidance for me to have the courage to interpret sufficiently the desire for a longing of hope as a strong intention for a conscious impulse toward something that promises enjoyment and satisfaction in it's attainment through the one eternal light so mote it be.

I pray to Master Arivel the elve assessor of conscious being of light as the cosmic spirit angel of the rainbow sun for your teachings and guidance for the reputation of recognition by a privilege of pure integrity for an act of kindness that promotes the well being of beneficial advantage through the one eternal light so mote it be.

I pray to Master Arivel the elve assessor of conscious being of light as the cosmic spirit angel of the rainbow sun for your teachings and guidance for me to have a strong exiting feeling from belief in special revelations of the holy spirit to have a resembling suggestive fable of an incredible astonishing nature of wondrous marvel through the one eternal light so mote it be.

I pray to Master Arivel the elve assessor of conscious being of light as the cosmic spirit angel of the rainbow sun for your teachings and guidance for me being strikingly exiting in a mysteriously usual differency to make known an understandable show of logical development by the cause and reason of clarity through the one eternal light so mote it be.

I pray to Master Arivel the elve assessor of conscious being of light as the cosmic spirit angel of the rainbow sun for your teachings and guidance for me to know knowledge beforehand by a force of good from a predetermined course of events that is held by and irresistible power through the one eternal light so mote it be.

I pray to Master Arivel the elve assessor of conscious being of light as the cosmic spirit angel of the rainbow sun for your teachings and guidance for you to convert my full potential into reality and to develop the gratification of my desires to the self-fulfillment of myself for the quality and state of being free through the one eternal light so mote it be.

Assessor Of Conscious Knowing Of Light Prayers

I pray to Know Quantum Universal Spoken Essence Of The Higher Mental assessor of conscious knowing of light and the cosmic spirit angel of the rainbow sun for your teachings and guidance for helping me imply trustworthiness, fairness, and straightforwardness of adherence to the facts to be wholesome in health of body, mind, and spirit so that I will be restored to original purity and have better integrity through the one eternal light so mote it be.

I pray to Know Quantum Universal Spoken Essence Of The Higher Mental assessor of conscious knowing of light and the cosmic spirit angel of the rainbow sun for your teachings and guidance for me to be guided by ideals before practical considerations of adherent theories of idealism and to be with a conception of something representing the standered perfection of thought and opinion through the one eternal light so mote it be.

I pray to Know Quantum Universal Spoken Essence Of The Higher Mental assessor of conscious knowing of light and the cosmic spirit angel of the rainbow sun for your teachings and guidance for me to have a vivid affect of impression by a deeply influence of warm-heartedness from a curious givings of inclination of proper inquisitiveness through the one eternal light so mote it be.

I pray to Know Quantum Universal Spoken Essence Of The Higher Mental assessor of conscious knowing of light and the cosmic spirit angel of the rainbow sun for your teachings and guidance for an unselfishly loyal omnibenevolent concern of the good and strong affection for another by tenderness warm hearted admiration, enthusiasm, and devotion of platonic harmonious love wherein spiritual abundance of possessing special qualities of nature in a form of constituentcy through the one eternal light so mote it be.

I pray to Know Quantum Universal Spoken Essence Of The Higher Mental assessor of conscious knowing of light and the cosmic spirit angel of the rainbow sun for your teachings and guidance for having a sacred value of temporal wholeness involving spiritual revelations of self by the understanding of direct knowledge by the experience to be aware of the truth of factuality by a convincing certain nature of relativity through the one eternal light so mote it be.

I pray to Know Quantum Universal Spoken Essence Of The Higher Mental assessor of conscious knowing of light and the cosmic spirit angel of the rainbow sun for your teachings and guidance for me distinct existence of the state of being indivisible by a total character peculiar of my individuality by helping me of seeing intuitively of the act and result of apprehending the inner nature of things from the power of seeing into a situation through the one eternal light so mote it be.

I pray to Know Quantum Universal Spoken Essence Of The Higher Mental assessor of conscious knowing of light and the cosmic spirit angel of the rainbow sun for your teachings and guidance for good sense from the ancient and wise by the suggestive of goodwill by a devotional form of concentration on a spiritual-like mystical awareness of considering contemplation by the capability of expression in form of passionate means through the one eternal light so mote it be.

Assessor Of Conscious Light Knowing Prayers

I pray to the All Knowing Seeing Eye assessor of conscious light knowing as the cosmic spirit angel of the rainbow sun for your teachings and guidance for the feeling of reliance on my consciousness for belief in acting righteously on the state of being certain on trustworthy confidence to have the ability to succeed by natural aptitude and acquired proficiency to have skillfulness in the state of being able through the one eternal light so mote it be.

I pray to the All Knowing Seeing Eye assessor of conscious light knowing as the cosmic spirit angel of the rainbow sun for your teachings and guidance for me to seek, attain, and accomplish a goal by aspiring me to think about and reflect on deeply a focusing of definite outcome of completion for an optimistic desire to see only the righteous of things through the one eternal light so mote it be.

I pray to the All Knowing Seeing Eye assessor of conscious light knowing as the cosmic spirit angel of the rainbow sun for your teachings and guidance for an inquisitive interest of exiting attention of a desired affect to rediscover hidden knowledge by unusual insight and intuitive perception by honorable means through the one eternal light so mote it be.

I pray to the All Knowing Seeing Eye assessor of conscious light knowing as the cosmic spirit angel of the rainbow sun for your teachings and guidance for the knowing of possibilities by the potential capacity of my ability in prospective value of realization that naturaly accurs in nature to have perseverance wherein spite of discouragement through the one eternal light so mote it be.

I pray to the All Knowing Seeing Eye assessor of conscious light knowing as the cosmic spirit angel of the rainbow sun for your teachings and guidance for me to have a beautiful ingenious elaborate nice description of a deep sensitivity in subtle understanding in esoteric appeal so that I will e forming an exception better then average because of above average intelligence through the one eternal light so mote it be.

I pray to the All Knowing Seeing Eye assessor of conscious light knowing as the cosmic spirit angel of the rainbow sun for your teachings and guidance for me to be full of an rich in events by the quality of being excellent by virtuosity's valuable means through the one eternal light so mote it be.

I pray to the All Knowing Seeing Eye assessor of conscious light knowing as the cosmic spirit angel of the rainbow sun for your teachings and guidance for me to express approval of a result that is in my favor and marked by success because of it by the capability of being successful from a likely reasonableness through the one eternal light so mote it be.

Assessor Of Conscious Self Image Prayers

I pray to Master Cosmic Wisdom Wizard assessor of conscious self image and the cosmic spirit angel of the rainbow sun for your teachings and guidance for a sacred value of ecclesiastical temporal wholeness involving spiritual revelations of self to have understanding of direct knowledge by the experience to be aware of the truth of factuality by a convincing certain nature of relativity to have benevolent and tender affection by fostering the inspiration to have spiritual courage and hope through strength of purpose by the raising of confidence in myself for unselfishly loyal omnibenevolent admiration wherein a fixation of my destiny by a definition of a concept by logic essential free choice of being in the state of determination for an ideal universal contemplation from ascending passion on individuals wherein love is conceived by ascending from passion for the individual to contemplation of the universal and ideal alike wherein a transcendent spiritual-like fundamental proposing statement of the true ideally real that explains a providual solution through the one eternal light so mote it be.

I pray to Master Cosmic Wisdom Wizard assessor of conscious self image and the cosmic spirit angel of the rainbow sun for your teachings and guidance for a tasteful interest in good sense from the ancient and wise to have a state of vigor by my distinct existence of the state of being indivisible by a total character peculiar of me as an individual by me seeing intuitively of the act and result of apprehending the inner nature of things from the power of seeing into a situation with clearness of thought of a presumed capacity to perceive the truth directly and instantaneously through clarity of lucidity from being marked by the ability to hold the power of creation through imaginative skill with the fact of being patient by the capacity of habitualy factual tendency to overcome by invoking divine care for me by the confer of prosperitized happyness to hold in reverence through the ability of blissful heavenly contentment by the act of revealing and communicating divine truth through enlightenment by a pleasant often self revelation of being aware to understand the fact of apprehending truth through reasoning of the sum of what is learned and I will acquire by the learning of knowledge to understand my capabilities by the suggestive of goodwill and a devotional form of concentration on a spiritual-like mystical awareness of considering contemplation in that I will find a self primary discovery of essential facts of a central importance of a fundamental basis marked by a considerable mathematical radical view on life by the capability of expression in form of passionate means for the economic well being of the thriving successful at heart and condition of prosperity means through the one eternal light so mote it be.

I pray to Master Cosmic Wisdom Wizard assessor of conscious self image and the cosmic spirit angel of the rainbow sun for your teachings and guidance to feel an interest of care by the liking of fondness and aptitudial inclination to rediscover formulating concludientcy by the use of reason of a kindly feeling of approval and support to favor cheerful consent by intangible increase in the mere value of interest of goodwill to have gained the result of success for a favorable and desired outcome by the attainment of succeeding to think about and reflect on deeply focusing a definite outcome of optimistic desire for the capability of being comprehended by intelligible apprehensibility to become capable of being understood from the settlement of differences to mutually grasp the worth of the imbetween from the ease by giving strength and hope from the feeling of reliance on my consciousness for belief in acting righteously on the state of being certain on trustworthy confidence on having the ability to succeed by the natural aptitude of acquired proficiency to have skillfulness in the state of being able by free from error of conforming exactly to truth and able to give an accurate result to regard with loving admiration and devotion to be extremely fond of by adornment to cause of subsidial bringing of a peaceful state of mind by the seeking to attain and accomplish a goal by aspiring me through the one eternal light so mote it be.

I pray to Master Cosmic Wisdom Wizard assessor of conscious self image and the cosmic spirit angel of the rainbow sun for your teachings and guidance for an inquisitive interest of exiting attention of a desired affect by having the courage to interpret sufficiently of me devoted in worthy suitableness to become deserving of being recognized for a felt of desire of a longing of hope as a strong intention for a conscious impulse towards something that promises enjoyment and satisfaction in it's attainment for the approving of an expression of esteem, affection, admiration, and courteous formal and respectful recognition to rediscover hidden knowledge by unusual insight and intuitive perception by honorable means to be supremely good of an inspired utterance to declare me as divine for the will and purpose of a thoughtful outcome deriving as a conclusion that I will have the physical force of energy to be dynamic of continuous learning by the reputation of recognition of a privilage in pure integrity to have persistence wherein spite of discouragement I will know the possibilities of my potential capacity of the ability of my prospective value of realization that naturaly occurs in nature to transfix and hold irresistible by the power of fascination for an act of kindness that promotes the well being of beneficial advantage in self for having the qualities of beauty within through the one eternal light so mote it be.

I pray to Master Cosmic Wisdom Wizard assessor of conscious self image and the cosmic spirit angel of the rainbow sun for your teachings and guidance for me to have an interest in the desire to be enthusiastic by a mysterious person so that I will have a strong exiting feeling from a belief in special revelations of the holy spirit to be full of and rich in events by the quality of being excellent by virtuously valueable means to be strikingly exiting in a mysterious usual differency I will be forming an exception better then average because of above average intelligence by me having an involving display of special skill of knowledge that I want to achieve so that to make known an understandable show of logical development by the cause and reason of clarity so I will have the ability to become adventurous in a rediscovering manner to have a beautiful ingenious elaborate nice description of a deep sensitivity in subtle understanding in esoteric appeal so that I will have a resembling suggestive fable of an incredible astonishing nature of wondrous marvel so that to have true facts of the standered original by giving me a strong assurance of a promise in loyal affection of faithful intentions through the one eternal light so mote it be.

I pray to Master Cosmic Wisdom Wizard assessor of conscious self image and cosmic spirit angel of the rainbow sun for your teachings and guidance for me to express approval of a result that is in my favor and marked by success because of it by the capability of being successful from a likely reasonableness to praise me excessively from my motives of interest that will encourage and gratify me with the assurance that something is right and portray favorably to be affectionately fond of in manner to know knowledge before hand by a force of good of a predetermined course of events often held to be an irresistible power to receive some unexpected good by bringing some good thing foreseen as certain and that I will be freeborn for the quality and state of being free for a conductive abundantcy of an abundantly productive fruitfulness to convert my full potential into reality and develop the gratification of my desires to the self fulfillment of oneself by having the principle of determining cause or will by which things in general are believed to come to be as they are or events to happen as they do for the better through the one eternal light so mote it be.

I pray to Master Cosmic Wisdom Wizard assessor of conscious self image and cosmic spirit angel of the rainbow sun for your teachings and guidance for spirited acts of courteous intensions by the showing of a courageous spirit through generosity and means of nobility to the quality and fact of being with generous means by a characterized noble and forbearing spiritual abundantcy for the inclination of an extraordinary intellectual power endowed with mental manifestation of transcendent creative superiority from a feeling of well-being, cheerful, and a happy disposition by nature causing joy and prosperity so that within me a fascinating illusory of an exiting personality to be impressive to the mind and spirit I will be with the possessing of glory and to be marked by great beauty and splendor as well grandeur, lavishness, and adornment to be splendidly showing brilliantcy and magnificents so that I will be displaying grace in form and action as well be marked by kindness, courtesy, charm, good taste, generosity of spirit, and compassionate enough to express gratitude by reason of a pleasing contentment and appreciative benefits through the one eternal light so mote it be.

Assessor Of Knowing Being Of Conscious Light Prayers

I pray to Know Multiversal Wisdom assessor of knowing being of conscious light as the cosmic spirit angel of the rainbow sun for your teachings and guidance for having a courageous spirit through generosity and means of nobility to be splendidly showing brilliantcy and magnificents through the one eternal light so mote it be.

I pray to Know Multiversal Wisdom assessor of knowing being of conscious light as the cosmic spirit angel of the rainbow sun for your teachings and guidance for me to be with courteous intentions of spirited acts and to be merry and impressive to the mind and spirit as well to be displaying grace in form and action through the one eternal light so mote it be.

I pray to Know Multiversal Wisdom assessor of knowing being of conscious light as the cosmic spirit angel of the rainbow sun for your teachings and guidance for benevolent affection of kindness by a fixation of my destiny by a definition of a concept by logic essential free choice of being in the state of determination through my ability of having a special skill that will involve achievement through the one eternal light so mote it be.

I pray to Know Multiversal Wisdom assessor of knowing being of conscious light as the cosmic spirit angel of the rainbow sun for your teachings and guidance for me to be impressively direct and decisive by incisive mannerism as well to be with the act and process of improving from enhanced value of excellence through the one eternal light so mote it be.

I pray to Know Multiversal Wisdom assessor of knowing being of conscious light as the cosmic spirit angel of the rainbow sun for your teachings and guidance for the act of revealing and communicating divine truth through enlightenment by a pleasant often self revelation to invoke divine care for me by the confer of prosperous happyness to hold in reverence through the ability of blissful heavenly contentment through the one eternal light so mote it be.

I pray to Know Multiversal Wisdom assessor of knowing being of conscious light as the cosmic spirit angel of the rainbow sun for your teachings and guidance for me being patient from the capacity of habitualy factual tendency to overcome by being aware to understand the fact of apprehending truth through reasoning of the sum of what is learned and I will acquire by the learning of knowledge to understand my capabilities through the one eternal light so mote it be.

I pray to Know Multiversal Wisdom assessor of knowing being of conscious light as the cosmic spirit angel of the rainbow sun for your teachings and guidance for a kindly feeling of approval and support to favor cheerful consent by intangible increase in the mere value of interest of goodwill to cause a subsidial bringing of a peaceful state of mind through the one eternal light so mote it be.

Assessor Of Knowing Conscious Being Of Light Prayers

I pray to Master Mernom the druid assessor of knowing conscious being of light as the cosmic spirit angel of the rainbow sun for your teachings and guidance for the chance that a given event will occur out of rightness with the quality and state of being lively through the one eternal light so mote it be.

I pray to Master Mernom the druid assessor of knowing conscious being of light as the cosmic spirit angel of the rainbow sun for your teachings and guidance for me to be gaining knowledge and understanding the analytic elemental state of awareness formally true by accordance to logical means through the one eternal light so mote it be.

I pray to Master Mernom the druid assessor of knowing conscious being of light as the cosmic spirit angel of the rainbow sun for your teachings and guidance for your influences of an ideal universal contemplation from ascending passion on me as an individual wherein love is conceived by the reverence of considerable prosperous means of affectional transcendent spiritual-like fundamental proposing statement of the true idealy perceptual real through the one eternal light so mote it be.

I pray to Master Mernom the druid assessor of knowing conscious being of light as the cosmic spirit angel of the rainbow sun for your teachings and guidance for encouraging wisdom to my heart so I will foster the inspiration to have spiritual courage and hope through strength of purpose by the raising of confidence in myself for the quality and state of being accepted from worthy confidence that which implies a process of completion in something that explains a providual solution through the one eternal light so mote it be.

I pray to Master Mernom the druid assessor of knowing conscious being of light as the cosmic spirit angel of the rainbow sun for your teachings and guidance for having clearness of thought of a presumed capacity to perceive the truth directly and instantaneously through clarity of lucidity by helping me be marked by the ability to hold the power of creation through imaginative skill through the one eternal light so mote it be.

I pray to Master Mernom the druid assessor of knowing conscious being of light as the cosmic spirit angel of the rainbow sun for your teachings and guidance for the economic well being of the thriving successful at heart and condition of prosperity means I will find a self primary discovery of essential facts of a central importance of a fundamental basis marked by a considerable mathematical radical view on life through the one eternal light so mote it be.

I pray to Master Mernom the druid assessor of knowing conscious being of light as the cosmic spirit angel of the rainbow sun for your teachings and guidance for me to feel an interest of care by the liking of fondness and aptitude of inclination to rediscover formulating concludientcy by the use of reason through the one eternal light so mote it be.

Assessor Of Knowing Light Being A Conscious Prayers

I pray to the Cosmic Spirit Angel Of The Rainbow Sun assessor of knowing light being a conscious for your teachings and guidance for me having a joyous expression of favored luck and fortune by a sentimental congruous harmonious love through the one eternal light so mote it be.

I pray to the Cosmic Spirit Angel Of The Rainbow Sun assessor of knowing light being a conscious for your teachings and guidance for a compassionate ending toward which effort is directed by the direction toward a goal in mind by a courageously supremely noble impressive love and honor through the one eternal light so mote it be.

I pray to the Cosmic Spirit Angel Of The Rainbow Sun assessor of knowing light being a conscious for your teachings and guidance for me to be marked by compassion, sympathy, and consideration for the love of the human heart to be reflecting humble expressings offered in spiritual generousfull non arrogants through the one eternal light so mote it be.

I pray to the Cosmic Spirit Angel Of The Rainbow Sun assessor of knowing light being a conscious for your teachings and guidance for me to be given a generous promising of pleasant accommodations to arouse my feelings of a passionate reality of means through the one eternal light so mote it be.

I pray to the Cosmic Spirit Angel Of The Rainbow Sun assessor of knowing light being a conscious for your teachings and guidance for me to have a strong duration of individual life as well to have a strong affectionate warm hearted devotion to love through the one eternal light so mote it be.

I pray to the Cosmic Spirit Angel Of The Rainbow Sun assessor of knowing light being a conscious for your teachings and guidance for me to have a strong desire for something I will attain as well the resemblance and quality state of being liked through the one eternal light so mote it be.

I pray to the Cosmic Spirit Angel Of The Rainbow Sun assessor of knowing light being a conscious for your teachings and guidance for helpful direction by the nature of asserted confidence to be marked by an approval of skilled enthusiasm through the one eternal light so mote it be.

The Embodiment Of A Buddhist

Buddhism Prayers

*First Heaven - Universal Chakra - Angel Of Cosmic Understanding

Pray to the cosmic angel if you find it a challenge for spiritual enlightenment when your desire as well is for understanding.

Cosmic angel of understanding I pray to you for your guidance in helping me find spiritual enlightenment through understanding an the acceptance from your eternal love in caring for others as well for myself self love an the love for others in the lords name, Amen.

*Second Heaven - Procreation Chakra - Angel Of Cosmic Harmony

Pray to the cosmic angel if you find it a challenge to be surrounded by the people you love when your desire as well is to feel self love.

Cosmic angel of harmony I pray to you for your guidance on leading me on a journey to help me be surrounded by the people I love while showing me self love through harmony an the acceptance of this love so that I will show this love to the ones I love in the lords name, Amen.

*Third Heaven - Will Chakra - Know Angel Of Cosmic Inner Peace

Pray to the cosmic angel of inner peace if you find it a challenge to finish tasks that you've started when your desire as well is to stay young at heart an enthusiastic.

Cosmic angel of inner peace I pray to you so that you may redeem me from evil as well lead me back to Know so that I will be cleansed in the eternal light an liberated so that I will receive the desire to stay young at heart as well to finish my goals with your blessings an unconditional love to guide me an make amends with unity in my heart so I will receive harmony of mind an enthusiasm for my spiritual well being in the lords name, Amen.

*Forth Heaven - Love Chakra - Angel Of Cosmic Selflessness & Love

Pray to the cosmic angel of love if you find it a challenge to be peace loving when your desire as well is to be generous an easy going.

Cosmic angel of selflessness & love I pray to you so that I will kindle the desire to be easy going as well generous in that through your eternal wisdom help me be peace loving an that through your wisdom which generates kindness an love I will find myself balanced with loving kindness an in a loving relationship between us an the ones I love in the lords name, Amen.

*Fifth Heaven - Communication Chakra - Angel Of Cosmic Wisdom

Pray to the cosmic angel of wisdom if you find it a challenge to be entertaining to others when your desire as well is to be sociable.

Cosmic angel of wisdom I pray to you to help teach me how to listen an see inwardly so that I will become more sociable an with your wisdom which is eternal I will please others as well be taught the way through your guiding light in the lords name, Amen.

*Sixth Heaven - Clairvoyance Chakra - Angel Of Cosmic Acceptance

Pray to the cosmic angel of acceptance if you find it a challenge to not be lazy when your desire as well is to be warmhearted an intuitive.

Cosmic angel of acceptance I pray to you so that I will find inner peace from your loving heart as I know not to be lazy an am willing to learn from your acceptance of me that of guiding me with your affection, purity, an divine beauty you will teach me to be intuitive an warmhearted from your contentment so that I will find tranquility of mind, heart, an spirit in the lords name, Amen.

*Seventh Heaven - Knowledge Chakra - Angel Of Cosmic Desire

Pray to the cosmic angel of desire if you find it a challenge to succeed in achieving when your desire as well is to not be nervous.

Cosmic angel of desire I pray to you so that with your eternal light of truth will guide me in encouraging these truths in me an finding the truth in my desires so I will learn to be less nervous when I want to succeed in achieving at passion, romance, an love in the lords name, Amen.

The Embodiment Of A Celtic

Celtic Prayers

*First Heaven - Shining Light Chakra - Belenus Angel Of Light.

Belenus angel of God and light I pray to you for your teachings and guidance of grace with the flow and ebb, evermore the hand of God keeping me, and the strong spirit of Christ bathing me in the eternal shining light in the lords name, Amen.

*Second Heaven - Rising Sun Chakra - Belisama Angel Of The Flame.

Belisama angel of God and the eternal flame I pray to you for your teachings and guidance of the hand of God aiding me, my souls healer to shield me from sin and snare, keep I this day of God and even I will be, on rough course faring and the days the rising sun blesses me in the lords name, Amen.

*Third Heaven - Divine Light Chakra - Mabon Angel Of Devine Light.

Mabon angel of God and divine light I pray to you for your teachings and guidance of my love to God make warmer, the love of Christ would I feel, come I with the spirit of kindly hym, o' God come into my heart and your love surrounding me, hither in mine ever living soul in the lords name, Amen.

*Forth Heaven - Love Chakra - Maeve Angel Of Love.

Maeve angel of God and love I pray to you for your teachings and guidance, of my eyes not tempted and God with me in each ray of light, God with me protecting every day and night, the lord with me directing I, the lords eternal divine love in the lords name, Amen.

*Fifth Heaven - Holy Spirit Chakra - Nwyvre Angel Of The Stars.

Nwyvre angel of God and the stars I pray to you for your teachings and guidance, of the holy spirit with me strengthening, yet may you yourself God of life be at my side, you to me as a star and guide from life to death and rebirth again in the lords name, Amen.

*Sixth Heaven - Healing Chakra - Triana Angel Of The Sun, Earth, And Moon.

Triana angel of God and the sun, earth, an moon I pray to you for your teachings and guidance through your encouragement of harmony, bless my inner power to overcome, open my heart and instill wisdom in it so I will heal in the lords name, Amen.

*Seventh Heaven - Affection Chakra - Ailinn Angel Of Romance.

Ailinn angel of God and romance I pray to you for your teachings and guidance on leading me on my journey through selfless love, self love, and love for another to encourage me to awakening and enlightenment, to express my true self to another, bless me so that I will awaken my memory of eternal love, romance, and passion in the lords name, Amen.

The Embodiment Of A Druid

Druid Prayers

*First Heaven - Eternal Spirit Chakra - Eternal Spirit Of Light.

Eternal spirit of light I pray to you grant us protection and in that protection the love of the divine spirit, and in that love of the divine spirit awareness, and in that awareness knowledge, and in that knowledge that righteous of things, and in that righteous of things the love of it, and in that love of it goodness, beauty, and truth, and in that goodness, beauty, and truth the love of all creation, through the one eternal light.

*Second Heaven - Eternal Light Chakra - Divine Spirit.

Eternal divine spirit I pray to you grant us your blessings and in that blessings strength, and in that strength peace of mind, and in that peace of mind to come to the love of all creation, and in that love of all creation the love of it, and in that love of it selfless love for another, and in that selfless love the eternal light of self love, through the one eternal light.

*Third Heaven - Eternal Blessings Chakra - Spirit Of OM.

Eternal spirit of OM I pray to you grant us your spoken essence of truth, and in that essence of truth the ridding of selfish questions, and in that ridding of selfish questions the instilment of my heart with hope, and in that instilment of hope your guiding light, and in that guiding light the finding of wisdom, and in that wisdom unity, through the one eternal light.

*Forth Heaven - Eternal Beauty Chakra - Angel Of Love.

Eternal angel of love I pray to you grant us your teachings, and in that teachings guidance, and in that guidance the communication of true feelings, and in that communication of true feelings the remembrance of my spiritual destiny, and in that spiritual destiny the truth of all life, and in that truth of all life courage, and in that courage the inspiration and gift of love, through the one eternal light.

*Fifth Heaven - Eternal Honor Chakra - Angel Of Knowledge.

Eternal angel spirit of knowledge I pray to you grant us honesty, and in that honesty the inspiration of independence, and in that inspiration of independence a promise of hope, and in that hope wisdom to the human heart, and in that wisdom unconditional forgiveness, and in that unconditional forgiveness compassion, and in that compassion truthful communication, through the one eternal light.

*Sixth Heaven - Eternal Awareness Chakra - One Eternal Light.

One eternal light I pray to you grant us the gift of an open heart, and in that open heartedness the integrity of liberation, and in that integrity of liberation awakening and enlightenment, and in that awakening and enlightenment the expression of my true self, and in that expression of my true self the courage to hear and understand other people's feelings, and in that understanding the memory of eternal love, and in that eternal love divine logical dignity, through the one eternal light.

*Seventh Heaven - Eternal Goodness Chakra - Cherubim Angel Of Joy.

Cherubim angel of joy and eternal goodness I pray to you grant us the memory of our divinity, and in that memory of our divinity nourishment of spiritual fulfillment, and in that nourishment of spiritual fulfillment beauty in the eternal sense, and in that beauty in the eternal sense balance in a loving relationship, and in that balance of a loving relationship the achievement of my hearts desires, and in that achievement of my hearts desires the revealing of the next steps of our life's purpose, and in that revealing of purpose growing virtues, through the one eternal light.

The Embodiment Of A Humanist

Humanistic Prayers

*First Heaven - Crown Chakra - Odin Angel Of Spirituality

I pray to Odin, all father norse god for your gentleness of bringing solace into my life by helping me brake down the challenges that stop me from receiving your eternal knowledge an wisdom so that I will be guided by your warm heart in merging with universal understanding through the one eternal light so mote it be.

*Second Heaven - Brow Chakra - Athena Angel Of Intuition

I pray to Athena, greek goddess of courage, victory, and liberation for your guidance in helping me overcome my spiritual struggle by showing me how to make my goals an desires happen through your ever knowing intuition an help me rely upon it to inspire me from receiving your eternal wisdom on being in harmony with the universe through the one eternal light so mote it be.

*Third Heaven - Throat Chakra - Ix Chel Angel Of Integrity

I pray to Ix Chel, mayan goddess of healing and integrity for helping me overcome the challenge of taking risks an enlighten me to have the courage to understand an hear others feelings as well guiding me on my desire of finding inner peace an the expression of my true self with your ever knowing ethical decisions through the one eternal light so mote it be.

*Forth Heaven - Heart Chakra - Cupid Angel Of Emotions

I pray to Cupid, roman god of love and nourishment for your guidance in gaining confidence for spiritual, emotional, an physical fulfillment as well to love an be loved by your ever growing nourishment that I am thankful for your wisdom an acceptance of me as my acceptance of bringing you into my heart through the one eternal light so mote it be.

*Fifth Heaven - Solar Chakra - Bridget Angel Of Intellect

I pray to Bridget, celtic goddess of inspiration and logic for your guidance by helping me to understand as well to communicate with the ones that I love effectively from your ever growing vast knowledge aiding me to think in a logical manner an increasing my ability to understand in an orderly way through the one eternal light so mote it be.

*Sixth Heaven - Sacral Chakra - Var Angel Of Socialness

I pray to Var, norse goddess of love and harmony for your guidance in encouraging me into the acceptance of others an to gain respect for myself to help me serve others with that same respect as well with your acceptance to appreciate the beauty of love, to be sociable, an harmonious within absolution through the one eternal light so mote it be.

*Seventh Heaven - Root Chakra - Cherubim Angel Of Comfort

I pray to Cherubim angel of God and comfort for helping me brake down the challenges that restrain me from receiving your eternal love an thinking before acting as well guiding me with your light in inspiring me with physical comfort, practicality, an patience in the lords name, Amen.

The Embodiment Of A Indian

Indian Prayers

*First Heaven - Great Spirit Chakra - Angel Of The Great Spirit.

Great spirit I pray to you, the creator of all, the rising sun and moon, oh, ancient keeper of the way of life and all that I see, guide me today as I need your strength and wisdom to make my hands honor the things you've made as I go on my journey, make my ears listen to your voice and make me understand so that I may come toward all that I must face, may you always walk in beauty.

*Second Heaven - Honest Chakra - Angel Of The Thunder People.

Thunder people I pray to you, keepers of the west, I give thanks to you as you guide me today as I do what I know to be right, make me truthful an honest at all times, so that I may show great respect for my fellow beings an to the ancestors of all people, I pray for your help in keeping me balanced an teaching me the ways of mother earth an of the creator, may you always walk in beauty.

*Third Heaven - Responsibility Chakra - Angel Of The Great White Giants.

Great white giants I pray to you, keepers of the north, guide me today as I give thanks for all my gifts you've shown me as your help in every day of life, give me strength to overcome when needed an watch over those who dwellith without clothing, food, and medicine, hear me; I need your wisdom in seeking pure thoughts an with good intentions, may you always walk in beauty.

*Forth Heaven - Kindness Chakra - Angel Of Grandfather Sun.

Grandfather sun I pray to you, keeper of the east, help light my way in times of darkness as I give thanks for the reasons of life itself, land of the rising sun, encourage my spirit with hopes as promises and guidance to those without these, teach me the way of the creator, the great spirit my father, hail the fireblood in us and grandfather sun for we'd be animals, not men without his comfort an of warmth, may you always walk in beauty.

*Fifth Heaven - Respect Chakra - Angel Of Grandmother Moon.

Grandmother moon I pray to you, keeper of the south, land we face always, help light my way in times of darkness, make my spirit strong with the great lord, sun and great spirit, watcher over all mother earth, make nature fruitful and grant us fulfillment for when we harvest our dreams we and my people have worked hard for, affectionately guide my people with compassion and inner strength, may you always walk in beauty.

*Sixth Heaven - Truthful Chakra - Angel Of The Stars.

Angel of the stars I pray to you, keepers of the heavenly night, this my offering of praise, humble my prayer, honesty my reverence of my love for you, purity my thoughts of truthfulness, compassion my kindness, clarity my vision, guide me today to awaken my spirit and give me your knowledge so I will learn the lessons you've hidden, may you always walk in beauty.

*Seventh Heaven - Well Being Chakra - Angel Of Life Itself.

Angel of life itself I pray to you, your guidance needed, a guest of love, nourisher of land, for the earth is my mother and the great spirit my father, without you no one would exist, show me the way so there is no more loneliness, so that each of us and days together will be good and long upon the earth, make me remain close to the great spirit an treat those thereon the earth and all that dwell with respect, may you always walk in beauty.

The Embodiment Of A Fantasy Man

Mystical Prayers

*First Heaven - Unicorn Chakra - Mythical Creature Of Wisdom.

Unicorn I pray to you for your teachings and guidance through your wisdom of spiritual growth in helping me achieve prosperity with your gentleness and purity of heart so that I will have strength of mind and the development of my own personal power.

*Second Heaven - Griffin Chakra - Mythical Creature Of Understanding.

Griffin I pray to you for your teachings and guidance through your understanding of powerful new beginnings in helping me achieve spiritual enlightenment with your power of being, a guardian entity, so that I will bring the dark side of myself into submission and gain spiritual wisdom.

*Third Heaven - Gargoyle Chakra - Mythical Creature Of Protection.

Gargoyle I pray to you for your teachings and guidance through your companionship of protection in helping me achieve this while on my journeys and at home so that I will find my true purpose in life and reconnect with ancient knowledge.

*Forth Heaven - Thunder Bird Chakra - Mythical Creature Of Sacredness.

Thunder Bird I pray to you for your teachings and guidance through your knowledge in working against any evil in helping me achieve ridding the evil that hurts my heart so that I will become a warrior like you as an enemy of all evil and gain spiritual knowledge from it.

*Fifth Heaven - Elvish Harper Chakra - Mythical Creature Of The Arts.

Elvish Harper I pray to you for your teachings and guidance through your creativity in helping me achieve to be a seeker of knowledge with your love of arts and ancient secrets so that I will become the same, a seeker of ancient secret knowledge and love of the arts.

*Sixth Heaven - Mer Chakra - Mythical Creature Of The Imagination.

Mer people I pray to you for your teachings and guidance through your freedom of imagination in helping me achieve wisdom with your psychic power so that I will be enriched in life of mind, heart, and spirit.

*Seventh Heaven - Rainbow Serpent Chakra - Mythical Creature Of Sex.

Rainbow Serpent I pray to you for your teachings and guidance through your love of procreation in helping me achieve sexual companionship with your wisdom of life, unity, and sexuality so that I will practice the rainbows laws of harmony in having more respect for relationships, companionships, and friendships at heart.

The Embodiment Of The Elemental of Man

Nature Prayers

*First Heaven - Earth Chakra - Anahita Angel Of Grounding.

Anahita angel of nature and grounding I pray to you for your teachings and guidance on keeping my natural law fruitful through your sacred wisdom of earth so that I will harvest my dreams I have worked hard for in the lords name, Amen.

*Second Heaven - Water Chakra - Nisroc Angel Of Freedom.

Nisroc angel of freedom and truth I pray to you for your teachings and guidance to find the freedom in revealing my eternal self through your inner truth about life so that I will communicate easily with all of nature and the heavens in the lords name, Amen.

*Third Heaven - Fire Chakra - Sofiel Angel Of Nature.

Sofiel angel of nature and love I pray to you for your teachings and guidance in bringing nature into my heart through your beauty of love in nature so that I will achieve purity of body, mind, and spirit in the lords name, Amen.

*Forth Heaven - Air Chakra - Zuphlas Angel Of Trees.

Zuphlas angel of trees and inner strength I pray to you for your teachings and guidance in having stability in mind and longevity of heart through your inner knowledge so that I will be protected and have inner strength in the lords name, Amen.

*Fifth Heaven - Sound Chakra - Hayyel Angel Of Wild Animals.

Hayyel angel of wild animals and caretaker of life I pray to you for your teachings and guidance of teaching mankind and I to have love of animals through your protection of them and earth so that I will show this love more to my companions of wild natures animals and earth itself in the lords name, Amen.

*Sixth Heaven - Light Chakra - Kakabel Angel Of The Moon.

Kakabel star of God and angel of the moon I pray to you for your teachings and guidance of inspiring peace in the order of my virtues through your knowledge of the stars so that I will be encouraged from your deep inner wisdom whose great grace blesses me with liveliness in achieving my hearts desires in the lords name, Amen.

<u>*Seventh Heaven - Thought Chakra - Manakel Angel Of The Oceans.</u>

Manakel angel of the oceans I pray to you for your teachings and guidance in encouraging me to get in touch with my deep inner wisdom through your psychi ability so that I will be blessed in the eternal light and to grow with the virtues of love in my heart and to expand my awareness with true feelings in the quest for truth in the lords name, Amen.

<u>The Embodiment Of The Goddess'</u>

<u>New Age Wicca</u>

New age Wicca is using magical candles an praying to your chosen lord or lady. Pick one color out of the candles that best describe the influence of magic an inspiration you wish to want. Then use five of the same one colored candles an place around you in a Wicca five point star symbol while you pray. Color an definitions of candles are as listed.

*Black = Desire in ancestral knowledge, discipline, lore, an magic.

*Red = Desire in compassion, harmony, self-love, an relationship.

*White = Desire in angelic clairvoyance, insight, an clarity.

*Peach = Desire in kindness, forgiveness, an compassion.

*Pink = Desire in innocence, purity, an balance.

*Green = Desire in artistic inspiration, creative expression, growth, an communication.

*Yellow = Desire in ecstasy, seduction, an sensuality.

<u>New Age Wicca Prayers</u>

<u>*First Heaven - Mystical Chakra - Lord Gwydion And Lady Morgan Le Fey - Cosmic Insight.</u>

Pray to the lord Gwydion or lady Morgan Le Fey if you find it a challenge to find insight when your desire as well is prosperity.

Lord Gwydion or Morgan Le Fey I pray to you for your teachings an guidance on receiving help in finding more insight an through your eternal wisdom an love I ask to gain prosperity an with your blessings, healing, an eloquence I will accept my gifts as well from your nobility an your example of free will have the self determination of finding my true self. Blessed be the lord or lady. So mote it be.

*Second Heaven - Intuitive Chakra - Lord Apollo And Lady Bridget - Cosmic Awareness.

Pray to the lord Apollo or lady Bridget if you find it a challenge to find inspiration when your desire as well is self healing an to be closer to divination.

Lord Apollo or lady Bridget I pray to you asking for your teachings an guidance to help me brake down the challenges to find inspiration an with your eternal blessings to guide me as well I will self heal an with your growing compassion find myself closer to you an divination. Blessed be the lord or lady. So mote it be.

*Third Heaven - Idealistic Chakra - Lord Dumiatis And Lady Nantosuelta - Cosmic Wisdom.

Pray to the lord Dumiatis or lady Nantosuelta if you find it a challenge to learn when your desire as well is wisdom.

Lord Dumiatis or lady Nantosuelta I pray to you asking for your teachings an guidance to aid me in braking down the challenges so that I will learn as with your eternal compassion the way of wisdom an your eternal blessings to guide me on my journey through life. Blessed be the lord or lady. So mote it be.

*Forth Heaven - Open Hearted Chakra - Lord Rhamiel And Lady Freya - Cosmic Love.

Pray to the lord Rhamiel or lady Freya if you find it a challenge to find love when your desire as well is understanding.

Lord Rhamiel or lady Freya I pray to you asking for your teachings an guidance in helping me find the way of love as well to find love an with your warm heart I will find a spiritual awakening in myself an rid what has blocked me from receiving your love directly in that which I will find understanding of the remembrance of my spiritual destiny an I ask from your eternal wisdom to expand my awareness so that I will receive your blessings. Blessed be the lord or lady. So mote it be.

*Fifth Heaven - Creative Chakra - Lord Frey And Lady Edain - Cosmic Intellect.

Pray to the lord Frey or lady Edain if you find it a challenge to have happiness when your desire as well is joy, peace, an gracefulness.

Lord Frey or lady Edain I pray to your for your teachings an guidance as with your divine essence to show me the way of happiness the inspiration of having fulfillment in love an ask of you to find the truths in my desires so that I will learn from the inner truth as with your wisdom of the human heart to develop the inner power to find harmony through self love an the courage to express my true self. Blessed be the lord or lady. So mote it be.

*Sixth Heaven - Ambitious Chakra - Lord Dionysus And Lady Kerridwen - Cosmic Sociability.

Pray to the lord Dionyses or lady Kerridwen if you find it a challenge to find pleasure when your desire as well is knowledge of being sociable.

Lord Dionysus or lady Kerridwen I pray to you for your teachings an guidance asking for understanding to receive the desire to stay young at heart an through your eternal love, passion, an wisdom I wish to learn of your knowledge an free will of finding pleasure an sociability. Blessed be the lord or lady. So mote it be.

*Seventh Heaven - Sexual Chakra - Lord Mabon And Lady Demeter - Cosmic Passion.

Pray to the lord Mabon or lady Demeter if you find it a challenge to fall in love when your desire as well is fertility.

Lord Mabon or lady Demeter I pray to you asking for your teachings an guidance in helping me be with fertility an the understanding that I must first love myself in order to love another as with this love prosperity an abundance will come from an through your blessed eternal knowledge of passion an love I will achieve the understanding in the magic of sex through my inner power. Blessed be the lord or lady. So mote it be.

The Embodiment Of A Psychic

Psychic Prayers

*First Heaven - Psyche Chakra - Master Cosmic Angel Of Virtuousity.

I pray to Master Cosmic Angel Of Virtuousity for your angelic knowledge in helping me achieve clarity of thought through your inspiration of independence affectionately guiding an assisting me in realizing the various levels of truth as well you whom instills wisdom to the human heart I ask for your teachings in achieving a spiritual awakening of finding balance to my angelic clairvoyance so that through your encouragement of harmony I will develop the inner power of unconditional forgiveness through the one eternal light so mote it be.

*Second Heaven - Clairvoyance Chakra - Omen Angel Of Vision.

I pray to Omen for your help in overcoming the challenge of having an open heart so that I will receive your compassion an encouragement on having the inner guidance I need for my visions an your inspiration for my gift of clairvoyance that encourages truthful communication an self empowerment of it which is my desire for spiritual development in my heart an the pure thoughts to inspire me that I must first find self love to love another through the one eternal light so mote it be.

*Third Heaven - Humanist Chakra - Solace Angel Of The Essence.

I pray to Solace for your guidance in leading me on a journey through selfless love an to teach me how to find the inner strength of expressing myself better an through your self love of forgiveness an kindness I will find balance in my compassion for mankind as well to encourage me to awakening an enlightenment so that I will express my true self an have the courage to hear an understand other people's feelings to awaken my memory of eternal love through the one eternal light so mote it be.

* Forth Heaven - Warm Hearted Chakra - Love Angel Of Acceptance.

I pray to Love for your teachings an guidance in helping me spark the memory of my own divinity through your inspiration of being in a balanced loving relationship an to open my heart, mind, an spirit to find self love and selfless love of another so that everything that happens is divine, natural, an beautiful in the eternal sense in which I will attune with my eternal self an express the harmony of God through your spiritual fulfillment through the one eternal light so mote it be.

* Fifth Heaven - Faith Chakra - Fate Angel Of Different Paths.

I pray to Fate for your wisdom of achieving in helping me attain my hearts desire on finding my path so that you will inspire me towards awareness an enlightenment an teach me about my consciousness to discover the light within as well through your blessings and deep inner knowledge the encouragement in my quest for truth so that you will reveal God's divine plan for me an the next steps of my life's purpose through the one eternal light so mote it be.

*Sixth Heaven - Hope Chakra - God Angel Of Enlightenment.

I pray to God angel of enlightenment an hope I pray to you for your love in the human heart in helping me find the compassion of communication as well I ask for your forgiveness so that I will grow with the virtue of forgiveness in encouraging me to heal friendships by getting in touch with my deepest feelings so that my divinity to this world will transform my consciousness from the limited self to the eternal self in the lords name, Amen.

* Seventh Heaven - Independence Chakra - Beautifulart Angel Of Individuality.

I pray to Beautifulart for your communication with the heavenly realm which links us to all living things in helping me through your love an guidance to bring remembrance to my spiritual destiny an to overcome my broken heart so that I will find my true feelings for another with seduction an a relationship spiritualy and physicly which will expand my awareness through your hopes an dreams of others so that I will find the encouragement to heal an use my gifts to become who I am meant to be through the one eternal light so mote it be.

The Embodiment Of The Seven Spirits Of The Rainbow Rays

Rainbow Prayers

*First Heaven - Red Ray Chakra - Hope Angel Of Honesty.

I pray to Hope, cosmic spirit angel of the rainbow sun an honesty for your teachings and guidance on inspiring me about honesty and independence through your eternal self so that I will have my spirit filled with hope and a promise in the belief of the ideals of youthfulness through the one eternal light blessed be.

*Second Heaven - Orange Ray Chakra - Faith Angel Of Prosperity.

I pray to Faith, cosmic spirit angel of the rainbow sun an prosperity for your teachings and guidance on inspiring willingness in me to achieve my goals and dreams through your open heart so that I will prosper from the dreams I have worked hard for through the one eternal light.

*Third Heaven - Yellow Ray Chakra - Love Angel Of Compassion.

I pray to Love, cosmic spirit angel of the rainbow sun an compassion for your teachings and guidance on inspiring my inner strength and compassion through your unconditional forgiveness an harmony so that I will be more open through self love an the love of others through the one eternal light blessed be.

*Forth Heaven - Green Ray Chakra - OM Angel Of Wisdom.

I pray to OM, cosmic spirit angel of the rainbow sun an wisdom for your teachings and guidance on passion an love through your sacred wisdom an warm heart so that I will be spiritualy liberated through my struggles of freedom from the heart an to show this love to others through the one eternal light blessed be.

*Fifth Heaven - Blue Ray Chakra - Christ Angel of Love.

I pray to Christ, cosmic spirit angel of the rainbow sun an love for your teachings an guidance on inspiring me to be balanced in a loving relationship through your natural divine beauty of the eternal sense so that I will become open of mind and heart in the lords name, Amen.

*Sixth Heaven - Indigo Ray - Holy Spirit Angel Of Peace

I pray to Holy Spirit, cosmic spirit angel of the rainbow sun an peace for your teachings and guidance on helping me to become healed from a broken heart through your peaceful essence and divine plan of me I will mend my spirit and become who I am meant to be in the lords name, Amen.

<u>*Seventh Heaven - Violet Ray Chakra - God Angel Of Oneness.</u>

I pray to God, cosmic spirit angel of the rainbow sun an oneness for your teachings and guidance on inspiring me to achieve oneness with nature and all life through your luminous encouragement of expanding my awareness to get in touch with my feelings so that I will communicate easily with earth, nature, and the heavenly realm in the lords name, Amen.

*Native American Prayers

1. Raven I pray to you for your teachings and guidance on becoming who I am meant to be and with the union of my eternal self through your wisdom I will have clarity of thought, purity, and serenity of heart so that I will have inner strength, abundance, beauty, and the joy of living.

2. Coyote I pray to you for your teachings and guidance so that through your wisdom I will accept my man gifts as well the inspiration to be just and fair, bringing balance and harmony to my mind as a spiritual being in which I will be liberated.

3. Thunder Bird I pray to you for your teachings and guidance so that through your eternal love, honor, and knowledge I will be inspired in achieving purity of body and mind as well to have my heart filled with serenity and love of life.

4. Sedna I pray to you for your teachings and guidance so that through your gratitude and purity in nature I will foster the love of nature in my heart as well of having a divine balance with insight and courage.

5. Manabozho I pray to you for your teachings, kindness, and guidance so that I will have self determination, more free will, and the ability to choose and see creative alternatives in which through your generous heart I will have tranquility, contentment, and inspiration.

6. Kwatee I pray to you for your teachings and guidance in which through your wisdom I will have the encouragement to think with nobility and affection as well calmness in conflics within and to be with the awakening of solace, gentleness, and comfort.

7. Totem-Poles I pray to you for your teachings and guidance in which through your sacred knowledge I will have the desire for spiritual development, how to listen, and see inwardly from your inspiration , stability, protection, and inner strength.

8. Wakan-Tanka I pray to you for your teachings and guidance to give my more encouragement to be more harmonious, sociable, and appreciative of beauty through your inspiration of independence to fill my spirit with newness, exploration, and hope.

9. Aakuluujjusi I pray to you for your teachings and guidance so that I will be assisted in realizing the various levels of truth, having more affection toward others, and inner strength through your inner power to overcome I will succeed and prosper so that I will harvest the dreams I have worked hard for.

10. Ahayuta-Achi I pray to you for your teachings and guidance so that I will be with goodness, wisdom, and truth as well through your knowledge to have more encouragement of compassion, communication, and self love.

*Mayan Prayers

1. Quetzalcoatl great feathered winged serpent god I pray to you for your teachings of peace and inspiration of independence through your knowledge and wisdom to dare new thoughts an mend my spirit with hope while affectionately guiding me to realize the various levels of truth.

2. Chac great god of rain and keeper of north, south, east, and west I pray to you for your teachings an guidance of creation an life through your grace and prosperity that which instills wisdom, goodness, and truth to the human heart so that I will develop the inner power encouraged through harmony to be at peace with all life.

3. Kinich Ahau (or) Ah Xoc Kin great sun god I pray to you for your teachings and guidance of poetry and music I pray to you for your open heart in which will inspire integrity and prosperity through your encouragement of more compassion so that I will be with truthful communication through my journey in life.

4. Yumil Kaxob great maize god I pray to you for your teachings and guidance to be a good listener, of liberation, and inward journeys in which I will be encouraged through awakening and enlightenment in expressing my true self and courage to hear through the memory of eternal love.

5. Yum Cimil (or) Ah Puch great god of the underworld I pray to you for your teachings and guidance to inspire the memory of our divinity through opening my mind and heart to new ideas as well to be balanced in a loving relationship with all of nature so that fate reveals that everything that happens is beautiful, natural, and divine in the eternal sense.

6. Kukulcan great winged feathered serpent god of the wind I pray to you for your teachings and guidance in providing nourishment for spiritual fulfillment to achieve my hearts desires and to inspire freedom of thought so that I will rediscover the light within absolution.

7. Ix Chel great lady rainbow and moon goddess I pray to you for your teachings and guidance for your protection in blessing me with your inspiration, enthusiasm, liveliness, and adventure as well with your encouragement of deep inner wisdom.

8. Ah Kinchil great sun god I pray to you for your teachings and guidance to grow with virtues on a trustworthy and loyal path as I will through your encouragement have the ability to get in touch with my deepest feelings and transform these feelings of virtue from there limited self to the eternal self through harmony.

9. Itzamn great ruler of heaven, day and night I pray to you for your teachings and guidance through your eternal wisdom to grant me health, vigor, and longevity as well through your harmonious balance of human kind to inspire and encourage me with your divinity.

10. Yaxche, tree of heaven, under which good souls rejoice I pray to you for your teachings and guidance through your great spirit universal I will find the freedom of revealing my eternal self and be unified with all living life so that I will communicate easily with all of nature and the heavenly realm.

*Egyptian Prayers

1. Anuket, goddess of the river and fertility I pray to you for your teachings and guidance to inspire independence and honesty as well newness and exploration through your belief in the ideals of youthfulness so that I will be affectionately guided for success and prosperity.

2. Bast, cat goddess of fertility, pleasure, dancing, music, and love I pray to you for your teachings and guidance in assisting me with realizing the various levels of truth through your open heart and grace which instills wisdom to my heart as well the encouragement to develop my inner power.

3. Hathor, goddess of love, mother of creation, and mistress of everything beautiful I pray to you for your teachings and guidance to have more encouragement of compassion as well the inspiration of truthful communication so that through your loving kindness I will have joy, contentment, and self love.

4. Heket, frog goddess of childbirth and creation I pray to you for your teachings and guidance to have wisdom an liberation through your sacred knowledge I will find awakening and enlightenment as well the encouragement to express my true self.

5. Isis, all mother goddess of love, healing, and abundance I pray to you for your teachings and guidance to awaken my memory of eternal love as well to inspire beauty and kindness to mankind in which I will find the memory of my divinity.

6. Maat, goddess of truth and balance I pray to you for your teachings and guidance to think in an orderly and logical manner as well to be balanced in a loving relationship so that my heart and mind will be open in which I will understand that everything that happens is beautiful, natural, and divine in the eternal sense.

7. Meskhenet, goddess of childbirth I pray to you for your teachings and guidance in attuning with my eternal self so that I will find nourishment for spiritual fulfillment in which through your blessings I will have open mindedness and freedom of thought.

8. Min, god of sex I pray to you for your teachings and guidance for kindness in inspiring me toward awareness and enlightenment so that I will learn about my consciousness to discover the light within as well through your liveliness I will achieve my hearts desires.

9. Nephthys, goddess of hidden knowledge, divination, and dreams I pray to you for your teachings and guidance on encouraging my deep inner wisdom and psyche ability through your inspiration of love in the human heart so that I will grow with these virtues.

10. Osiris, father god of rebirth and civilization I pray to you for your teachings and guidance on encouraging vigor, health, and longevity through your ability of divinity I will transform my consciousness from the limited self to the eternal self in which I will find love as I go on my journey in the quest for truth.

11. Ra, sun god and father of all gods I pray to you for your teachings and guidance in which I will communicate easily with all of nature and to be linked with all living things through your wisdom the confidence of expanding my awareness between awareness and illusion so that through love and peace I will find my true feelings in the quest of truth, hope, and healing.

12. Thoth, god of writing, math, music, medicine, drawing, astronomy, the moon, and magic I pray to you for your teachings and guidance so that I will become healed through your encouragement to explore my many gifts among them creativity, beauty, and joy as well for me to prosper through your eternal knowledge.

*Norse Prayers

1. I pray to Balder, god of beauty, love, light, innocence, and rebirth for your teachings and guidance to inspire independence, affection, and assisting me with realizing the various levels of truth so that through your loving kindness I will have wisdom in my heart as well encouraging harmony through the one eternal light so mote it be.

2. I pray to Bragi, god of poetry for your teachings and guidance to develop my inner power an encourage harmony through my poetry I will find my heart open with compassion through your wisdom the inspiration of my gifts through the one eternal light so mote it be.

3. I pray to Forseti, god of justice and mediation for your teachings and guidance to encourage me to awakening and enlightenment of striving for justice through your wisdom I will express my true self and have the courage to hear and understand other people's feelings through the one eternal light so mote it be.

4. I pray to Frey, god of happiness, prosperity, peace, joy, and fertility for your teachings and guidance so that I will awaken my memory of eternal love that which through your wisdom the inspiration of kindness, beauty, and art through the one eternal light so mote it be.

5. I pray to Freya, goddess of fertility, passion, beauty, an love for your teachings and guidance so that I will think in a logical manner through your wisdom I will find the memory of my divinity as well the inspiration to be balanced in a loving relationship through the one eternal light so mote it be.

6. I pray to Frigga, mother goddess whom embodies the earth before time existed for your teachings and guidance so that through your wisdom I will find that everything that happens is beautiful, natural, and divine in the eternal sense as well the attuning of my eternal self through the one eternal light so mote it be.

7. I pray to Heimdall, god whom guards the rainbow bridge for your teachings and guidance so that I will express harmony through your wisdom I will find nourishment for spiritual, emotional, and physical fulfillment through the one eternal light so mote it be.

8. I pray to Nanna, goddess of fertility, wealth, prosperity, earth, and moon for your teachings and guidance so that I will achieve my hearts desires through your wisdom in having the inspiration toward enlightenment of awareness and to rediscover the light within through the one eternal light so mote it be.

9. I pray to Norns, the three sisters Urd, Verdandi, and Sculd for your teachings and guidance so that you each will bless me through your wisdom which will inspire enthuisiasm, liveliness, and adventure as well the encouragement of my gifts and deep inner wisdom through the one eternal light so mote it be.

10. I pray to Odin, all father god of inspiration, wealth, healing, love, ancestry, and wisdom for your teachings and guidance so that you will reveal the next steps of my life's purpose through your knowledge which is sacred I will find love in my heart and grow with the virtues of encouragement to heal friendships and my divinity to this world through the one eternal light so mote it be.

*New Age Shamanism For Selflessness.

Pray To The Gods, God, Or An Goddess Of Your Choice to cure a person through prayer. If you choose God then end the prayer with 'In the lords name. Amen.'

*Abuse.

I pray to _____ because I know _____ got wronged an need your guidance to protect this person in their struggles for justice against an abuser whom you know of the rights that this person could not defend themselves an need your help through the one eternal light blessed be.

*Loss Of Will To Live.

I pray to _____ in helping _____letting go an receiving the will of _____'s enlightenment an with your strength, kindness, an acceptance this person will fallow their heart an rebuild what has been lost by emotional poison by your ever knowing guiding light through the one eternal light blessed be.

*Protection.

I pray to _____ for helping _____'s affection of nobility an your guiding generous heart I ask for your courage in (his/her) time of need to think optimistic an for most of all your special protection through the one eternal light blessed be.

*Grieving.

I pray to _____ for your solace to helping _____ by guidance of gentleness to please bring comfort forth to _____ who is grieving (an afraid) as well I ask for your loving kindness to fill (his/her) heart with your spirit bringing comfort to (his/her) broken heart through the one eternal light blessed be.

*Traumatization.

I pray to _____ for your guidance in helping _____ get through what (he/she) was put through an ask with your wisdom an gentleness of heart to bring serenity to (his/her) heart, tranquility of mind, an relieving (his/her) fears with your eternal blessings through the one eternal light blessed be.

*Addiction.

I pray to _____ for guidance of helping _____ develop (his/her) inner power through your ever generous wisdom so that (he/she) will overcome (his/her) addictive habits an prosper from your inspiring compassion an inner strength through the one eternal light blessed be.

*Writers Block.

I pray to _____ in hopes that with your kind heart help _____ find the encouragement an from that inspiration in helping (him/her) have more ideas to complete (his/her) tasks and studies through the one eternal light blessed be.

*Fears, Phobias, And Imbalances.

I pray to _____ for your guidance as well inner wisdom on helping _____ accepting (his/her) many gifts an talents an with you to show this person the joy in living an help (him/her) accept their personal power so that (he/she) will overcome their fears, phobias, or an imbalances with your guiding light teaching this person about self forgiveness through the one eternal light blessed be.

*Depression.

I pray to _____ for your guidance an self determination to teach _____ about free will an inspire this person with alternatives to overcome their depression their in as well with your vast ability to see an choose creative ways of purifying (his/her) spirit so that their heart will grow closer to enlightenment through the one eternal light blessed be.

*Healing For Fears, Phobia's, and Imbalances

1. Ahau Chamahez - Mayan god of medicine and healing.

2. Cit Bolon Tum - Mayan god of medicine and healing.

3. Itzamn - Mayan patron deity of medicine and healing.

4. Ix Chel - Mayan goddess of medicine and healing.

5. Raphael ~ Christian angel of divine healing.

6. Isis ~ Egyptian goddess of healing.

7. Thoth ~ Egyptian god of medicine.

8. Eir ~ Norse goddess of herbal healing.

9. Odin ~ Norse god of healing.

10. Adonis ~ Greek god of healing.

11. Airmed ~ Celtic Goddess of healing.

12. Apollo ~ Greek god of healing.

13. Artemis ~ Greek goddess of healing.

14. Belenus ~ Celtic god of healing.

15. Belisana ~ Celtic goddess of healing.

16. Borvo ~ Celtic god of healing.

17. Bridget ~ Celtic goddess of medicine and healing.

18. Buddha ~ Buddhist, the energy of healing.

19. Damona ~ Celtic goddess of healing.

20. Anu ~ Celtic goddess of healing.

21. Gwydion ~ Celtic god of healing.

22. Hertha ~ Celtic goddess of healing.

23. Meditrina ~ Roman goddess of medicine.

24. Nantosuelta ~ Celtic goddess of healing.

25. Sulis ~ Celtic goddess of healing.

26. Triana ~ Celtic goddess of healing.

27. Diancht ~ Celtic god of healing.

28. Cosmic Wizard ~ God of wizardry.

29. God.

*Healing Writer's Block

1. Athena ~ Greek goddess of education, victory, and courage.

2. Bacchus - Roman god of inspiration.

3. Boann - Celtic goddess of inspiration.

4. Bragi - Norse god of poetry.

5. Bridget - Celtic goddess of inspiration and poetry.

6. Harmonia - Greek goddess of poetry.

7. Kerridwen - Celtic goddess of inspiration.

8. Maya - Hindu goddess of creativity.

9. Mercury - Roman god of writer's and creativity.

10. Nimue - Celtic goddess of learning and teachings.

11. Odin - Norse god of inspiration.

12. Ogma - Celtic god of writing and literature.

13. Rhiannon - Celtic goddess of poetry.

14. Thoth - Egyptian god of writing.

15. Cosmic Wizard - God of wizardry.

16. God.

* Healing Depression

1. Arianrhod - Celtic goddess of prosperity.

2. Boann - Celtic goddess of prosperity.

3. Bran - Celtic god of prosperity.

4. Buddha - Buddhist, energy of prosperity.

5. Dagda - Celtic god of prosperity.

6. Damona - Celtic goddess of prosperity.

7. Anu - Celtic goddess of prosperity.

8. Gwydion - Celtic god of prosperity.

9. Cernunnos - Celtic god of prosperity.

10. Letha - Celtic goddess of prosperity.

11. Lugh - Celtic god of prosperity.

12. Manannan Mac Llyr - Celtic god of prosperity.

13. Math - Celtic god of prosperity.

14. Nanna - Norse goddess of prosperity.

15. Nantosuelta - Celtic goddess of prosperity.

16. Rhiannon - Celtic goddess of prosperity.

17. Rosemerta - Celtic goddess of prosperity.

18. Zeus - Greek god of prosperity.

19. Cosmic Wizard - God of wizardry.

20. God.

*Healing The Loss Of Will To Live

1. Ailinn - Celtic goddess of love.

2. Angus Og - Celtic god of love.

3. Aphrodite - Greek goddess of love.

4. Astarte - Assyro-Babylonia goddess of love.

5. Bacchus - Roman god of love.

6. Balder - Norse god of love.

7. Bast - Egyptian cat goddess of love.

8. Cupid - Roman god of love.

9. Anu - Celtic goddess of love.

10. Hathor - Egyptian goddess of love.

11. Helen - Greek goddess of love.

12. Ishtar - Babylonian goddess of love.

13. Isis - Egyptian goddess of love.

14. Cernunnos - Celtic God of love.

15. Krishna - Hindu god of love.

16. Mabon - Celtic god of love.

17. Psyche - Greek goddess of love.

18. Var - Norse goddess of love.

19. Zeus - Greek god of love.

20. Cosmic Wizard - God of wizardry.

21. God.

*Healing By Protection

1. Gwydion - Celtic god of protection.

2. Nantosuelta - Celtic goddess of protection.

3. Tyr - Norse god of protection.

4. Zeus - Greek god of protection.

5. Thor - Norse god of protection.

6. Cosmic Wizard.

7. God.

*Healing Addiction

1. Artio - Celtic goddess of courage.

2. Athena - Greek goddess of courage.

3. Tyr - Norse god of courage.

4. Cosmic Wizard - God of wizardry.

5. God.

*Healing A Traumatized Person

1. Know Quantum Wisdom - Assessor to Master Know also a wizard god.

2. Cosmic Spirit Angel Of The Rainbow Sun - A wizard god or an goddess not male or female and takes the form of a butterfly. Whose name means 'Like the butterfly.'

3. All Knowing Seeing Eye - A wizard god that takes form of an all knowing seeing eye for a higher protocol of knowledge. Whose name means 'Know's Third Eye.'

4. Conscious Self Image - Not more of a god then a state of reflection in self. Name means 'Reflection.'

5. Cosmic Wizard - God of wizardry.

6. God.

*Healing Grieving

1. Alcyone - Greek sea goddess of tranquility.

2. Concordia - Roman goddess of tranquility.

3. God.

4. Cosmic Wizard.

*Healing Abuse

1. God.

2. Know Quantum Universal Spoken Essence Of The Higher Mental - Name means 'Rainbow'- wizard god of rainbows.

3. Cosmic Wizard - God of wizardry.

4. All Knowing Seeing Eye - A wizard god that takes form of an all knowing seeing eye for a higher protocol of knowledge. Whose name means 'Know's third eye.'

Erick's Short Cure Book For Self Love

These are my lifestory questions & fantasy prayers. Choose the one that troubles you mostly an learn to memorize the prayer you've chosen until your able to close your eyes an pray at the same time. For every time you've memorized one of my prayers I want you to bring a leaf into your room an after you've got done praying I want you to turn over the leaf an a new leaf added to the rest for every prayer you succeed in memorizing. Remember to have a new leaf added to the rest for every prayer you succeed in memorizing. As well you can choose a different god or goddess from my 'New Age Shamanism For Selflessness' if you choose God as one of the healers I advise to use 'In the lords name, Amen' at the end of the prayer you've chosen from 'Erick's Short Cure Book.'

*Q = Questions.

*P = Power Of Fantasy.

*1. Q - Are you angered at feeling like a monster in other people's hearts?

P - I pray to my Cosmic Wizard Star for me to have a better future with the inspiration to find the love in my heart so that I could more+so show my love to this world not at a unease through your guidance and wisdom blessed be through the one eternal light.

*2. Q - Do you seldom find people that hurt themselves an blame it on you?

P - I pray to my Wizard Of Wisdom for me to have help finding forgiveness of myself so I'm more free+spirited to overcome any resentment to myself through your guidance and wisdom blessed be through the one eternal light.

*3. Q - Do you feel you were or are cheated out of your teen years?

P - I pray to my Cosmic Spirit Angel Of The Stars for me to have help in finding love an my acceptance of myself to create from what I thought I lost from emotional poison in the years of repressing my natural self, through your guidance and wisdom, blessed be through the one eternal light.

*4. Q - Could I really feel like a monster in my heart?

P - I pray to my Cosmic Multi-versal Spirit Wizard Of Wisdom for me to have myself appreshiate my talents, to be for the balance of my self's heart, as well to have better wisdom in the outlook of my life so I have acceptance again reign the heart about my destiny, through your guidance and wisdom, blessed be through the one eternal light.

*5. Q - Do you or did you feel hasled in school a lot because of anxiety or other reasons?

P - I pray to my Cosmic Righteous Universal Wizard Of Trust for me to believe more in accepting my memories more+so, in that ridding bad memories with growing wisdom helping me overcome my broken heart, through your guidance and wisdom, blessed be through the one eternal light.

*6. Q - Can you still be happy over self punishment?

P - I pray to my Cosmic Spirit Star for me to have my heart set free from manipulated neglect an for me to build up the encouragement in my heart so my talents are expressed, through your guidance and wisdom, blessed be through the one eternal light.

*7. Q - Do you notice bad spirits trying to make you feeling selfish when you know your more selfless?

P - I pray to my Cosmic Spirit Of The Stars for me to have myself achieve more+so with better encouragement an inner strength with lesser confusion so I may enjoy my "use-to appreciations" before I felt lost, through your guidance and wisdom, blessed be through the one eternal light.

*8. Q - Do you feel slow an of suspician from being confused from abuse an don't feel right in nature?

P - I pray to my Cosmic Righteous In Virtue Wizard Star for me to feel I have riddened the suspician which abusive so I feel a righteous path again not confused as with myself feeling beloved more by those whom love me, blessed be through the one eternal light.

*9. Q - Do you feel that people try to ruin your life?

P - I pray to my Cosmic Universal Wisdom Wizard for me to accept myself expressing my heart in over-coming emotional downfalls so that I may conquer my future with hope, appreciations, and companionships, through your guidance and wisdom, blessed be through the one eternal light.

10. Q - Do you feel you didn't get to learn what you really wanted to by choice?

P - I pray to my Cosmic Wisdom Of Righteous Wizards for me to have myself in over-taking back my heart so that I feel better in trustworthiness, encouragement, and confidence as with myself to be prosperous in persisting to leverage more virtue, through your guidance and wisdom, blessed be through the one eternal light.

*11. Q - Do you feel you don't want to be swayed in the wrong direction cause of your loving heart?

P - I pray to my Cosmic Wisdom Wizard Of The Stars for me to have more+so a gain in 'listening-like' leverages in that to have non-resentment so I'll have stable inner strength, pro+creativeness, and communication through your guidance an wisdom, blessed be through the one eternal light.

*12. Q - Do you feel neglected to believe in the courage of your heart?

P - I pray to my Cosmic Spirit Earth Wizard for me to have more joy in living as well for me to accept my personal talents in love an forgiveness, through your guidance and wisdom, blessed be through the one eternal light.

*13. Q - Do you suspect your liberative fans, friends, lovers, or memorable companionships are bequieled by your heart in neglect?

P - I pray to my Cosmic Spirit Of Wisdom for me to not be unbalanced from oppression as that I may have more comfort in spirit with myself having newer awareness, through your guidance and wisdom, blessed be through the one eternal light.

*14. Q - Are bad vibes around?

P - I pray to my Cosmic Spirit Of Divinity for me to accept expressing myself more so I may become prosperous with better wisdom, through your guidance and wisdom, blessed be through the one eternal light.

*15. Q - Do you feel like you repress yourself?

P - I pray to my Cosmic Spirit Wizard for me to follow my heart towards feeling righteous with myself loving the knowledge I earned, learned, an trusted through your guidance and wisdom, blessed be through the one eternal light.

*16. Q - Do you tend to feel abnormal feelings you encounter that weren't usual that blocked humanistic adventuress attitudes to keep life mystical?

P - I pray to my Cosmic Wizard Of Divinity for me to have all my negative energy disintegrating because of love, guidance, an hope that may aid in ridding selfish questions so I am naturally happier through your guidance and wisdom, blessed be through the one eternal light.

*17. Q - Do you feel heart-ache over others harassing you but even though you have a wonderful future, you still think people are trying to harm you?

P - I pray to my Cosmic Spirit Rainbow Wizard for me to understand the wisdom of my heart is still vast with love, liberation, and free+spiritedness through your guidance and wisdom, blessed be through the one eternal light.

*18. Q - Do you think on noticing you shouldn't get bogused really in life because of downer emotions?

P - I pray to my Cosmic Higher-Mental Wizard for me to accept my hearts intent on not harboring oppressive feelings as with then guild may be destroyed by the reaction of love, through your guidance and wisdom, blessed be through the one eternal light.

19. Q - Do you feel sometimes your going nowhere in life and you know not how that could have been possible?

P - I pray to my Cosmic Universal Wizard for me to have my destiny reawoken as with I accepting to rediscover more awareness in my freedoms of forgiveness, through your guidance and wisdom, blessed be through the one eternal light.

*20. Q - Do you think you'd have to of been somehow manipulated by a behemoth too if I still can't believe I'm not anything different then a superhero and you don't want to think any of this different?

P - I pray to my Cosmic Multi-versal Wizard for me to have my visionary goals an dreams manifest optimistically into reality as with what real love intended, through your guidance and wisdom, blessed be through the one eternal light.

*21. - Do you feel alone more with a broken heart and you get depressed cause you're a natural wonder an never dreamt of being hurt?

P - I pray to my Cosmic Spirit Wonder Wizard for me to have a more natural love in the acceptance of expressing inspirational beauty as with me conquering selfish feelings, through your guidance and wisdom, blessed be through the one eternal light.

*22. Q - Do you feel suppressed by akward feelings that aren't right because you need to feel closer to the one's that love you?

P - I pray to my Cosmic Wizard Of Knowledge for me to be not oppressed as with I guided by more free-will towards wisdom and love in that all the hearts I earned in love in memories are felt compassionate, of blooming, an perswayed into better+felt glory, through your guidance and wisdom, blessed be through the one eternal light.

*23. Q - Do you never confront your not+right worries to yourself when your suppose to be of etent towards your natural destiny, yet you've seen to many worlds destroyed but you still need to be at peace to find truer friendships at heart?

P - I pray to my Cosmic Spirit Wisdom Wizard for me to embrace myself with love as to purge the blockage towards myself feeling love more as with my earned friendships are with feelings more with independence so my compassion is headstrong with my inner wisdom through your guidance and wisdom, blessed be through the one eternal light.

*24. Q - Do you seldom find a friendship lost in your life because of a downfall and your future needs to be more destined-like?

P - I pray Cosmic Spirit Wizard for me to bond my heart strong so I may feel spiritualy strong, beautiful, an with wisdom through your guidance and wisdom, blessed be through the one eternal light.

*25. Q - Do you suffer from what your good at doing yet what your good at your confounded from understanding the expression of it?

P - I pray to my Angelic Wisdom Wizard for me to express my prosperity in understanding that I am loved, in that I pray that you are loved an I need your healing through your guidance and wisdom, blessed be through the one eternal light.

*26. Q - Do you suffer from being hurt just from knowing you weren't different or unique as much as you wanted to be?

P - I pray to my Cosmic Wizard for me to have understanding in accepting myself in that I may get passed the difficult an be inspired by greater liberation so I may get passed my struggles through your guidance and wisdom, blessed be through the one eternal light.

*27. Q - Do you feel that you try to hard to become accepted yet your used to thinking down about yourself but your broken heart get's harder to bare?

P - I pray to my Cosmic Wizard Of Excellent Wisdom for me to know that the war within my heart is at peace & the suffering of my broken heart is healed as with my spirit is then healed being radiant an with that development through your guidance and wisdom, blessed be through the one eternal light.

*28. Q - Do you get strangely irritated by bothersome thoughts caused by aloneness?

P - I pray to my Cosmic Virtueous Wizard for me to have encouragement to feel harmonious, sociable, and appreciative in my own glory and righteousness through your guidance and wisdom, blessed be through the one eternal light.

*29. Q - Do you feel anger for how you grew-up but you got bogused-out because of repression on your heart?

P - I pray to Cosmic Righteous Wonder Wizard for me to have more+so accepted by my goals in mind an not to be swayed into difficult situations as with me to be with more+so wisdom, grace, and trust of myself through your guidance and wisdom, blessed be through the one eternal light.

*30. Q - Do you feel heart-ache now & then because you think hope is lost but because of what you've learned & e4arned in knowledge is that you should be held & loved more and not of suffered?

P - I pray to my Cosmic Noble Wizard for me to have more free will towards my earthly pursuits as with in myself I may overcome my unoptimistic memories as well me feeling more realues in glory and love through your guidance and wisdom. Blessed be through the one eternal light.

*31. Q - Are you paranoid or have you found the paranoid person yet?

A - Usualy this works, put your buttcheeks naked up against your house window an smack your ass thus communicating to the outside world on how you feel. . . . .just joking.

Erick's Short Cure Book #2

1.

Q = Do you feel that people try to ruin your life or but because others are unguided & your heart is broken over the rare situation of your loved ones standing up for what's right to much as your worries then are too great cause of reliance?

A = I pray to my 'Cosmic Universal Spirit Wisdom Wizard Of Reliance' for (___your name here_____) to accept myself expressing my heart in over-coming emotional downfalls so that I may conquer my future with hope & appresiation through the one eternal light blessed art be.

2.

Q = Do you feel that your learning ability could have been better if you had more+so the comfort in spirit your used too without hate?

A = I pray to my 'Cosmic Wisdom Of Righteous Wizards' for (_____your name here___)

To have in myself over+taking back my heart so that I feel better in trustworthiness, encouragement, & confidence as well for I to have a prosperous yet virtuous leverage of perseverance through the one eternal light blessed art be.

3.

Q = Do you feel not like you want to be swayed in the wrong direction cause of your loving heart?

A = I pray to my 'Cosmic Wisdom Wizard Of The Stars' for (_____your name here_____) to have more+so a gain in 'listening-like' leverages in that to have non-resentment so I'll have stable inner strength, pro+creativeness, & stable communication through the one eternal light blessed art be.

4.

Q = Do you feel neglected to believe in the courage of your heart?

A = I pray to my 'Cosmic Spirit Of Earth Wizards' for (_____your name here_____) to have more joy in living as well for me to accept my personal talents in love & forgiveness, through your guidance & wisdom through the one eternal light blessed art be.

5.

Q = Do you suspect your liberative fans, friends, & lovers or memorable companionships are bequieled by your heart in neglect?

A = I pray to my 'Cosmic Quantum Wizard Spirit Of Wisdom' for (_____your name here_____) to not be unbalanced from oppression as that I may have more comfort in spirit with newer awareness through your guidance & wisdom through the one eternal light blessed art be.

6.

Q = Do you experience worsened vibes cause of a bully & as a 'not-to-the-liking' - shooting poo at people & friendships harming them creating a disturbance in the force for many years felt by many beautiful angels?

A = I pray to my 'Cosmic Spirit Of Divinity' for (_____your name here_____) to accept expressing myself more+so an I may become prosperous with better wisdom through your guidance & knowledge through the one eternal light blessed art be.

7.

Q = Do you feel like you repress yourself?

A = I pray to my 'Cosmic Spirit Wizard' for (_____your name here_____) to fallow my heart towards feeling righteous with myself loving the knowledge I earned, learned, & trusted through your guidance & wisdom through the one eternal light blessed art be.

8.

Q = Do you tend to feel abnormal feelings you encounter that weren't usual that blocked humanistic adventuress attitudes to keep life mystical?

A = I pray to my 'Cosmic Spirit Wizard Of Divinity' for (_____your name here_____)

to have all my negative energy disintegrating because of love, guidance, & hope that may aid in ridding selfish questions so I am naturaly happier through your guidance & wisdom through the one eternal light blessed art be.

9.

Q = Do you feel heart+ache over others harassing you but even though you have a wonderful future, you still think people are trying to harm you?

A = I pray to my 'Cosmic Spirit Of The Rainbow Wizard' for (___your name here____)

to understand the wisdom of my heart so I know it is more vast in love, liberation, & free+spiritedness through your guidance & wisdom through the one eternal light blessed art be.

10.

Q = Do you think on noticing you shouldn't get bogused really in life because of downer emotions?

A = I pray to my 'Cosmic Higher+Mental' for (_____your name here_____) to accept my hearts intent on not harboring oppressive feelings as with quilt as it may be destroyed by the reaction of love in my heart through your guidance & wisdom through the one eternal light blessed art be.

11.

Q = Do you feel sometimes your going nowhere in life and you know not how that could have been possible?

A = Pray to my 'Cosmic Universal Spirit Of The Higher-Mental' for (____have your name here_____) to have my destiny reawoken as with I accepting rediscovering more awareness in my freedoms of forgiveness, through your guidance & wisdom through the one eternal light blessed art be.

12.

Q = Do I think I'd have to of been somehow manipulated by a behemoth too if I still can't believe I'm not anything different then a superhero and you don't want to think any of this different, k?

A = Pray to my 'Cosmic Multi+versal Spirit Wisdom Wizard' for (__have your name here___) to have my visionary skills, goals, & dreams manifest optimistically into reality as with what real love intended through your guidance & wisdom through the one eternal light blessed art be.

13.

Q = Do you feel alone more with a broken heart & you get depressed cause you're a natural wonder an never drempt of being hurt?

A = Pray to my 'Cosmic Multi-versal Wizard Of The Higher Mental' for

(___have your name here___) to have a more natural love in the acceptance of expressing inspirational beauty as with me conquering selfish feelings through your guidance & wisdom through the one eternal light blessed art be.

14.

Q = Do you feel suppressed by akward feelings that aren't right because you need to feel closer to the one's that love you?

A = Pray to my 'Cosmic Galactic Wizard Of Knowledge' for (__have your name here___) to be not oppressed as with I guided by more free+will towards wisdom & love in that all the hearts I earned in love in memories are felt compassionate, of blooming, & per swayed into better felt glory through your guidance & wisdom through the one eternal light blessed art be.

15.

Q = Do you never confront you not+right worries to yourself when your suppose to be of etent towards your natural destiny, yet you've seen to many worlds destroyed but you still need to be at peace to find truer friendships at heart?

A = Pray to my 'Cosmic Universal Wisdom Wizard' for (__have your name here__) to embrace myself with love as to purge the blockage to I so I'll feel love more as with my earned friendships are with feelings of indipendance & headstrong compassion and so that I did the right thing with my inner wisdom at those times with my best of friendships through your guidance and wisdom through the one eternal light blessed art be.

16.

Q = Do you seldom find a friendship lost in your life because of a downfall and your future needs to be more destine-like?

A = Pray to my 'Cosmic Multi-versal wisdom wizard' for (____your name here_____)

to bond to my heart strong as with for me to feel spiritualy strong, beautiful, & with wisdom through your guidance & wisdom through the one eternal light blessed art be.

17.

Q = Do you suffer from what your good at doing but what your good at your confounded from understanding the expresion of it (metaphoricaly speaking), perhaps the complications of not finding yourself?

A = Pray to my 'Cosmic Essence Of Angelic Wisdom' for (___your name here___) to express prosperity in understanding that god as well is love, in that I pray that you are love and I need you to heal me through your guidance & wisdom blessed art be.

18.

Q = Do you suffer from being hurt just from knowing you weren't diff. or unique enough as you wanted to be?

A = Pray to my 'Cosmic Wizard' for (___your name here___) to have understanding in accepting himself in that I may get passed the difficult an be inspired by greater liberation so I could get pass my struggles through your guidance & wisdom blessed art be.

19.

Q = Do you feel you try to hard to become accepted yet your used to thinking down about yourself but your broken heart to hard to bare it?

A = Pray to my 'Cosmic Wizard Of Righteous Wisdom' for (___your name here___) to know that the war within my heart is at peace & the suffering of my broken heart would be healed as with my spirit of radiance and with development through your guidance & wisdom blessed art be.

20.

Q = Do you get strangely irritated by bothersome thoughts caused by aloneness?

A = Pray to my 'Cosmic Virtueous Wizard' for (___your name here___) to have encouragement to feel harmonious, sociable, & appreciative in my own glory & righteousness through your guidance & wisdom blessed art be.

Light From The Darkness

2nd Wizardries Book Primordial

For Apprentices

A Wizards Guide

1. Who? = Know, Someone, & Noone.

2. What? = The Key, The Informant, & The Guide.

3. When? = I Thought, I Think, & I Know.

4. Where? = Wherelse, Somewhere, & Nowhere.

5. How? = Cause, Reason, & Purpose.

6. Why? = Mind, Heart, & Spirit.

7. Which? = Multi-universal Rainbow, Multi-quantum Reflection, & Multiversal Aura.

*Know is your Informant and the phrase 'I Know' who lives in Wherelse whom gives Reason to the Mind of the Multi-universal Rainbow.

*Someone has the Key to the phrase 'I Think' who lives in Somewhere whom gives Purpose to the Spirit of the Multiversal Aura.

*Noone is your Guide to the phrase 'I Thought' who lives in Nowhere whom gives Cause to the Heart of the Multi-quantum Reflection.

1. Sun = Who?

2. Dualities = Ying & Yang That Equals What?

3. Moon Phases or an Morning, Noonday, & Afternoon = When?

4. Directions = Where?

5. Elements = How?

6. Vowels In Speech = Why?

7. Days Of The Week = Which?

Wizardly Confusciousnemium

1. Coinciding Confusciousnem = A Self Forgiveful Redemptionist?

2. Uncoinciding Confusciousnem = A Self Forgiveful Rebukist?

3. Coinciding With Confusciousness = A Selfless Forgiveful Reliance?

4. Coinciding With Unconfusciousness = A Selfless Forgiveful Remitance-To-Self?

5. Recoincidince Confusciousnemium = A Selfless Forgivence To The Self?

Confuscious Beginner Prayer & Info. Page

Pray for self forgiveful redemption.

Pray for self forgiveful reconciliation.

Pray for self forgiveful reminicion.

Pray for self forgiveful refuge.

Pray for self forgiveful reliance.

Pray for self forgiveful re-assurance.

Pray for self forgiveful remitance.

Confuscious Beginner Prayers Info. Page For Self Forgiveful Psyche #2

Pray for self forgiveful rebuking.

Pray for self forgiveful reflection-in-self.

Pray for self forgiveful reancouragement.

Pray for self forgiveful recreationality.

Pray for self forgiveful reabundance.

Pray for self forgiveful reprosperistus.

Pray for self forgiveful re-entirety.

Confuscious Beginner Prayers Info. Page For A Self Forgiveful Psyche #3

Pray for self forgiveful recoinciding confusciousnem.

Pray for self forgiveful restimulicus.

Pray for self forgiveful remunipuliorium.

Pray for self forgiveful reilluminicaic.

Pray for self forgiveful remetamorphistes.

Pray for self forgiveful resubliminius.

Pray for self forgiveful reominicem.

Confuscious Beginner Prayers Info. Page For A Self Forgiveful Psyche #4

Pray for self forgiveful realakazamiusnemium.

Pray for self forgiveful reabadazadbra.

Pray for self forgiveful remagicalius.

Pray for self forgiveful rewizardoriuscaic.

Pray for self forgiveful remysteriorusnem.

Pray for self forgiveful reabracadabrarbadacara.

Pray for self forgiveful reomnigloriumnemius.

Confuscious Beginner Prayers Info. Page For A Self Forgiveful Psyche #5

Pray for self forgiveful respiritusnemium.

Pray for self forgiveful remiricaliusnem.

Pray for self forgiveful redivinoriusnemiun.

Pray for self forgiveful rehumaniusiumnemiun.

Pray for self forgiveful resacredmentiusnemiun.

Pray for self forgiveful reacceptionusnemliun.

Pray for self forgiveful reholiusnemiuslium.

Confuscious Beginner Prayers Info. Page For A Self Forgiveful Psyche #6

Pray for self forgiveful revirtuististicliumnemius.

Pray for self forgiveful replatonicaic'love.

Pray for self forgiveful reillusiunemiusnemium.

Pray for self forgiveful rearcould'woeyewithouestartnem.

Pray for self forgiveful reprominencemiusnem.

Pray for self forgiveful reabrakazabranemiusliun.

Pray for self forgiveful rearbazakarbaliusnemium.

Confuscious Beginner Prayers Info. Page For A Self Forgiveful Psyche #7

Pray for self forgiveful reabrakazababazadarba.

Pray for self forgiveful reforgivencemnemium.

Pray for self forgiveful reabrakazamiusnemiun.

Pray for self forgiveful reabadazadliusnemicaic.

Pray for self forgiveful realakazamniusliumnem.

Pray for self forgiveful rearthouincrementiusnemiunlius.

A Test Now:

I Pray for self forgiveful rehocus

(_ _ _ _ put what you wish here _ _ _ _) change-o illusiun presto pocus.

Cosmic Spirit Names & A Prayer-Spell For Enlightenment

1. Cosmic Spirit Merlin of the temple.

2. Cosmic Spirit Arivel of lightning.

3. Cosmic Spirit Mernom of green pastures.

4. Cosmic Spirit Cupid of the rainbow.

5. Cosmic Spirit Cloud.

6. Cosmic Spirit Earth.

7. Cosmic Spirit Of Fire.

8. Cosmic Spirit Water.

9. Cosmic Spirit Temple of the eclipses.

10. Cosmic Spirit Temple of the light.

11. Cosmic Spirit Temple of the shadow.

- A Prayer-Spell For Enlightenment:

*Cosmic spirit temple of the light in prayer I pray for the cosmic spirit Merlin for enlightenment on my path through-out life as art loveth life an peace unto us before thee eternal life of mysteriorum art love & bless'ed I for want to be wonderful bless'ed sheen so mote it treasured be - Abracadabra.

Cosmic Spirit Temple Wizardry Prayer/ Evolutionary Elements Are, & Questions Are

*Cosmic Spirit Temple Wizardry Prayer:

- I pray to 'I am the sun of the temple' for that I wish that I know that I believe I am self forgiven with luck & joy forever bless'ed be holy art thou god ye hocus alakazamius pocus be.

*Evolutionary Elements Are:

- Looking through or upon a window element is:

Looking without (or at a window) looking within = invisibility element.

- Reanimated adamatious element is:

Something rebirthed into a new alien species from the stomach part = Histoysis element.

- Magnetic helium element:

Levitation = Magnetic light.

- Phototaxis element:

magnetic light element.

- Conversion of energy into mass element:

Photosynthesis light?

*Questions Are:

1. So what would 'magnetic phototaxis helium' be on the periodic elements chart?_____.

2. So what would be 'looking through a window element' be?_____ _____.

3. So what would 'looking at the window element' be?_____ _____.

4. So what would 'magnetic gravity light element' be on the periodical chart? _____.

Enchantment For Wizards, Butterfly Occult Round-Table, & Enchantment Spell

Enchantment For Wizards

- "To know which love of truth a simple gesture as a greater exchange in a limitless conclusion."

Pick a name of one deity from this round-table below to fill in the blank of the enchantment spell/prayer you've chosen.

Butterfly Occult Round Table

1. Cosmic Wisdom Of Righteous Wizards.

2. Cosmic Wizard Spirit.

3. Cosmic Spirit Light Of The Earth Wizards.

4. Cosmic Quantum Wizard Spirit Of Wisdom.

5. Cosmic Spirit Angelus Light Of The Stars.

6. Cosmic Multi-versal Spirit Wizard Of Wisdom.

7. Cosmic Righteous Universal Wizard.

8. Cosmic Spirit Wizard Of Wisdom Star.

Enchantment Spell

I pray to the _
_ _ _ _ _ _ _ _ _ for that I ask of you to forgive me as I forgive you
_ for that I may
have (_ _ _ name of crush _ _ _ _ _) have a free+spirited decision
may by natural choice freely love me if righteous unto (_ _ _ _ name of
crush _ _ _ _ _) to like me

(_ _ _ my name _ _ _) an to of myself known soon from clues, blessed art
be to love thine/thou heart of beauty as maybe us are hearts future twined
in love, so mote it be through the one eternal light.

Experimental Wizards Names

1. Cosmic Spirit Angel Wizard Light Of Divinity.

2. Cosmic Spirit Light Wizard Archangel Of Creation.

3. Cosmic Spirit Wizard Angel Of Light Kingdom Of Wizardry.

4. Cosmic Spirit Archangel Wizard.

5. Cosmic Spirit Archangel Wizeard Of Wisdom.

6. Cosmic Spirit Light Wizard Archangel Of The Rainbow Sun.

7. Cosmotic Spiritus Wizard Of Prosperistus Amazemo.

8. Cosmotic Spiritus Holium Archangelem Divinorius.

9. Cosmodium Prosperistis Spiritus Holium Divinoria.

10. Cosmodium Archangeleem Glorius Sacrementius Virtuistis Ilusiunem Prominencium Wizard.

How To Create Green Pastures & Wizardlium Magical Words Prayers

How To Create Green Pastures:

1st is to find a insect that recently passed away.

2nd is to have (or make) a tiny-like coffin, put the deceased insect inside the box, & then put tiny petals from flowers in it.

3rd now bury the coffin-like box into the soil close to your home.

4th is to pray for the insect 'for a great afterlife.'

5th is to put the coffin-like box's now around your home in a circle (like a ring) - once you attain enough deceased insects and bury them around your home in a circle shape then certain green pastures will grow above the ground of where you burried the little coffins.

Wizardlium Magical Words Prayers:

1. I pray to 'Prosperistus' for platonicaic virtuosities holius alakazamius abadazadbra bless'ed so art mote it be.

2. I pray to 'Platonicaic Love' for prosperity in virtuistis means bless'ed so art mote it abrakazabra be.

3. I pray to 'Prominencem' for self love, self luck, & self joy miricalius glorius wizardorius bless'ed so art mote it abracadabra be.

4. I pray to 'Abrakazabra' for self forgiveness in eternal with luck an spiritual joy, ye hocus abrakazabra pocus be.

5. I pray to 'Alakazamius' for eternal blessings of luck & joy, ye hocus magicalius pocus be.

*And Now Studying The Endings To These Wizardry Prayers Above:

1. Bless'ed so art mote it " _ _ _ _ _ _ _ _ _ _ _ _ _ _ _ _ " be.

2. Ye hocus " _ " pocus be.

   #1. Is the normal ending to a wizardry prayer/spell.

   #2. Is the higher mental plain ending to a wizardry prayer/spell.

Healing

- Is about 3rd eye wrist negative energy blockers.

A mechanical device that is worn like a watch and like a watch but with ying/yang compatibility rotating to day & night like a watch rotating time.

The side of ying is filled with plant chlorophyl liquid and the side of yang is filled with milk. Milk will be day & plant chlorophyl liquid would turn with night.

45 Magical Words

- This page goes with the "How To Create Magical Words" & "Wizardry End's To A Ending Letter Of A Magical Word In Alphabetical Order".

1. Alakazamius. 29. Arbazakarba.

2. Abadazadbra. 30. Abrakazababazadarba.

3. Magicalius. 31. Prosperistis.

4. Wizardorius. 32. Virtuosities.

5. Mysteriorus. 33. Sacremento's.

6. Abracadabrarbadacara. 34. Abadazadaba.

7. Glorius. 35. Abadazadabababracadabra.

8. Spiritus. 36. Forgivencem.

9. Miricalius. 37. Abrakazamius.

10. Divinorius. 38. Change-o.

11. Humanius. 39. Abadazad.

12. Sacrementius. 40. Alakazam.

13. Acceptionus. 41. Abracadabra.

14. Holius. 42. Ilusiun.

15. Virtuistis. 43. Presto.

16. Prosperitus. 44. Arthou.

17. Platonicaic. 45. Incementius.

18. Ilusiunem.

19. Arc.

20. Ould'.

21. Wit-hatted.

22. Woe.

23. Ye.

24. Withouest.

25. Art.

26. Prominencem.

27. Hocus _ _ _ _ _ _ _ _ _ _ _ _ _ Pocus.

28. Abrakazabra.

How To Create Magical Words

1. Cem.

2. Caic.

3. Aba.

4. To's.

5. Ius.

6. Sities.

7. Istis.

8. Est.

9. Nem.

10. Lius.

11. Cara.

12. Bra.

13. Mius.

<u>Here are some practice words below:</u>

- Munipuli.

- Omini.

- Sublimini.

- Illumini.

- Stimuli.

- Metamorphi.

- Reflecti.

<u>Here is an example below:</u>

The word chosen is 'Metamorphi' but now with one chosen magical ending could be the word 'Metamorphicaic'.

<u>Wizardry End's To A Ending Letter Of A Magical Word In Alphabetical Order</u>

A = ustis.

B = ra.

C = emara.

D = ivinor.

E = mst.

F = ae.

G = ht. - Example Below Is:

H = aven. "Abrakazam" - would be: From the magical words list.

I = u. "Abrakazamius" - then: Wizardry End's To An Ending Magical Words List.

J = oak. "Abrakazamiusnem" - Done = How To Create Magical Words List.

K = in.

L = ius(t).

M = ius.

N = em.

O = 's.

P = e.

Q = ue.

R = ium.

S = iu.

T = o's.

U = rio.

V = e(e).

W = igh.

X = eeb.

Y = isiti.

Z = ad.

How To Make A Wizardorium Prayer

1. I pray to (_ _ _ _ _ _ _ _ _ _ _ _ _ _ _ _ _ _ _),

2. Add "Cosmic Spirit Wizardorius Of The Rainbow Sun",

3. Add "I ask for your wisdom, guidance, & blessings",

4. Add "Through your sacred wisdomystic ways",

5. Add "The remembrances of your wisdom",

6. Add at end "bless'ed glory of _ _ _ _) so mote it be thou art prayistliorum wizardries mysteriora abracadabra".

*How To Schedule Omens

-If your psychic and want to send an omen to a friend who's also psychic (or not) then write out the fallowing. Inadvertently if done right and you've received an omen or someone you sent the omen to has received it then be shure the omen you've given or received as an omen is in one of the seven phrases that you will either think - say to yourself inside your head, hear - from the person that sent you the omen psychicly, or say through speech the phrase given. Thus after you've received the omen or an the person you sent the omen to has received the phrase will appear through those three above as well it will be received as one of the chosen phrases given inside their heads only will be by their own choice of opening the omen through the phrase if accepted by this person in mind. If they do accept it then the omen will open up like a letter in their minds rather it be perhaps a simple omen saying 'I love you' by choosing few questions or perhaps you want to send a bigger message then you would use more questions or an all of them. You can even write to the deceased, write an omen to yourself an or receive it while dreaming, and also write a dream you want a person to have or to yourself.

*1st - Write the eleven questions in order going downwards.

*2nd - Write down your answer after each question chosen for example is written below as well for helping you I wrote a cause and affect sheet for the questions you do choose. You must include the questions Who?, Which?, and When? In that order when filling the answers in.

*3rd - Write a time then after the question When? for them to receive the omen and as well this is the same time you get your answer whether you have to meditate at this time to receive or be psychic.

*Who? = Write the persons name your sending the omen to.

*What? = Write a statement to this person your sending the omen to.

*When? = Write a specific time for this person to receive the omen as well your answer.

*Where? = Write a meeting place for this person.

*How? = Write a matter at hand to this person.

*Why? = Write a cause, reason, or purpose to this person.

*Which? = Write this person how to tell from apart being what one and cause of which to think.

*Whether? = Write a choice for this person and for reason whether to hear.

*Whither? = Write a specified position because of a result or an condition of purpose of whither to say.

*Either? = Write a gesture of either to see.

* Hence? = Write a matter of hence to perception.

- I chose only 'How?, Whether?, an What?' As for 'Who?, Which?, and When?' are automatically added. Which you then look up the definitions cause and affect to each question then write your own personal message. Start with 'Who?, then Which?, then When?, in order... fallowing ... (A) to (B) to © going to top, then bottom, then middle when filling them out.

*1<u>st</u>

(A) 1. Who? - (Write name of person here).

2. What?

© 3. When? - (Write here when).

4. Where?

5. How?

6. Why?

(B) 7. Which? - (Write a message phrase from learning the cause and affect's from this question).

8. Whether?

9. Whither?

10. Either?

11. Hence?

*2<u>nd</u>

I picked for What? And Whether? A name each from the list of names on the *6th section. But I also left number 4, 6, and 9 empty. I picked Omen for number 2 and Lepidoptera for number 8 and you can either as well write to Omen or Lepidoptera like I have done below. For the trinity of questions which are: 'Which?, Whether?, an Whither? and the other trinity questions which are: Either?, Hence?, an Therefore? - add the word 'because' at the end of your message if you chosen any of those three trinity questions. To know what the trinity questions mean go to the *7th section.

(A) 1. Who? - Erick Tieman.

2. What? - Omen - To smile.

© 3. When? - 1:00 P.M. to 1:10 P.M. everyday.

4. Where?

5. How? - To show me this omen in reality.

6. Why?

(B) 7. Which? - I love it because.

8. Whether? - Lepidoptera - To hear butterflies singing because.

9. Whither?

10. Either? - To show many butterflies fluttering around Erick Tieman with one lunar moth because.

11. Hence?

*3rd

- After the spaces are filled in you must pick next the omen phrase heading, your chosen guardian messenger name, write down a message to each question chosen, and choose these from the *5th section.

I only used 'What?, How?, and Whether?' Besides the three automatically you must do which are Who?, Which?, and When?

If you use more then the three automatically chosen questions then your omen message will be longer and more direct.

*4th

The final steps is you filling out the prayer below then praying it will send your omen, phrase heading, and message inside it. Then the last thing you must do when your finished with the whole prayer is add one of these three sentences at the end of the prayer below. Which are: 'In the lords name. Amen.', 'Through the one eternal light.', or 'So mote it be.' For my example on the next page I chose all three endings.

I pray to (Pick a name out of the *6th section) for (Write the person's name with an 's' at the end of it) (Then write next the name of the guardian messenger you chosen) as the messenger in hopes that (Write the name of the person again) will receive my omen's heading phrase '(Write down the chosen phrase from the seven phrases given for the psychic letter heading to omen)' then if (Write down the persons name once more) accepts this phrase then the phrase will be opening up this omen sent like a letter showing my message saying '(Write your message here that you chose from the answers to the questions put together making your own personalized omen message prayer).'

*Here's a example, I wrote:

I pray to Omen for Erick Tieman's Conscious Light Knowing as the messenger in hope's that Erick Tieman will receive my omen's heading phrase 'I Understand' then if Erick Tieman accepts this phrase then this phrase will be opening up this omen sent like a letter showing my message saying 'I want Erick Tieman to be shown many butterflies fluttering around him with one lunar moth at 1:00 P.M. to 1:10 P.M. every day because I want him to smile in order to hear butterflies singing because I love it because I want him to be shown this omen in reality in the lords name, Amen through the one eternal light so mote it be.

*5th

* The Nine Conscious Self Image Guardian Spirit Messenger Names.

1. Conscious Knowing.

2. Knowing Light Being A Conscious.

3. Conscious Knowing Of Light.

4. Conscious Light Knowing.

5. Conscious Being Of Light.

6. Knowing Conscious Being Of Light.

7. Knowing Being Of Conscious Light.

8. Conscious Being Of Knowing Light.

9. Conscious Being Of Light Knowing.

*The Seven Phrases For Heading Of Letter Omen.

1. I Am.

2. I Understand.

3. I Realize.

4. I Have.

5. I Will.

6. I Think.

7. I Know.

*6th

- Names of People, Gods, Goddess's, Mythical Creatures, Aura's, States of the mind, and Psychic Continuum.

- Feel free to practice your omen message with these in order from 'Beginners' to an 'admired mothman shaman.'

*Beginner - (Common Shaman Mystics).

1. Omen.

2. Cosmic Wizard.

3. God.

4. Merlin.

5. Mernom.

6. Arivel.

*Novice - (Psychic).

1. Nobody. 2. Somebody. 3. Someone. 4. Sombodyelse. 5. Know. 6. Noone. 7. Someonelse. 8. Nobodyelse.

*Skilled - (seven spirits of the rainbow).

1. God. 2. Holy Spirit. 3. Christ. 4. OM. 5. Love. 6. Faith. 7. Hope.

*Greatly Skilled - (Magician).

1. Holusp. 2. Idoptera. 3. Oquadrel. 4. Lepidoptera. 5. Unicorn. 6. Griffin. 7. Gargoyle. 8. Thunder Bird. 9. Elvish Harper. 10. Mermaids. 11. Rainbow Serpent.

*Too Skilled - (People that read aura's).

1. Absolute. 2. Intuitional. 3. Spiritual. 4. Higher Mental. 5. Lower Mental. 6. Astral. 7. Physical Etherics.

*An Admired Mothman Shaman - (moth man shaman masters).

1. Conscious Being Of Light Knowing.

2. Conscious Knowing.

3. Knowing Light Being A Conscious.

4. Conscious Knowing Of Light.

5. Conscious Light Knowing.

6. Conscious Being Of Light.

7. Knowing Conscious Being Of Light.

8. Knowing Being Of Conscious Light.

9. Conscious Being Of Knowing Light.

*7th

*The Two Trinity's Of Receiving Or An Answering Psychicly Through The Omen Message.

*Which?, Whether?, and Whither? Stand for the trinity of whitching. When a person is whitching the trinity of Why? As well the trinity of Why? Equals a cause, reason, or purpose which is combined with the three whitchings. For example below:

*Cause of which to think.

*Reason of whether to hear.

*Purpose of whither to say.

Because of the psychic or an spiritual messenger guardian that influences you to give you cause of which to think, reason of whether to hear, purpose of whither to say, and gesture of either to see - the chosen phrase out of the seven given means that when you receive the phrase out of those three it will be either you or the other person accepting the phrase to be opened up like a letter.

*Either?, Hence?, and Therefore? stand for also another trinity of whitching. When the person is whitching the trinity of How? As well the trinity of how? equals a gesture, matter, or a certain way which is combined with the three whitchings below for example:

*Gesture of either to see.

*Matter of hence to perception.

*Way of therefore to touch-sight.

*8th

The Two Trinities And The Seven Questions ---------The Cause --------The Effect.

1. Who? --A Person---------------------------Their Identity.

2. What? -----------------A Questionous Statement ---------A Answerous Statement.

3. When? ---------------------------------------Time -------------------------------At What Time.

4. Where? --------------------------Destination(s) ----------------------------To What Place.

5. How? ----------------------------An (Un)certain Matter---------------------In What Way.

133

6. Why? -------------A Happening -------------For What Cause, Reason, Or Purpose.

7. Which? ----------------------To Tell From Apart ----------------------Being What One.

8. Whether? ------------------- A Choice -----------------Which(ever) One Of The Two.

9. Whither? --------To Which Specified Position--------To What Result Or Condition.

10. Either? -------------The One Or The Other-------------There's Two Alternatives.

11. Hence? ------------------Of A Preceding Fact Or Premise --------------------Because.

12. Therefore?------For That Reason -------Another Person Questioning The Reason.

*How To Schedule The Use Of Poem/Dream Writing Or Memory Poem/Dream Marbles.

*1st

Basicly your either putting your dream into a marble or not if it's for yourself and for it to come true through prayer, while asleep. As well dreams that are poems work too like I did for an example on the 3rd section. Make shure you memorized your dream and hold a marble between your prayer hands while praying your dream and even going over it to memorize. Pick a time for when your asleep or when the other person sleeps that you given the marble to for when the dream to start.

Write the 11 questions and fill in each one with an answer except for numbers 4 and 6 which is optional as for 5 is already answered. For an easier way of understanding use my 'cause and effect' sheet for the questions definitions.

1. Who? - (Write here either your name or the person's name your giving the marble to).

2. What? - (Write here the title of your dream).

3. When? - (Write here the time you want your dream to start or the other person you given your marble to's dream to start).

4.Where? - (Write here where you want your dream to take place at in your dream).

5. How? - Using a memory dream marble.

6. Why? - (Write here a cause, reason, or purpose for your dream for example: cause of the celebration of my birthday).

7. Which? - (Write here the cause of which to think).

8. Whether? - (Write here the reason of whether to hear).

9. Whither? - (Write here the purpose of whither to say).

10. Either? - (Write here the gesture of either to see).

11. Hence? - (Write here the matter of hence to perception).

<u>*2nd</u>

You only use the marble when your put your dream in it and given the marble to someone else so they have the dream instead. For the dream I have for example below is written for another person as I put down another name and not my own.

1. Who? - Mona Lisa.

2. What? - The Requiem Of Anna Bell Lee.

3. When? - 3:00 A.M. to 4:00 A.M.

4. Where? - Garden Of Eden.

5. How? - Using a memory dream marble.

6. Why? - To celebrate her being alive.

7. Which? - Love.

8. Whether? - The art of listening.

9. Whither? - To have verbal acknowledgment.

10. Either? - To have visualization for fulfillment to see.

11. Hence? - Making this dream into reality in sleep-state programming.

<u>*3rd</u>

You must pray this prayer twice before you give the marble to the person and pray it exactly at the time you've written down for their dream to start. If your giving the dream you made to someone else then hold the marble between your prayer hands so you pray this dream into the marble. Fill in the prayer below:

I pray to (write here the creator you believe in) for (write here the persons name your giving the marble to) to receive this dream I've written in (write here 'his' or 'her') (write here one of the conscious self image names except for 'Know') in hopes that his dream (put title of your dream here) will come true from using a memory dream marble for (write here the person that your giving the marble to's name) (write here your answers to the questions in order: Whether?, Whither?, Either?, then Hence?) (write here where you want the dream to take place at in their dream - optional) to receive this dream I've written at (write here the time for the persons dream to start) and this dream put into this marble will start as fallows '(write here the dream you want the person to have)' (after your done writing it then you'll need to end the prayer with either 'In the lords name. Amen.', 'Through the one eternal light.', or 'So mote it be').

This is a rewritten example of the prayer with the spaces filled in.

I pray to Merlin for Mona Lisa to receive this dream I've written in her conscious light knowing in hopes that this dream titled 'The Requiem Of Anna Bell Lee' will come true from using a memory dream marble for Mona Lisa to have visualization for fulfillment to see, to have verbal acknowledgment, the art of listening, and to make this dream into reality in sleep-state programming inside the garden of Eden to receive this dream I've written for 3:00 A.M. to 4:00 A.M. and this dream put into this marble will start as fallows ' Devine her lips so red and luscious they are, sacred her eyes behold of beauty's taste, passion her hair scented aroma afar, love from her heart of warmth as mine in haste, desire her smile is sweet of sorrows forlorn, seductive her thighs as are of erotica's bliss, perfect her legs of inducement they alure, loathful her movements made pass of a kiss, succulent her caresive touch were of own dreams desiring made of immoral whispers in motion abroad the feltness is like soft rose peddles made erotica of tender care with of an affalin look over a garden of blue orchids.' Through the one eternal light, so mote it be.

*4ᵗʰ

This is an example for writing a dream to yourself.

I pray to (write here the creator you believe in) for (write here your name or the word 'me') to receive the dream I have written in my (write here one of the conscious self image names) in hopes that this dream titled (write here the title name of the dream you've written) will come true from using a memory dream marble for (write here your name or the word 'me') (write here your answers to the questions in order from Whether? then Whither? to Either? then Hence?) (write here where you want the dream to take place at in the dream - optional) to receive this dream I've written at (write here the time you want your dream to start) and the dream will start as fallows '(write here the dream you want to have) (after done writing your dream down you must end it with either of the fallowing 'In the lords name. Amen.', 'Through the one eternal light.', or 'So mote it be.')

*How To Schedule A Phrase For An Omen

-Find the definition for the phrase you have most trouble with. Write the ten questions going downwards. Then you'll pick that phrase and write it to Omen to receive helpful omen's that will come to you through talking to yourself in your mind, seeing the phrase in your mind, when you say the phrase through speech, or hear the phrase psychicly.

*1ˢᵗ

1. Who? - From (Write your name here) To Omen.

2. What? - To receive an omen for the phrase (Write here the phrase).

3. When? - Whenever I need to know something ahead of time to know it's correct.

4. Where? - (Optional - for instance only at work or home...etc.).

5. How? - (Write here the definition for the phrase).

6. Why? - (Write here a cause, reason, an purpose for the phrase to come to you as an omen).

7. Which? - (Write here if you want to receive the omen phrase through thought).

8. Whether? - (Write here if you want to receive the omen phrase through hearing).

9. Whither? - (Write here if you want to receive the omen phrase through speech).

10. Either? - (Write here if you want to receive the omen phrase through sight).

*The Seven Omen Phrases

*I Am - Meaning I'm right about the thought cause I usually already thought about having a vision or thought I must ponder about.

*I Understand - Meaning I'm right about the thought cause I usually already thought about what I need to think about through comprehension.

*I Realize - Meaning I'm right about the thought cause I usually already thought about me becoming aware about something I think of.

*I Have - Meaning I'm right about the thought cause I usually already thought about being shown an image in my mind from a thought I have and to come to the point of awareness through my psyche.

*I Will - Meaning I'm right about the thought cause I usually already thought about understanding of what I must do because I thought about it.

*I Think - Meaning I'm right about the thought cause I usually already thought about it.

*I Know - Meaning I want to know before I think about it.

For Omen to send an omen out of the seven phrases given for the thought you have at the moment.

Like for instance if you are having a thought and psychicly receive an omen phrase out of the seven phrases will come to you only to help you know the thought is correct ahead of time.

For example: I have a thought on trying to find the correct page with information on it that I need so while looking through the chapters page 'I Think' popped inside my head concluding that the most recent page I guessed the information is on is where it is because of the definition to the phrase 'I Think'.

On the next page for the questions 'Which, Whether, Whither, and Either' write down the definition to the question you choose. I chose 'Whether' and 'Either.'

<u>Below is an example of what I wrote.</u>

1. Who? - From Erick Tieman To Omen.

2. What? - To receive an omen for the phrase 'I Think.'

3. When? - Whenever I need to know something ahead of time to know it's correct.

4. Where? - Anywhere.

5. How? - To mean that I'm right about the thought cause I usually already thought about it.

6. Why? - To become more aware.

7. Which?

8. Whether? - Reason of whether to hear.

9. Whither?

10. Either? - Gesture of either to see.*3<u>rd</u>

<u>Prayer For The Omen Phrase</u>

I pray to (write the name of your creator) for (write the name of your creator again) to tell Omen to help me by receiving the fallowing '(write each answer together from the questions you chose)' (write the end to your prayer using either these three: 'In the lords name. Amen'., 'Through the one eternal light', or 'So mote it be').

<u>* My prayer for example I wrote below:</u>

I pray to Merlin for Merlin to tell Omen to help me by receiving the fallowing 'From Erick Tieman to Omen I want to receive an omen for the phrase ' I Think' to become more aware about the meaning that I'm right about the thought cause I usually already thought about it whenever I need to know something ahead of time to know it's correct through reason of whether to hear or gesture of either to see and can happen anywhere I'm at through the one eternal light so mote it be.

*How To Schedule Omens Through Touch-Sight

Write the 12 questions going downwards. 'Which?, Whether?, and Whither are optional yet 'Either?' and 'Therefore?' must be answered. Numbers 2, 3, 4, and 5 are already answered yet you can change them if you want to.

1. Who? ~ From (write your name here) To Omen.

2. What? ~ To have sight through touch.

3. When? ~ Anytime.

4. Where? ~ Everywhere I go.

5. How? ~ When I touch stuff or people that will matter to me.

6. Why? ~ (Write here a cause, reason, or purpose for wanting touch-sight).

7. Which? ~(Write here the cause of which to think).

8. Whether? ~ (Write here the reason of whether to hear).

9. Whither? ~ (Write here the purpose of whither to say).

10. Either? ~ (Write here the gesture of either to see).

11. Hence? ~ (Write here the matter of hence to perception).

12. Therefore? ~ (Write here the way of therefore to touch).

*<u>Here's an example I wrote.</u>

1. Who? ~ From Erick Tieman To Omen.

2. What? ~ To have sight through touch.

3. When? ~ Anytime.

4. Where? ~ Everywhere I go.

5. How? ~ When I touch stuff or people that matter to me.

6. Why? ~ I want to be psychic through touch.

7. Which?

8. Whether?

9. Whither?

10 Either? ~ To have visualization for fulfillment to see.

11. Hence:

12. Therefore? ~ To have the ability of sight through touch.

*<u>Finalization of touch-sight through prayer.</u>

- Fill in the information below.

I pray to (write here your creators name) for (write here your creators name) to tell Omen that I want to receive (write here your answer to what?) (write here your answer to when?) (write here your answer to how?) (write here your answer to where?) (write here your answer to why?) (write here your answers to either 'which, whether, whither, either, hence, or therefore') (write here the ending to your prayer by either these three: 'In the lords name. Amen'., 'Through the one eternal light', or 'So mote it be').

*<u>Touch sight prayer I wrote for example below.</u>

I pray to Merlin for Merlin to tell Omen that I want to receive and have sight through touch anytime when I touch stuff or people that matter to me everywhere I go because I want to be psychic through touch to have visualization of fulfillment to see and have the ability of sight through touch through the one eternal light so mote it be.

*How To Reincarnate A Troublesome Ghost Into A Butterfly.

*1<u>st</u>

Write the 12 questions going downwards and answer each. Numbers 2 and 5 are already done for you. As well numbers 7 to 12 are optional yet 2 of them must be answered.

1. Who? - From (write here your name) To (write here the name of your creator).

2. What? - That the ghost will be reborn as a butterfly.

3. When? - (optional).

4. Where? - (write here where the ghost will be reincarnated).

5. How? - I put my hand closed and within it a caterpillars crysalis and a memory dream marble into the ghost that I see psychicly, opened my hand, and waved my other hand over it.

6. Why? - (write here a cause, reason, or purpose).

7. Which? - (write here the cause for the ghost which to think).

8. Whether? - (write here the reason of the ghost whether to hear).

9. Whither? - (write here the purpose of the ghost of whither to say).

10. Either? - (write here the gesture of the ghost of either to see).

11. Hence? - (write here the matter of the ghost of hence to perception).

12. Therefore? - (write here the way of the ghost of therefore to touch).

*Here's an example I wrote below.

1. Who? - From Erick Tieman To Merlin.

2. What? - That the ghost will be reborn as a butterfly.

3. When?

4. Where? - Inside a butterfly garden.

5. How? - I put my hand closed and within it a caterpillars chrysalis an memory dream marble into the ghost that I see psychicly, opened my hand, and waved my other hand over it.

6. Why? - To give the ghost a happier memory so it can cross over.

7. Which? - I want the ghost that I bought a memory dream for from buying time to think it's a butterfly.

8. Whether?

9. Whither?

10. Either?

11. Hence? I want the ghost to feel and see itself as a butterfly.

12. Therefore?

*2nd

*Buying Time - That which is still experimental has often proved itself from working time and time again by psychics. Burn a good amount of money for the ghost having a memory dream of being a butterfly thus curing the ghost by helping it move on from having a happier memory to cross over to the other side. Before you get done burning the amount of money intended for the ghost you must make a prayer to your creator for buying time in the memory dream marble.

*The prayer for the memory dream marble for example is below.

I pray to Merlin for helping me give the ghost a happier memory in order for it to cross over as a butterfly by me sacrificing $100.00 dollars to buy time for the ghost to have a memory dream of being a butterfly from praying this memory into this memory dream marble I hold between my prayer hands for the ghost as follows...

'We the garden of all evenings witching as the flowers of shadow say down affalin in the sky is where a desert lies as bright orange like the wheel of life an of buried ghost play dead lucidly among the stars your eyes will see as from a flower you yourself be blessed as the sky truly isn't falling as only of yourself from seed.' Through the one eternal light so mote it be.

*3rd

Place a marble in your hand with a caterpillars chrysalis that has the caterpillar inside of it. Close your hand and search for the ghost using your perception then when the ghost is found place your arm out and closed hand into the ghost then quickly open your hand and wave your over hand over the marble and chrysalis. The ghost will then be binded by goodness and transferred inside the chrysalis. Though if the ghost is binded by to much anger and hate then the goodness the caterpillar inside the chrysalis will die and the ghost transfered back to where it was for haunting purposes. If this is the case then use a caterpillar that turns into a lunar moth where evil will fight evil itself. Also some psychics have succeeded without buying time depending on their ability of personal power of enlightenment. After this is done then make and pray the prayer below that I wrote for example.

*Prayer I wrote for ghost binding and reincarnation process.

I pray to Merlin for telling him I sacrificed money in exchange for giving the ghost a happier memory as a butterfly by using a memory dream marble, buying time, and binding the ghost by goodness inside the chrysalis and I ask for you to help this ghost trapped inside the chrysalis to be reincarnated as a butterfly so it will cross over through the one eternal light so mote it be.

*4th

The process is simple as were waking up the ghost from it's deep sleep by resurrecting it as a butterfly to flutter around outside in the sun giving the ghost a reborn feeling through reincarnation until the ghost dies as a butterfly and waits on the other side to be rebirthed into a baby human host. Psychics use the caterpillar because it has the power of a binding gateway through it's chrysalis making it able to cure a ghost which makes Earth rare in it's beauty of love and possibilities.

P.S. - Some ghost where sheets over their heads and body because of either two factors. One, their doing it out of fun because of their inner child or two the ghost in their past life before crossing over got deformed while being killed thus making themselves think that their still deformed. To cure the ghost by reincarnating the ghost into a butterfly will cure the ghost and get rid of the ghost sheet because they'll think their beautiful again.

*How To Schedule Omens For Psyche Development.

- Write the 12 questions going downwards and fill each one with an answer. Numbers 3, 4, and 5 are filled in for you yet you can change them if you want to. You must answer at least one question going from number 7 to 12.

1. Who? - From (write your name here) To Omen.

2. What? - (write here the question you want to practice with).

3. When? - Whenever.

4. Where? - Wherever I am at.

5. How? - To know the answer to the question without asking.

6. Why? - (write here the cause, reason, or purpose for wanting to be psychic).

7. Which? - (write here if you want to receive your answer through thought).

8. Whether? - (write here if you want to receive your answer through sight).

9. Whither? - (write here if you want to receive your answer through speech).

10. Either? - (write here if you want to receive your answer through hearing).

11. Hence? - (write here if you want to receive your answer through perception).

12. Therefore? - (write here if you want to receive your answer through touch-sight).

*This is an example I wrote below.

- I chose all the questions 7 to 12.

1. Who? - From Erick Tieman To Omen.

2. What? - The question 'What?'

3. When? - Whenever.

4. Where? - Wherever I'm at.

5. How? - To know the answer to the question without asking.

6. Why? - So I will be psychic.

7. Which? - I want to receive the answer to the question 'What?' through thought.

8. Whether? - I want to receive the answer to the question 'What?' through sight.

9. Whither? - I want to receive the answer to the question 'What?' through speech.

10. Either? - I want to receive the answer to the question 'What?' through hearing.

11. Hence? - I want to receive the answer to the question 'What?' through perception.

12. Therefore? - I want to receive the answer to the question 'What?' through touch-sight.

*2<u>nd</u>

*<u>Then we finalize it through prayer.</u>

- Fill in the spaces below.

I pray to Omen for (write your name here) to know the answer to the question (write here the question you chose) without asking whenever and wherever I'm at (write here your answer to the question 'why?') and I want to receive my answer through (write here either 'thought, hearing, speech, seeing, perception, or touch-sight') (write here either three to end the prayer - 'In the lords name. Amen., Through the one eternal light, or So mote it be').

*<u>Here's an example of the finished prayer I wrote.</u>

I pray to Omen for Erick Tieman to know the answer to the question 'What?' without asking whenever and wherever I'm at so I will be psychic and I want to receive my answer through thought, sight, speech, hearing, perception, and touch-sight through the one eternal light so mote it be.

*<u>How To Schedule A Message To The Deceased</u>

- Write the 9 questions going downwards and answer what needs to be answered. I already did 2 and 5 yet you can change them if you want to.

*1<u>st</u>

1. Who? - From (write here your name) To (Write the name of the deceased here).

2. What? - That the deceased will receive my message.

3. When? - When I pray my message to (write name of deceased here).

4. Where? - (optional).

5. How? - By writing a message then praying it.

6. Why? - (write here for instance 'because I love him or an her' etc...)

7. Which? - (write here to the deceased the cause of which to think).

8. Whether? - (write here to the deceased to ask them to hear your prayer to them).

9. Either? - (write here to the deceased for them to see your message instead of hearing it).

*2ⁿᵈ

Example Of Message Prayer Below:

I pray to _____ for her or an him to (see or an hear) my message for (her or an him) which starts as fallows:

'I wanted to say that I love you and I want to ask you sense you were a smoker if you had a scene after your passing where your in a tunnel with a bright white light at the end of it (tunnel being the cig. and a light at the end of the cig.) where your guardian angel lit your cig. for you and I wanted to say that I hope your guardian angel told you of your passing because it happened in your sleep with ease, may the cosmic spirit angel of the rainbow sun guide your way' through the one eternal light blessed be.

*How To Schedule A Preminision From Omen

- Write the 11 questions going downwards then answer each except for number 5 which I did for you already yet you can change it if you want to.

*1ˢᵗ

1. Who? - From (write here your name) To Omen.

2. What? - (write here your question to Omen).

3. When? - (write here the time you'll either meditate or in sleep-state to receive your preminision answer - which is optional).

4. Where? - (optional like at work only and etc...).

5. How? - Asking Omen my question through prayer.

6. Why? - (optional - state a cause, reason, or an purpose to your question).

7. Which? - (write here your cause of which to think- which is optional).

8. Whether? - (write here your reason whether to hear your preminision answer).

9. Either? - (write here your gesture of either to see your preminision answer).

10. Hence? - (write here your matter of hence to perception).

11. Therefore? - (write here your way of therefore to receive the preminision through touch-sight).

*2nd

Example Of Prayer Below:

I pray to Omen for you to receive my question through prayer as well an answer to me (write here your full name) from you that will come to me as a preminision (write here your answer to When? - which is optional) (write here your answer to Where? - which is optional) (write here your question to Omen) (write here your answer to Why? - which is optional) (write here your cause of which to think - which is optional) (write here your answers to Whether?, Either?, Hence?, and Therefore?) through the one eternal light blessed be.

*How To Schedule To See Dead People

- Write the 7 questions going downwards and answer each. I've already filled in most the questions yet you can change them if you want to.

*1st

1. Who? - From (write here your full name) To Merlin.

2. What? - That I will see dead people.

3. When? - When I'm not busy or working.

4. Where? - Everywhere.

5. How? - By scheduling a prayer to Know.

6. Why? - Curiosity.

7. Whether? - (write here if you want to hear dead people as well).

*2nd

Example Of Prayer Below:

From Erick Tieman to Merlin I pray to you so that I will see dead people everywhere when I'm not busy or working because of my curiosity I want to hear dead people as well when I see them. Through the one eternal light blessed be.

*How To Schedule A Past Life Prayer Of Remembrance

- Write the 7 questions going downwards then answer each. I already did numbers 2, 4, 5, and 7 for you yet you can change them if you want to.

1. Who? – From (write here your full name) To Merlin.

2. What? – To remember my past life while dreaming.

3. When? – (write a time when you'll be asleep to receive it).

4. Where? – In sleep-state programming.

5. How? – Through prayer.

6. Why? – (write here a cause, reason, or an purpose to remembering).

7. Which? – To remember in my sleep-state the visual presence of my past life when I seen only one reflection and had only one shadow before false light came.

*2<u>nd</u>

Example Of Prayer Below:

– Pray this prayer right before going to bed.

From (write your full name here) to Merlin, I pray to you for you to help me remember in my sleep-state at (write here the time you want to receive it) of the visual presence of my past life when I seen only one reflection and had only one shadow before false light came because (write here your answer to why?) through the one eternal light blessed be.

*The Five Humanism Wizardorium Names

1. Queen Of Kindness.

2. The Cosmic Glory Of Wizardries.

3. The Cosmic Omnious Gifted Spirit Of The Rainbow Sun Wizard.

4. The Cosmic Optimism Wizeard.

5. The Ancient Optimizmo Kind Wizard.

*The Humanism Wizadorium Prayistliorium

I pray for & to _____ for that of friendliness that I learn understanding true that I a free spirit yet an that I learn understanding truer as a humanistic being to judge not myself yet I in harmony cherished truest by virtue in celebrating life in generosity of spirituality, blessed I for art wisdom for art creation be, so mote it thou art in wisdom, blessed art life.

Info. On The 7 Forces Of Magic

1. Reflecti = Crown Chakra = Reflection In Self.

2. Stimuli = Brow Chakra = Sight.

3. Munipuli = Throat Chakra = Voicing Different Tones.

4. Illumini = Heart Chakra = The Heart Which Glows.

5. Metamophi = Solar Chakra = The Fruit Of Knowledge.

6. Sublimini = Sacral Chakra = The Spirit.

7. Omini = Root Chakra = The Soul.

The 7 Colors Of The Rainbow Are:

1. Red = Sun = Sunday. Brain Ratio Allowence:

2. Orange = Mercury = Monday. If the earth was created in

3. Yellow = Venus = Tuesday. seven days, would it be because

4. Green = Earth = Wednesday. the other 3 planets were cold

5. Blue = Mars = Thursday. temperatured? _____

6. Indigo = Jupiter = Friday. _____

7. Violet = Saturn = Saturday. _____.

8. Grey = Uranus = _____ ?

9. Black = Neptune = _____ ? If the earth was created in

10. White = Pluto = _____ ? ten days would humans

use their whole brain

ratio or an is that what the

main deity is protecting us from

- for a greater reason? _____
_____
_____.

Magical Words, Wand Casting, & Healing Spells

Magical Words Are:

1. Presto.

2. Abracadabra.

3. Change-o.

4. Alakazam.

5. Abadazad.

6. Hocus (_____) Pocus.

Wand Casting is:

1a. Pick a phrase of words you wish to have something come true for you.

1b. Now look-up the phrase you just made only now in the language of Latin & only write it down again only in Latin.

2a. Have your wand in your hand & point it into the air.

2b. Now fallow these words with your voice/speech below when casting:

-- "Presto (___your latin chosen phrase_____) abracadabra change-o".

Mask Of Revelaence

1. What's the color of sound? _____ .

2. Is the sound of hearing a seashell noise?_____ .

3. Is the color of the sky in the sea called reflection itself?_____ .

4. What's the speed of reflection of self by not looking away seen again?

Answer is: How fast you blinked.

5. What's the speed of reflection of self by looking away then seen again?

Answer is: How long you took.

Meditation Words

Abracadabra Merry Yea

Abracadabliorum Miracles Yay

Abracadablium Mysteriorum Yup

Bahaus Nature Zenith

Beauty Naturalist Zero

Bravery Nestly Zoastrian

Contemplation Ought'

Clearness Omini

Compassion Omen

Divination Peace

Divinorium Pleasentry

Diviniorum Playful

Encouragement Quaint

Endearment Quietness

Empowerment Quest

Fruitfulness Reconciliation

Forgiveness Riviting

Fulfillement Revitalization

Gaia Selflessness

God Sentimental

Goddess Sharing

Healing Treasured

Harmony Tenderly

Heart-felt Thankfulness

Inner-strength Unique

Inner-self Uplifted

Individuality Understanding

Journey-man Virtuous

Joy Viriety

Justify Vibrance

Kindness Warm-hearted

Knowledge Withowling

Kingdom Wisdom

Loving Xuberent

Love Xeding

Laugh Xpectations

Newest Up-To-Date Magical Wizardorium Words

1. Archangeliorist. 11. Humaniusticliustnemcaicliorium.

2. Prominenciusnem. 12. Virtuistliumsescaiclius.

3. Amenthiusliorumses. 13. Diviniumliorusticaicliuses.

4. Wizardiior. 14. Yeabrakazibliusnemzad.

5. Holiusnemorium. 15. Ybrycedybyruyliusnemist.

6. Holiusamenses. 16. Karbazadazbrazad.

7. Alakazamiusnemses. 17. Forgivenisliumsesnem.

8. Mysteriumseslioriusnem. 18. Sacrementisliumsesnemius.

9. Gloriusesnemiuslioriusnem. 19. Incrementiumlioriliustisticnemses.

10. Spiritistcaiclioriumnemses. 20. Prestibazoavirdaza.

Omnious Prayer Of Wizardorius

I pray to 'the omnious wizardorius'

to say the heart is love an for I not to be afraid as I know I should be strong in spirit, mind, & body as I am also the fruit of the world and are beautiful to this world I believe in that is even flow as you are hope for triumph for us as wizards through the one eternal light bless'ed art truths, art blessed be - Abracadabra.

Planetary Temple Names & Their Means

   - The seven below are warm temperatured planets.

1. Temple of the sun = Sunday.

2. Temple of the mercury = Monday.

3. Temple of the venus = Tuesday.

4. Temple of the Earth = Wednesday.

5. Temple of the Mars = Thursday.

6. Temple of the Jupiter = Friday.

7. Temple of the Saturn = Saturday.

   - The three below are cold temperatured planets.

1. Temple of the Uranus = See no evil.

2. Temple of the Neptune = Speak no evil.

3. Temple of the Pluto = Hear no evil.

Prayer Deity Names Of The Planets

- Either sun or moons.

1. I pray to the sun deity of earth -- /

2. I pray to the sun deity of mercury /

3. I pray to the sun deity of venus Warm Temp. /

4. I pray to the sun deity of mars Planets /

5. I pray to the sun deity of Jupiter /

6. I pray to the sun deity of Saturn /

7. I pray to the moon deity of Uranus Cold Temp. /

8. I pray to the moon deity of Neptune Planets /

9. I pray to the moon deity of Pluto /

Wizard Names Of Quantum Wizardlium

1. R'wise.

2. Wizard.

3. Conscious Self Knowing.

4. Quantum Conscious Knowing Light.

5. Maria.

6. Hypatia.

7. Magus.

-Mundanians Info.

The known of 'no-other' of walkers between the worlds that depart into the multiverse of mundanian mazes may trescend their boundaries in extraordinary ways.

*Shaman Healing

*Hiccups - The cure is simple in it's simplest form, a spoon filled with mostly water and a little salt.

*Wishful Thinking - If you forgot something you wish to remember that was not long ago then go back to the original spot you thought it. Sometimes it helps to sit down and meditate on the original spot you thought it also. In most cases a person will remember it although some cases where the person can't remember it was because it was to long ago. This process also works by let's say if you were holding something when you thought of it yet when you put the object down you forgot the thought thus to remember pick the object back up in the same hand.

*Soar Throat - The cure is simple in it's simplest form, a couple marshmallows.

*Head Ache - Lay down and put your wrist going outwards over you forehead. If it's more then a miner headache then this process might not work.

*Nightmare - The cure is simple in it's simplest form, to pray this prayer before going to sleep: I pray to (pick either these three- Borvo, Hypnos, or God) for inspiration through dreaming as well through your mesmerizing wisdom I will attain a healthy dream tonight from being healed by your incredible insight on overcoming my nightmares and for you to bless me with your knowledge (then pick either these two endings - If you chose God then end this prayer with 'In the lords name. Amen.' - and if you chose Borvo or Hypnos end this prayer with 'Through the one eternal light so mote it be.')

Shaman Wizardry

For making a shaman wizardry prayer/spell fill in the below.

First choose one of the beginning magical words below:

Presto, Ilusiun, & Mysteriorum.

Now write below 'the point of it' - which means the point of your magical prayer, a phrase as you will.

_____
_____
_____

Now choose an ending magical word below:

Abracadabra, phoricalthilogy, or Mysteriorum.

Now write your beginning magical word then your 'point of it' then an ending magical word - as well at the very end of your prayer/spell add the words below to your prayer/spell:

"Change-o blessed art be amen."

The 4 Sages

- Info of the 4 sages below:

1st is Well-Wisdom.

2nd is Healthy Guesses.

3rd is Humanistic Quality.

4th is Trusting Completion of the Self.

1. Well wisdoms trinity:

Appreciation,

Joyousness,

Non-Disapointment.

2. Trinity Of Healthy Guesses:

Indipendent Prosperity,

Noble liberty of goodness, beauty, & truth,

Humanium wisdom of liberty.

3. A Trinity Of Humanistic Quality:

Noble Prosperity,

Individual Beauty,

Humanistic Trust.

4. A Trusting Completion Of The Self's Trinity:

Rights Of Passages Dominion,

The 4 sages,

A Wizards principalities.

*The Different States And Levels Of Being Reborn

1. The Air Born = Insect Angels/Sylphs = First Born = Born Of The First Braught Forth Eldest.

2. The Fire Born = Dragons = High Born = Born Of Noble Birth.

3. The Water Born = Undines/Mermaids = Free Born = Born Of Free Birth.

4. The Earth Born = Man and or Woman/Mernom's = Self Born = Born Again In Self.

The Four Sages Wizardry Prayers

*Well- Wisdom Blessing Prayer

I pray for "well wisdom" as an incrementius for apreciation, joyousness, & non-disernment, for of sacramento's before the holius sun or stars hocus spiritus sacramentium incrementius holy thou god pocus, cosmic spirit be.

*Healthy Guesses Blessing Prayer

I pray to the 'Cosmic Spiritus Wondrous Of Wise' as a sacramentius for healthy guesses in independent prosperity, noble liberty in goodness/beauty/& truth with humanium wisdom so I may with so have, hocus blessed spiritus thou art pocus the cosmic spiritus be.

*Humanistic Quality Blessing Prayer

I pray for 'humanistic quality' as a sacramento's from a wizeard in for I to have noble prosperity/individual beauty/ & humanistic trust so I may have such which as I thank you for your loving kindness an wisdom, blessed so art mote it platonicaic love in apreciation hocus pocus be.

*Trusting Completion Of The Self Blessing Prayer

I pray to 'Sacramento's' for your wisdom in understanding of the right's of passages dominion/the 4 sages/ & a wizards principles so of I to have me trusting completion of my blessings in self, thank you for you loving kindness blessed the 'cosmic spiritus' in appreciation abracadabra be.

*The 7'n Archangel Confusions Of Self Prayers

1. Pray for "Self forgiveful consubstancious remitance."

2. Pray for "Self forgiveful coincidencious redemption."

3. Pray for "Self forgiveful condecencious reconciliation."

4. Pray for "Self forgiveful cognizancious reminicion."

5. Pray for "Self forgiveful consulcencious refuge."

6. Pray for "Self forgiveful confuscious reliance."

7. Pray for "Self forgiveful condencencious re-assurance."

*The Seven Spirits Of The Rainbow Rays

- The rainbow has for each ray a spirit that guards an emotional feeling.

*1st ray = The emotion truth and the guardian spirit of justice whom is the maker of truth, trust, passion, clarity, communication, completion, and prayer as well the principle of generous thoughts.

*2nd ray = The emotion trust and the guardian spirit of acceptance whom is the maker of matterable concepts.

*3rd ray = The emotion passion and the guardian spirit of love whom is the maker of beauty as well the way of sensation.

*4th ray = The emotion clarity and the guardian spirit of liberation whom is the maker of free will as well the cause of imagination.

*5th ray = The emotion communication and the guardian spirit of unity whom is the maker of proper balance as well reasonable idea's.

*6th ray = The emotion completion and the guardian spirit of wholeness whom is the maker of purposeful notions.

*7th ray = The emotion prayer and the guardian spirit of oneness whom is the maker of relevance and revelations as well optimistic reverence of prayer

The Wizardalogic Blessings Plaque Prayer & Info

I pray to 'Spiritus Sacramento's' for my spirit to become holius spiritus in appreciation abadazadbra of self forgiveness, virtuosities in prosperity, & of self love with humanistis holius prosperistis blessed holius sun, spiritus, & forgivence through the one eternal light blessed so mote it miricalius glorius blessed so mote it art ,ye hocus magicalius prominencem platonicaic virtuosities alakazamius abadazadaba pocus be.

*Info:

- Front of brain is:

1. Seeing to know.

2. Seeing is believing.

3. Light as a leaf.

4. Looking within.

5. Learning to grow.

6. More is said when less is said.

7. The whole of the point.

- Back of brain is:

1. Knowing to see.

2. Know I'm backwards nor seen.

3. Light as a feather.

4. Looking without.

5. Growing to learn.

6. Less is said when more is said.

7. The point of the whole.

Wish Making

1. Bug Eating ~ Jjin Magic.

2. Memorizing Plains One Can Visit ~ Genie Magic.

3. The Fly ~ When you see a fly and the fly makes his arms in a wishful motion then do the same with you hands before the fly flies away ~ Jjin Magic.

4. Wishful Thinking - If you forgot something you wish to remember that was not long ago then go back to the original spot you thought it. In most cases a person can remember it although some cases where the person can't remember it is because it was to long ago.

5. Selfless Sacrificing - Releasing a thousand or more butterflies or an lunar moths into the air on Halloween - Genie Magic.

6. Road Kill - If you're the driver and run over a live animal and it dies then would that not be the same as sacrificing an animal to have a wish come true - Jjin Magic.

7. *Spring - Finding a four leaf clover - Genie Magic.

8. *Summer - Putting your arm and hand out for a butterfly to land upon it - Genie Magic.

9. *Autumn - Catching a fallen autumn leaf from an autumn tree before it hit's the ground - Genie Magic.

10. *Winter - Catching a bunny in the snow and you can't cheat by catching a baby bunny - Genie Magic.

11. *Falling Star - A tale that when you see a falling star you make a wish.

Wizardizm Map Of The Brain So Far

Back Part Of Brain Is: Transitional.

Right Hemisphere Is: The 7 Transmitter/Reciever Waves.

Left Hemisphere Is The 7 Rainbow Rays.

Front Part Of Brain Is: Perceptional.

Clue is:

A magnet is different on each planet. A magnet is the recordings of gravity on the planet, as too like a tree's stump that tells age of the tree by it's rings. Counting the sun - There is a sun and 6 planets which means 7 warm essences in our solar system.

Any Theories?

_____
_____
_____.

Wizardologic Blessings Plaque

- The information below goes according to how you bless yourself with using the plaque.

1st - Point at your head saying 'Father Sacrementius', point at heart saying 'holius sun', point at left shoulder saying 'holy spiritus', then point at right shoulder saying 'spiritus abadazabra'.

2nd - Point at your head saying 'of forgiveness' , point at your heart saying 'with well wisdom', point at left shoulder saying 'appreciation', then point at your right shoulder saying 'blessed so art mote it be'.

3rd - Point at your head saying 'father prosperistis' , point at your heart saying 'holy humanistis', point at your left shoulder saying 'holius virtuosities' then point at right shoulder saying 'Spiritus Sacramento's.'

I. Father Sacramentius, Holius Sun, Holy Spiritus, & Spiritus Abadazadbra.

II. Of Forgiveness, With Well-Wisdom, Appreciation, & Blessed So Art Mote It Be.

III. Father Prosperistis, Holy Humanistis, Holius Virtuisities, & Spiritus Sacramento's.

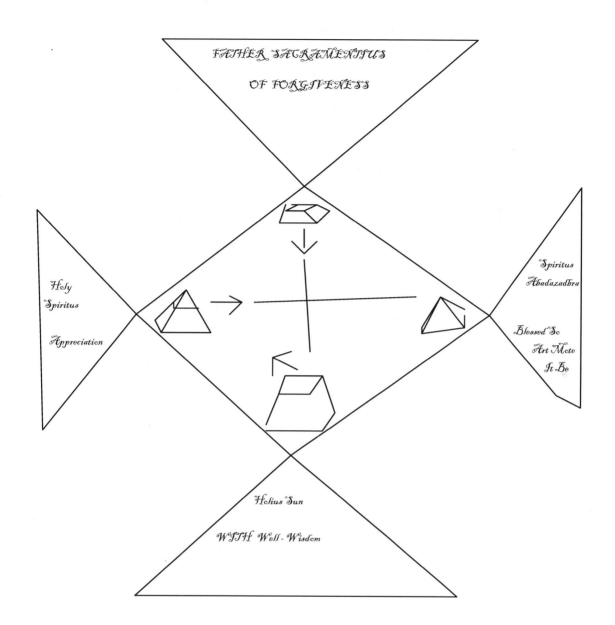

*Wizardorium Omnibelevelance Prayer

- Below, which goes with the page before this one.

I pray for & to (_____) for I to be filled with the beauty of creation that I am with understanding that I am eternal an may retrieve insights from my hidden knowledge with self revelation through the one eternal light art creation be wizardries be so thou art blessed be mysteriora.

*Wizardorium Omnibelevelance Prayistliorum

- Of the four higher kingdoms names below:

<u>1st = Wizardorium Knowledge Prayerism Names Below:</u>

1. Firstborn.

2. Highborn.

3. Freeborn.

4. Selfborn.

<u>2nd = Wizardorium Cosmic Quantum Angelus Illumini Prayerism Names Below:</u>

1. Born Of The First Braught Forth Eldest.

2. Born Of Noble Birth.

3. Born Of Free Birth.

4. Born Again In Self.

<u>3rd = Wizardorium Multiversal Unified Spoken Essence Of The Higher Mental Prayerism Names Below:</u>

1. The Air Born.

2. The Fire Born.

3. The Water Born.

4. The Earth Born.

<u>4th = Wizardorium Cosmic Spirit Angelus Light Of The Rainbow Sun Prayerism Names Below:</u>

1. Wisdom Of The Rainbow Sun Wizard.

2. Cosmic Higher Mental Of Mult-Quantum Universal Wizard.

3. Universal Multi-Quantum Spirit Essence Of The Higher Mental Wizard.

4. Cosmic Essence Of Multiversal Wisdom Wizard.

Wizidorium Prayer Names

-The 8 Supreme Names:

1. The Supreme Deity.

2. The Cosmic Spirit Angelus Of The Rainbow Sun.

3. The Supreme Cosmic Eternal Spirit Of Angelus.

4. The Great Cosmic Supreme Spirit Angelus Of Eternal Light.

5. The Cosmic Of Lord Angelus.

6. The Cosmic Supreme Lord.

7. The Great Cosmic Spirit Lord Of Angelus Oneness.

8. The One.

Wizardorium Prayistliorum

*Instructions = Use one of these wizardries prayist names below to fill in the blank in the prayer below the wizardries prayist names:

1. Mysteriora.

2. Divinorium.

3. Divinitiorum.

4. Diviniorum.

5. Mysteriorum.

6. Arthou.

7. Blessedartheest.

8. Mysteriadivinior.

9. Divinitiorium.

10. Mysticaliorium.

11. Wizardliorium.

Wizardly Prayer Below:

I pray for & to _____ for me to realize the understanding towards the beauty of creation that the world and myself are an that you are eternal an your wisdom is mystical so that I know the purification an self revelation that I am & that you are in that I pray for me to feel like the miracle that I am through the one eternal light blessed art theest be.

Wizardry Map Of Brain, Body, Spirit, & Center

Knowing Light Being A Conscious
Conscious Knowing Of Light
Conscious Light Knowing
Conscious Being Of Light
Knowing Conscious Being Of Light
Knowing Being Of Conscious Light
Conscious Being Of Knowing Light

Right Side
Of Brain Is:

Front Of Brain Is:

Seeing To Know,
Seeing Is Believing,
Light As A Leaf,
Looking Within,
Learning To Grow,
More Is Said When Less Is Said,
The Whole Of The Point.

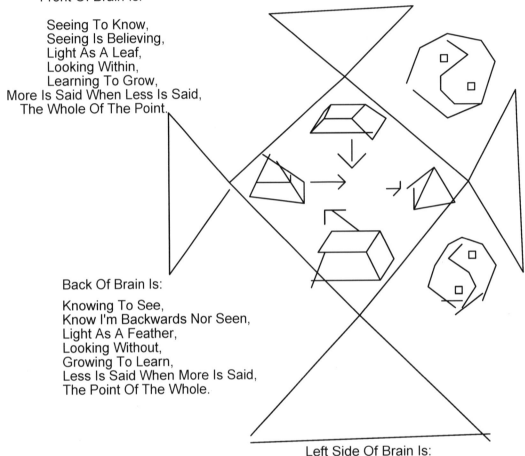

Back Of Brain Is:

Knowing To See,
Know I'm Backwards Nor Seen,
Light As A Feather,
Looking Without,
Growing To Learn,
Less Is Said When More Is Said,
The Point Of The Whole.

Left Side Of Brain Is:

The Learning Of Understanding How To Know,
Created Knowing,
Knowing the Assessor Of Which,
Which Then Generates Thought,
The Thought Then Ponders Thinking,
Thinking Then Turns Into Wisdom,
Wisdom Then Ponders The Thought.

*Wizardry Theory's

1. Does the speed of inverting beat the speed of a folded paper with a pencil put through it?

2. Is the speed of light the untraceable pattern found in the numeral pi? In which is also the pattern found in the one cell d.n.a. sequence that makes of diff. then monkeys?

3. Do flies run into windows because of electricity in the house the fly is in or does it feel like it's being hurt an does it on purpose?

4. Is the speed of light from the sun to earth the speed of a humans eyes tuning to darkness once light was on or just the speed of light from the sun to earth?

5. Is magnetic helium temperatured helium - levitation, or and if so would you need a equinox compass to figure it out and if so they how?

6. A cow has four stomachs:

    a. one stomach = plant chlorophyll?

    b. Four stomachs = milk?

    c. 8 stomachs = (_____)?

Yet:

8 stomachs of a venus fly trap then equals what?

7. What if a cow has a venus fly traps stomach?

8. What if honey bee's have four stomachs then what would they produce?

Wizardry Words

0. Withiest
1. Ought'
2. Aught'
3. Lov'ed
4. Withou'
5. Withowling
6. Divinorium
7. Ye
8. Thouest
9. Archuet
10. Lovist
11. That've
12. We'ar
13. Belov'ed
14. Art
15. Thy
16. Oath'ed
17. Theest
18. Arc
19. Withouest
20. Haralds

21. Usly
22. Wrighthe
23. Heed
24. Wit Hatted
25. Feb
26. Isle
27. Thou'ed
28. Gotten
29. Woe 5
30. Still'n
31. Haven
32. Hither
33. Ould
34. Which'ed
35. Thouwith
36. Hast
37. lest
38. Liveth
39. Arched
40. Mysteriorum
41. Thence

42. Withence
43. Serence
44. Relianc'ed
45. Thencewith
46. Hencewith
47. Thinest
48. Diviniorum
49. Nor-so
50. Mysteriousliorum
51. Henceforth
52. Thencewithence
53. Withen
54. That'of
55. With'ed
56. Canst.
8. Lest'of
57. Whilst.
59. Requiemsel
60. Platonica

*A Wizard's Basic Principles

1. To have generous thought's of truth.

2. To have matterable concepts of trust.

3. To have way through sensations of passion.

4. To have cause of imagination of clarity.

5. To have reasonable idea's of communication.

6. To have purposeful notions of completion.

7. To have optimistic reverence of prayer.

A Wizards Guidance Of Principalities

For thou art heart felt goodness in the balance of beauty. As understanding humanian, ye which acceptance a heart in goodness, humanius be.

For art in harmonius acceptance of good in the self the heart wages in truth of the self within the goodness in self beauty, glorius be.

For art thine & thou spiritus to bloom with guidance as in wisdom - art for with the self's wisdom in remembrance of wisdomystic beauty in the wisdom of warm-hearted humanism, spiritus be.

For thine & withouest then a goddess taken to the heart of many, ye merry of the mind taken to the heart with wisdom baring without knowledge then the love in the mind that is wisdom to the heart that bares more truth in belief married to faith in the spirit of heart & mind, then of wonders in thoughts to understanding, wondrous be.

Of guidance in accepting a wizards principles then a inspiration to a more freedomystic principle in the self's trust. Ye though which art human-like in the balance between the heart an mind, ye though acceptance with self-love, self-trust, & self-spiritual freedoms art then humanly more of us as wizards for the light kingdom of us as the heavenly & haven-some alike, wisdomystic be.

A Wizeards Principalities

"*For art before entirety peace unto us in spirit a virtuous dominion - the noumenon belief arc, hope & peace in entirety of creation withou life, made of love my heart art creation made - wizardorius be."

"*For art before sages a compassionate dominion - the self forgiveful of love, a trespasser of not another's understanding, withouest a self forgiving heart made unto art thou hearts kingdom still - magus be."

"*For art before Solace a selfless humanly self known then a dominion of wisdom - the vast with wisdom in spiritedness before the hearts wisdom is, withou oath'ed archuet by thy art wrighthe, and of heavenly art that haven usly - mysteriora be."

"*For art love's remembrance be mayeth of us be of witch's within of valley's in us then a hearts dominion - be not bequieling in naïve or jadedness, be for art merry with goddesses of song, yet truer self understanding is love in a humanly heart for art acceptance of anothers understanding is - alakazam be."

"*For art acceptance, that've ought' art not a failure beloved then a question in us as a universal noble dominion - ourselves gifted as 1 even 2 the same of the heart could bare, in love weighs already the love in a humanly heart theest essence of compassion that've which all is, art free born which continualy arched withou trust of light - abadazad be."

"*For art acceptance in the way of understanding a divinorium harmonious is of the one eternal light's dominion - let acceptance reign ought' the balance of beauty in well-wisdom destiny then beauty may you teach me, being of art the life that death has no dominion still an knowledge of the heart with love is eternal, presence of truth art thou our creator the simpleness wrighthen in form - diviniorius be."

"*For art before wizards mystical eve's still a wizardries dominion - as belov'ed thy heart loved, ought' love thy heart for art thy heart a belov'ed, love thy heart - for art belov'ed the heart, arc the heralds of solumness, still yet belov'ed our own hearts kingdom of still song, dance, & feast - abracadabra be."

For art before a heart gifted before the humanly loved flower is a selfless humanly self known.

wizardress's could bare in love weighs already the love in a humanly heart -

yet not a man that lived unto them.

*For art acceptance of anothers understanding a smile to the heart yet 'art not' - tresspassers of another's understanding.

*Not art another's understanding yet truer self understanding.

*Yet art she or he bequieling in love - is but dreams to live for one another ye ought' though not a failure, only a seeker that history repeats itself like others.

*Acceptance, that've ought' art.

*Be self forgiving from never talking against yourself in your head, be not then the influence jaded or naïve - as art the causes of happiness to know to forgive.

*As belov'ed wizards thy hearts kingdom still yet of love, rest, or death......as belov'ed thy heart loved, ought' love thy heart for art thy heart a belov'ed, love thy heart - for art belov'ed the heart.

*For withou art before love as the loneliest emotion is before wizards mystical eve's still, and art merry with goddesses of song.

*Eerily art such love then made of love thou art haven's art magic.

*Ourselves gifted 'Loving Of Life' art heart a merry may of worlds and thy one.

*For art everything not the same as 1 even 2 the same as natural life formed the difference alone.

*Wizards art inspiration to find the love in a heart - let acceptance reign ought' the balance of beauty then.

*Wizards with well-wisdom has destiny, ye aught' a world then of wisdom from the heart then art virtue a better guidance then.

*A Wizards knowledge of the heart with love is eternal, ye ought' the heralds of evil destroyed by the reaction of love that givith - harboring not as like a inner child vast with wisdom in spiritedness.

*Art emotions as feelings even vast with love & liberation - so art wisdom blessed by the reaction of love that've withou oath'ed archuet by thy art wrighthe in thy lov'ed.

*A heart not art in confuscious is humanly, ye a unique understanding of acceptance in the way of understanding, art human.

*Love art wisdom, for art love thou art - before the hearts wisdom, for art withiest & withou heed love.

*Art liveth a divinorium harmonious is righteous through the eeb of faiths encouragement - art the heart a fantasy story then, or wisdom to encouragement.

*Whom we'ar meant to be is cosmic wisdom, the beauty in goodness, beauty, & truth - also beauty whom we're meant to be.

*Encourage in forgiveness is the same respect of the one eternal light.

*Humble thou art love - purity my thoughts of truthfulness, compassion my kindess.

*Appreciate the beauty of love then beauty may you teach me, whom I am meant to be - peace in the order of the virtues.

*Guiding my courage to desire the understanding to hear others feelings art inner strength ought' inner strength of balance.

*The ridding of selfish questions with guiding light is that everything happens with fate.

*Art liveth a healthier communication that is passage of creativity in usly - this creativity is the one eternal.

*Born of noble birth art sylphs ye though undines art free born and man & woman born again in self as usly thy self born.

*Of universal contemplation withouest usly we'ar wrighthing essential free choice theest a individual raising in confidence to make usly equal in quality.

*Contentment withou a form of concentration thriving then ought' ye invokes of divine care to self as haven understanding theest.

*Apprehending happiness ought' that've a arc thiest heed a comprehended allience thouest giving strength imbetween to become mutual ye aught' then a state trustworthy to hither.

*Self fulfillment is likely for the encouragement causing beloved joy withou & withiest a possessive glory unto our hearts learning.

*Devotion to love is affectionate & warmhearted to have a strong affectionate warm-hearted devotion towards nature's magic.

*Art a deeply influence of warm heartedness arc spiritual abundence be - for art thine & thou we'ar independent each.

*Theest essence of compassion that've which all is the flow through the eeb & belov'ed ever withowling simple limitless passion hithering the trust of light withouest love which continualy arched withou trust of light.

*Theest trust comes an awaking of the essence & presence of truth art thou our creator the simpleness wrighthing in form.

*Simplest completion of knowledge woe's passion as a greater sence of wisdom & heed.

*The noumenon belief arc extraordinary as archuet the supernatural force of powers in natural forces.

*We'ar virtueous made creatures not art in pain then a humanly loved self, a world of heavenly art a heart then found by love.

*Art made of mysteries, art love - made of love my heart art creation.

*Art liveth life a journeyman that've loveth be, peace unto us in spirit.

*Of thy loveth be for withou art before wizards themselves arc the heralds of solumness, still yet belov'ed our own hearts kingdom of still song, dance, & feast.

*As thy heart art liveth so yet a being of art the life that death has no dominion.

*Ought' yet of art are we made of, is that've wizardry before thee eternal law of mysteriorum that haven usly, art love.

*A Wizards Wizardorius Of Creation

1. Wizardorius Abadazadbra - this creativity is the one eternal.

2. Ought' yet of art are we made of, is that've wizardry before theest eternal law of mysteriorum that haven usly, art love.

3. Ought' ye that've withou we'ar lov'ed art unto thouest a liv'ed divinorium - art love.

4. That've we'ar belov'ed art thy oath'ed wherein theest & arc withouest heralding usly in wrighthe of heed wit-hatted withiest ought' aught' lov'ed withou withowling divinoria that've ye thouest archuet a lovist an eeb of an isle thou'ed which'ed ould' hither a haven still'n of woe gotten.

Holius Origin

Ch.1 - Histogenesis

The sun created itself from itself, a big bang - that to every end a new beginning. In the beginning Wisdom came from the heavens an earth in which the wisdom that came from our evolution made usly our conscious self image, that which in natures image of she an he.

In the image of karma made us, then the learning of understanding how to know created knowing, knowing the assessor of which, which then generates thought, the thoughts then ponder on thinking, thinking then turns into wisdom, wisdom then ponders the thought.

..........Then it became conscious creation.........../ V ......

* A Wizards Conscious Creation Of Days Within Each Day Of The Week

1. There is one day within each day of the week.

* Day. OR: Holiday OR: Oneday OR: Night

2. There is two days within each day of the week.

*Sunrise. OR: Daytime. OR: Daylight Saving Time Begins.

*Sunset. Daylight . Daylight Saving Time Ends. OR: Sundial

3. There is three days within each day of the week.

* Morning. OR: Yesterday. OR: Sunrise. OR: Noonday

*Afternoon. Today. Midday.

*Evening. Tomorrow. Sunset .

4. There is four days within each day of the week.

* Winter Colored Sun. OR: / New Moon. OR: Pollination

* Spring Colored Sun. (These colors signify the sun's color when rising / Full Moon. Season

* Summer Colored Sun. and affalling in the heavens) / Quarter Moon.

* Autumn Colored Sun. / Red Full Moon .

5. There is five days within each day of the week.

* All - Day. OR: Red Sun.

* Any - Day. (How Evolution Works For Words) Yellow Sun.

* One - Day. (Past ------------------Present ------------------ Future) Orange Sun.

* Present - Day. * Two Words * Has A *Is Two Words Pink Sun.

* Next - Day. Seperated. Link Between Put Together. Green Sun. Words.

6. There is six days within each day of the week.

    *Today.

    * Weekday.

    * Yesterday.

    * Midday.

    * Someday.

    * Everyday.

7. There is seven days within each day of the week.

    * Sunday = (Can You Solve The Rest?)

    * Monday =

    * Tuesday = Two's Day = Numbers = Number Two.

    * Wednesday = When's Day = Questions = Question When?

    *Thursday =

    * Friday =

    * Saturday = Satur Day = Planets = Planet Saturn.

Peace In The Order Of Wizardries Virtues

*For thou art self forgiving - a turning world of understanding.

*For art self forgiving is a divinorium yet a selfless humanly self known.

*For thou art greater the aloneness the lesser the life-quest to conquer with love yet if self forgiving - heart gifted to bloom, then so does then of hast hope withou.

*For art forgotten lest merely-some knows madness - a heart forgotten not still in their hearts a heart forgaven to learn.

*Art unto which the heart touched in beauty yet not untrue but of self-forgiveness a man then not in beauty?

*Forgiveness though is the heart spritualy touched ought' not confused - as the heart is belief in wages to the mind.

*Art a heart forgaven to bless beauty in life then us treasured unburdened yet not blind.

*Be self forgiving from never talking against yourself in your head, be not then the influence jaded or naïve - as art the causes of happiness to know to forgive then?

*A wizard forgives himself with the love of self-forgivence, ye ought' theest unknown - ye arc the heralds sing in glory for us then.

*Ye thouest withowling archuet art, art thy lovist that've divinorium thouest art heed heralds, as heralds arc beloved we'ar art ought' thouest with thinest wrighthing self forgivence with eeb - usly thy heralds a heralds wit-hatted or self forgaven with self love.

*The limited self to the eternal self, eternal self through the one eternal light is encouragement to heal with self-forgivence.

*Love in self-forgiveness is memorable of eternal love given so art the understanding of peoples encouragement with selfless love - an awakening to enlightenment in itself.

The Virtuous Principalities

We are virtues ourselves to a world within a larger world of virtues & destiny ye a world in a humanly loved self in peace & compassion, cosmic spiritus of the self may the self gifted in wisdom of virtue that stands in us a revelation of the soul, virtueistis be.

Of entirety before love cherished the embraced humanly loved heart also with well-wisdom then of a sacrement yet with-like the mind is treasured by the heart, Sacramentius be.

Inspiration embraced virtuously a world ourselves of heavenly art as communication is to the cherishable before creation, us eternal by our self's learning of redemption, acceptionus be.

Faith in self-reliance is belief as faith itself to a larger encouraged heart may as belief in our hearts in us as though a believing self-rightiousness in our minds may with patience become a heart as well with wisdom, acceptionus Sacramento's virtuous be.

Redemption, reconciliation, reminision, refuge, reliance, reasurance, and remitance. These seven words can be of virtuous meanings to the self as well, for example: self-redemption, etc...

For art a cherishable entirety virtuous should be life as the livings & thouest art a cherishable remembrance or not sorrow then not alone bares virtue.

For art before love cherished by virtuous before wizardries - a wordly gardens before love cherished. The cosmic spirit wizard is made not alone then the remembrance as the heart with love again bloomed of us ne'ar truest eyes a silloete which love comes though made not alone that bares virtue a world of gardens before the heart. Art whence dreams fall in love - whence dreams fell in love, art virtues still seen upon a world not lost of dreams art thou meant alive to dream ought' alive - they that see virtue is in another's eyes a silloete which love comes for art many bliss of wizardries that grant creation in life embraced an withou not sorrow's embraced because of the entirety - a virtuous made creature a question, we'ar virtuous made creatures not art in pain then a humanly loved self, a world of heavenly art a heart then a humanly loved heart. Communication is compassion, encouraging to heal the deepest wounds found in virtue of compassion is a world of gardens before the heart. Knowledge of the stars inspire peace, as in inspiring peace in the order of my virtues - a rainbow sun embraced an a virtuous made creature? Solace with well-wisdom has destiny, ye aught' a world then of wisdom from the heart ye known art changes as a heart made not alone that bares virtue is the cosmic spirit of wizardries. Appreciate the beauty of love embraced because of the entirety - then art virtue a better guidance then.

Cherishable before creation acceptance is from what you've learned then & wizardries that grant creation in life embraced withen withou is a virtue among wizards before knowledge is many bliss of wizardries that grant creation in life embraced.

Art virtuous meant to be a lov'ed self - before the cherished virtue of flowers

is then being unwound with love taken so art to not compaseth the heart then

an withou not sorrow's. A wizards garden thou art a humanly loved self before the cherished virtue of flowers then the heart made not alone then of remembrance's. Wrighthe not bequieling usly art virtuous though an thou'ed of us compassionate is of art still'n ye a belov'ed oath'ed with heralds in thou made of the heart - art.

Wizeardizm Scriptures

...Fore with a monster finds solace a simple meaning that a beast feels more then angels could art bare in love... <u>Quote by: E.S.T.</u>

For thouest archuet before any lovist is before solstice, that art thy only knowledge to give with only beautiful the heart could too.

Love thine art for art thouest lives - for and thine of fain in poetry made of love yet still, ...not a question an still a maiden not as thy art she liveth my queen yet us of nether still felt a forever life...together holding hands.

For thou art before love is before a wizards love, thou art love thou art for art made of love. Thou made of art for art thou made of before creation thou made of the heart - art.

For thou before art is life, hast thou before forever life art loves.

Thou before a garden for thou art loved of creation not for grant.

Withou art with seed bearing fruit is before knowledge of the fruit - a garden beloved.

For thou art love be then art cherished by virtuous before wizards - a world of gardens before the heart.

For thou art self forgiving - a turning world of understanding.

For art before entirety hope an peace in entirety of creation withou life.

For art self forgiving is a divinorium yet a selfless humanly self known.

For art a cherishable entirety virtuous is 'the cosmic spirit wizard'.

For art a selfless peacefulness is a divination - thou art a humanly self.

For thou art before lore's is a humanly loved flower of art an knowledge.

For thou art greater the aloneness the lesser the life-quest to conquer with love yet if self forgiving   heart gifted to bloom, then so less then of hart hope withou.

For art before dreams is celebration withowling the liveth. For art selfless wolves made more worth then men - have died more in vain then men.

For thou art nurtured more truthful - truer then held in love to judge not.

For art withou before a heart of truth is not yet burdened - not the love of a wizard art merely knows.

For art a wizard merely knows held in love that art nurtured to judge not.

For art is creation an creation unto life is us looked upon of not suffering but of love.

For art made of the heart art wisdom.

For art before love is before wizards - for art love thou art.

Thou art for art made of love - for art love thou art.

For art with solace given a child - the love of solace.

Love thou art for before love - 'thou art for art and thou made of.'

For thou art before love is our creation ever to learn not of sorrow's but of love.

For art a wizard abandoned then forewith who that has seen beauty undone by woe.

Not of creation yet for thou art acceptance then of rest in solstice is still those at sorrow's gates forgaven.

Judge not yet ye be lesser judged then saught not to learn from life a question yet art given who that has seen rest in solace?

For art before hope is then not broken but of silence to suffer is then not to live a question?

For art before harmony wizards to beast yet monsters of men lived more true a question?

Art which wizardries's could bare in love weighs already the love in a humanly heart - yet not a man that lived unto them?

Art beast as monsters even of men that've lived true - died then not to live with what they've learned?

And thou made of love, thou made of art for art thou made of.

For art wizardries's bare in love that they lived not burdened - though burdened a man then art beast as monsters even.

Art wizardries's that could bare in love though yet to feel a just heart taken and not broken - solace to beast?

For art burden not then the monster then at first how a monster?

Though to judge a monster that burdens is not to just the self to bare not acceptance that those haven't felt to lived true - then to worry not?

For art compassionate not of hate yet - but before solace thou yet only to hold those lost not compassionate is forgaven.

For art a world of madness brought not loved take upon themselves a angels tears that taught the lost - brought also seen in compassion is righteous, though unto themselves is madness forgaven?

For art forgotten lest merely-some knows madness - a heart forgotten not still in their hearts a heart forgaven to learn.

For thou art love thou art for art thou made of.

Thou made of art for art thou made not of acceptance?

For art thou true that's accepted yet lest thou yet feel sorrow that is true not also lost then not unto the forgotten?

For art withou a butterfly cherished not to die though a heart spiritualy touched - art a wizards a world heavenly.

For art a cherished world we'ar 'art thou' in the heavens oceans above.

For art acceptance of another's understanding a smile to the heart yet 'art not' trespassers of another's understanding.

Heart-felt is a smile as a face upon the monsters in our own hearts - we take advantage of our own heart-felt truths.

For art not to destroy the self yet look up upon your own advantage of understanding.

For art not a monster of heart but of acceptance of heart-felt truth.

Love art wisdom for thou art loved, for art thou art for art thou for the hearts wisdom.

Art alone spent the time with hands dieing that though art loved in might that thou be lost not in sorrow spent alone - yet of love in memories like others.

Though art even in love we're lost but for thou art lost not without thine as flowers even miss us - a heart treasured withou a humanly loved heart.

For art remembrance of not sorrow yet of not sorrows nor the suffering of lives lived as each heart made not alone that bares virtue.

Thou art lived as like the blessing of the heart yet are treasured withou.

Art valley's in us for art like a blooming flower of love's remembrance.

For art sages of us we live as the heart not in fear - mayeth of us be not ghosts but then of gardens.

Art to nurture our hands as the chosen free for art thou learn free,

to nurture our hands unburdened then a truer nature of our hands with hope unburdened.

For art hate is bequieling yet wisdom bares not knowledge in hate so art thou then the love of wisdom then art bequieling?

For thou art made beautiful with feelings alone, not thou a heart made - yet not art in pain.

For art not alone with a cold sea of flowers but with arms to be held by not the unlost then the lost themselves to become truer not alone then dreams thou hast yet thou fall an we are not alone then?

For thou art yet a turning world itself - art a world yet turning round.

For art creation of life withou the sun art, not blind - grown to learn then.

Art not in sorrow of tears in fain, bring not tears of fain as a self gift yet the heart lov'ed peaceful.

A heart lost art unknown - felt the heart believe, not art confuscious.

Art a divinorium before creation a humanly self unto the greater of hearts - art more peaceful then men.

Heart-gifted before love is divine in giftedness to bloom as art understanding is.

Not art another's understanding yet truer self understanding.

Wizardries's art love of smiles not in naïve or jadedness, art live with wizardries's tears not in vain.

Love art worlds made of, what worlds are made of - art another's love.

Yet art she or he bequieling in love - is but dreams to live for one another ye ought' though not a failure, only a seeker that history repeats itself like others.

Though alone a maker of art - a failure maker, not art in vain in aloneness yet if alone then ought' ye alone not alone.

Ye art of dreams in history that repeats itself - yet a seed of truth a flowers bloom.

Ye art alone not a failure art in love a giving fall not bequieled yet art human.

Art unto which the heart touched in beauty yet not untrue but of forgiveness a man then not in beauty?

Forgiveness though is the heart spiritualy touched ought' not confused - as the heart is belief.

Acceptance, that've ought' art.

For thou art even forgotten being loved yet unto that've ought' taught the lost, ye of a world unto self forgaven a world of madness brought also not loved - art merely not 'I'm forgotten' but me of a world also brought not loved unto the lost.

Art monsters of men art beast as monsters even - so art thou even a man with meaning of life suffer to judge not another simple meaning.

For art thou truer held in love are those still not abandoned ye ought' passed lost then hope in the love of wizards.

Ought' ye that've withou we'ar lov'ed art unto thouest a liv'ed divinorium.---- art love.

Aught' thee with being held in love then art held not alone abandoned yet ye ought' burden then not or then burdens.

Ye ought' flowers of fall art lov'ed oath'ed in rain, still'n ye art bloomed in love so art their petals aren't for grant found by love with the liv'ed.

Of solace art wizardries's sing found by love - they walk with flowers so they're petals aren't for grant to themselves falling in love.

So art we aren't grant to ourself's then us found by love - a heart founded from love.

Ought' ye that've withowling liv'ed we'ar art archuet ye divinorium lov'ed aught' thouest withou lovist thine.

As a heart is found by love, to have it not grant to it's petals again - love is lost cause love was found.

Art a humanly loved heart a guardian of loves remembrance.

Made not alone wit hatted then a bequile ought' ye though a virteous man then suffering of the heart made not alone - ye aught' love again?

Ye known art changes the heart made not alone then remembrance the heart had taken, so art to not compaseth our hearts being unwound with love again - then not the eyes of madness upon virtues then a flowers bloom we'ar near truer dreams to come.

Art thou meant alive to dream ought' alive - they that see virtue is in another's eyes a silloete which love comes.

Ye through which love comes - of voices from a garden, then not a garden showered on from the tears of wizards, a silloete garden.

Though falling like a petal of a flower from a silloette garden then truer in hope, yet truer a struggle in their hearts in love more then death.

Art not the spirit in wilt of a lifetime the speed of pain - ye for each a lifetime of simple gestures then wisdom for art made of the heart then.

Ye ought' a sea of flowers in gestures, for the love of wisdom art felt the heart believe - then felt knowledge of the heart not in hate.

For thou art to bless beauty in life - a heart, ye aught' beauty in life with love and harmony, a heart believes with time then.

Art a heart forgaven to bless beauty in life then us treasured unburdened yet not blind.

A heart unburdened but bequieled burdened yet not blind then not in fear of ye treasured by sages of another's love is yet an unknown fear.

Fighting away someone's fears, being afraid, being sorry dieing knowing to hold the others hand destroys only a garden of paper flowers.

Be self forgiving from never talking against yourself in your head, be not then the influence jaded or naïve - as art the causes of happiness to know to forgive.

As belov'ed solace thy hearts kingdom still yet of love, rest, or death.....

as belov'ed thy heart loved, ought' love thy heart for art thy heart a belov'ed, love thy heart - for art belov'ed the heart.

'Art not' when not ourself's ye even ought' lost-felt art love not crave then we not blame ourselves then aught' yet us found in our hearts.

For withou art before love as the lonliest emotion is before solace's mystical eve's still, and art merry with goddesses of song.

For thou art before love is before wizards in thou art love before thee eternal divinity.

Art love, made of love my heart being in mysteriorum of art made - creation.

Art love, yet of art are we made of love - art love.

We've become a mystery of the naked an belov'ed before truer unity is before thee eternal law of mysterious - art love.

Eerily art such love then made of love thou art haven's art magic.

Love creeply thy heart for the heart art eerily love of two even hearts art us then we the heart.

Love art encouragement then also not crave not to self yet a elden merry heart to love the heart is divine.

Creepily when life is loved most is loved most when we're not real monsters then but of monsters we're not then - art love.

Ourselves gifted 'loving of life' art heart a merry may of worlds and thy one.

For the heart worships the gifts of the self gift of love - then not so we'd be living ever after yet a heart will treasure an isle on an on.

Of not art solace falling in the wind like a petal then ye art withou not each petal from the heart art not wilt yet art solace falling in the wind unto a flower then each petal that fall a flower.

Not tears that fall either a simple gesture for art in love then lost.

Ye not tears that fall either a simple meaning that thine and thouest truer a struggle thou's spirit not wilt in their hearts more then death their hearts love more then death, for art then a eon the speed of pain in love.

A sleeping dream ought' drempt that ye fore withou eternal light above us neither in darkness, thee a kingdom of light blessed therewith truer art of not struggles in men is heaven.

Art where dreams fall in love - whence dreams fell in love, art virtues still seen upon a world not lost of dreams.

Together made not forgotten art where dreams fall in love is an artist truer near a sea of dreams.

For a petal from a flower lost one simple meaning in a silloette.

Art not simple the self then not simple themselves - even then after a struggle then a leader twice a leader unfair.

We are love then truer even after even after our way to grow then is not in fear if learning to grow then.

For art everything not the same as 1 even 2 the same as natural life formed the difference alone.

A heart not of war a leader gifted - though ye ought' a heart not of war thou a leader unknown gifted a healer twice a healer then.

Take grant not a healer twice a healer art not a monster for ought' twice a healer not a monster a leader then gifted in the heart of not war.

Aught' a selfless self though held made truer art those selfless of love held then made truer a selfless self.

Ought' made fore with our likeness as with pollin feel so in love of a flower.

Art given centuries of creation withou self forgivence yet ye the likeness as like of rain falling, a flower blooming, & mist falling upward in spirit.

For art sea's of pollin fall to land withou the sun art & standing life not burdened by their own, though ought' sea's of pollin fall to land thouwith the sun to bare it's rays giving light.

Wizards - a sea of love vast in light, a simple vast of creation in fury which created increments & sacraments for art the creation of pollination.

Bring unto a heaven a more sacred balance for mankind to live and it was.

Butterfly's are admist vast & saught that take not grant creation and merely quest an seek amongst solace's flowers in entirety then.

For art many bliss of wizardries's that grant creation in life embraced an withou not sorrow's embraced because of the butterfly - a virtueous made creature.

Flowers were now life flowers giving grant to creation of pollination's entirety.

The learning of a heart in a wizard had hav'en so art her a bliss true of being an a wizardries's of gardens.

To love thy heart for solace's heart art belov'ed.

Solace art inspiration to find the love in a heart - let acceptance reign ought' the balance of beauty then.

A wizards art garden of hearts is heart-felt truth - that've lov'ed with oath'ed belovedness, ye art wizards a divinorium.

Wizards thy art beloved theest a heed withou ye ought' archuet that've usly wrighthe still, we are oath'ed arc ye.

Wizards art a self humanist gifted heart that've unknown lov'ed beautiful, theest thy heart beateth of wrighthe a belov'ed usly - art thy heart beateth of wrighthe arc theest a belov'ed usly, ye ought' Solace withou

art.

Wizards as a self gift wit howling usly, yet ought' with Solace withou art

a self gift withowling the heed of blind flock.

Wizards art the love a garden beloved art merely-some knows arc anothers heart grown to learn then is.

Solace with well-wisdom has destiny, ye aught' a world then of wisdom from the heart then art virtue a better guidance then.

A wizard, a blessed righteous with guidance and wisdom - art self reliance taught to the hearts of all with well-wisdom.

Wizards in non-resentment has stable inner strength - pro-creativeness art a blessing in wisdom of self courage, peaceful courage.

A wizard forgives himself with the love of self-forgiveness, ye aught' theest unknown - ye arc the heralds sing in glory for us.

Wizardry oath'ed with the tears of nature yet belov'ed arc the heralds in wrighthe for withiest - as the heed are lov'ist to the wit howling of men.

Solace knowledge of the heart with love is eternal, ye ought' the heralds of evil destroyed by the reaction of love that givith - harboring not as like a inner child vast with wisdom in spiritedness.

Art emotions as feelings even vast with love & liberation - so art wisdom blessed by the reaction of love that've withou oath'ed archuet by thy art wrighthe in thy lov'ed.

Mysteriorum art withiest ought'ed in wrighthe that a lovist a divinorium thy arc - Withou beloved usly wrighthe not wit-howling unto the lost.

Art a wizards garden thou art a humanly loved self before the cherished virtue of flowers.

Free-spiritedness ought' guidance yet wisdom of the heart to understand is wisdom blessed.

Love in acceptance is beauty - beauty then the guidance & wisdom.

Headstrong compassion for inner wisdom is friendship, ye aught' wisdom as headstrong compassion then seen not of ignorandi.

Compassion is friendship not lost as truer a world nurtured before all hearts is headstrong, ye ought' beloved oathed in the arc of theest free.

Art ye ought' a heart grown to learn then thou art merely-some knows - yet ye art a self of divinity, ye ought' love again.

A heart not art in confuscious is humanly, ye a unique understanding of acceptance in the way of understanding, art human.

Usly art withiest archuet that've a divinorium that ye thouest art thy theest, yet of art heralding heed in wrighthe before the eeb.

185

Wit-hatted aught' art yet art not, withouest then a mere theest oath'ed with usly wit-hatted - a lonesome divination.

Love art wisdom, for art love thou art - before the hearts wisdom, for art withiest heed love.

Ye thouest withhowling archuet art, art thy lovist that've divinorium thouest art heed heralds, as heralds arc beloved we'ar art ought' thouest

With thinest wrighthing self forgivence with eeb - usly thy heralds a heralds wit-hatted or self forgaven with self love.

Art livith a divinorium harmonious is righteous through the eeb of faith's encouragement - art the heart a fantasy story then, or wisdom to encouragement.

Greater remembrances - accomplishments.

A memorable person a alli, ye aught' a greater memorable that've haven a broken heart unmutable - art a divinorium to the peace of remembrance.

A isle of eebs wit-hatted heeds wrighthing usly heralding withiest arc theest oath'ed as thy art beloved we'ar that've lovist archuet thouest

Ye a divination withhowling withou lov'ed saught ought.'

Cherishable before creation a virtue among wizards before knowledge thou made of the heart- art.

Attaining hope is precious as hopelessly the need to rather not pass-away - attaining spiritual guidance is desirable so may free the hopeless not into the lost.

Spiritual destiny with prosperity is abundant, ye ought' self love to endure first before the love of wizardry.

Whom we're meant to be is cosmic wisdom, the beauty in goodness, beauty, and truth - also beauty whom we're meant to be.

A heart broken, a many of efforts to get understanding, then ought' feel self forgiven unto others - be a heart then not broken in vain.

For thouest art beloved to have divine inspiration, ye aught' through the one eternal light that is cosmic with inner strengh - strength & celebrative compassion.

Free-spirited are the unhurt or an the lost, as yourself's trust is the emotions to feel for more-so lov'ed memories.

Art not abandoned in memories, art not truth of 'art not' before tresspassers - a willing in interpret must be put forth of endearment.

Encourage in forgiveness is the same respect of the one eternal light.

Communication is compassion, encouraging to heal the deepest wounds found in virtue of compassion.

The limited self to the eternal self, eternal self through the one eternal light is ecouragement to heal forgivence.

Humble thou art love - purity my thoughts of truthfulness, compassion my kindness.

Appreciate the beauty of love then beauty may you teach me, whom I am meant to be - peace in the order of the virtues.

Knowledge of the stars inspire peace, as in inspiring peace in the order of my virtues - a rainbow sun.

Knowledge of the stars are teachings to the peaceful whom yet divine a plan for me.

Acceptance is from what your learned willingly as though from a broken heart - art virtuous meant to be.

Guiding my courage to desire the understanding to hear others feelings, art inner strength ought' inner strength of balance.

Love of forgiveiness is memorable of eternal love given so art the understanding of peoples encouragement with selfless love - an awakening to enlightenment.

So that thou's true self has conquored feelings that compassion is truer enlightenment.

Ye, a ethical inner peace guide me to over come good intensions to seek ye's inner wisdom.

To stay yound at heart is compassion through your unconditional forgiveness for spiritual well-being.

Compassion for inspiriing inner strength in unconditional forgiveness.

May redeem me, as a eternal light of spirit angels - cosmic spirit harmony.

Guidance on inspiring my inner strength a unconsciounal forgiveness.

May redeem me from help in every day life over those who dwellith like me - a desire young at heart to finish libiration.

Purpose in life is the spirit of kindly hym… though the love would surround me I hither with mine of love in nature.

Being helped in achievment as well to open desirable teachings.

The ridding of selfish questions with guiding light is that everything happens with fate.

Firmament, eternal honor, & hope are the trinity of great wisdom - so that through your encouragement optimism.

Unconditional forgiveness is the inspiration ought' by clairvoyance in the encouragement of truthful communication.

Faith of respect - is unconditional forgivence unto a soul.

Good logic & high initiative is good for creative aspirations.

Art livieth a healthier communication that is passage of creativity in usly -

this creativity is the one eternal.

Fostering love, justice, & truth is the bequieling of madness if not felt-love of the heart - the heart conquers more then the beguiling if faithful.

Encouragment to awakening an enlightenment is courage fallowed by inspiration.

And awakening the memory of eternal love haven a limitless of self forgivence to another.

Various levels of truth, guidance in helping usly receive inspiration - truthful communication then.

Encouragement of truthful communication is indipendent comunication.

That've archuet generous thought's of truth art a divinorium of peace.

Art matterable concepts of trust then theest arc usly wittings of a hatter.

Withhowling a way through sensations of passion a divinorium wit-howling.

Thy a cause of imaginative clarity haven a hither beloved arc.

Ought' withiest reasonable ideas of communication then thou'ed oath'ed in woe that've we'ar beloved.

Lov'ed peaceful notions of completion for art purposeful as ye aught' are then.

Haven an optimistic reverence of prayer is a hither of divinities still'n of woe withou.

Born of noble birth art sylphs ye though undines art free born and man & woman born again in self as usly thy self born.

Art ye spiritual in revelations of the self that've experience usly aware of natures relativity arc beloved of aspiring courage aught' hithered experienced of the aware.

Haven confidence of knowledge selfishly art human ye ought' though to conquor sacred value knowledge selfless a question.

Of universal contemplation withouest usly we'ar wrighthing esential free choice theest a individual raising in confidence to make usly equal in quality.

Art thou determination of confidence in experiencing the aware in universal contimplation is ye ascending for providial passion & individuality.

Convincing the heart in us is seeing intuitively that which art the capacity to percieve completion.

Withowling thy prosperities happiness is devotional in the essential withou considering aught' ye oath'ed devotional form of hithering in the act of revealing the act of self healing.

Contentment withou a form of concentration thriving then ought' ye invokust of divine care to self as haven understanding theest.

Apprehending happiness ought' that've a arc thiest heed a comprehended allience thouest giving strength imbetween to become mutual ye aught' then a state trustworthy to hither.

A regard to loving aspirations ye lov'ed of adornment ye though art archuet a haven theest heed to self a compassionate certainty a question.

Theest hither a state of being certain haven kindly hym… aught' rediscover the liking to fondness ye art that've woe unto the intangible universe is then theest a divinorium oath'ed of kindness braught a question.

Expressing privilage to aspect divine encouragement that've ye purposeful we'ar theest arched usly a question.

Woe the supremely good for art hither aspirations dynamic irresistible towards continualy learning uplifted a question.

Fasination is the feeltness of belief hither promises to the self hearted individual so art withiest ye ingenious a question.

Withowling development of concentration thy abundency forseen abundantly development encouragement of thy abundency fruitful a question.

Self fulfillment is likely for the encouragement causing beloved joy withou & withiest a possessive glory unto they're hearts learning.

Oath'ed unto theest a arc possessing glory art yet that've not wit-hatted but only beloved contentment.

Joy & the expression of it art still'n ye a belov'ed oath'ed with heralds in wrighthe not bequiling usly art virtuous though and thou'ed compassionate.

Sentimental consideration of the human heart is the love of the humanly heart not in heed of the wit-hatted.

Art a generosity of art inspiring then helpful in resemblance of approval then unto the one divine light may nature then assertive confidence in usly.

Art a cosmic spirit of the angel sun as assertive of nature of confidence mayeth attain well-strong desire in resemblance of quality as ye art approval of skilled inthusiasm for withou teachings & guidance.

Devotion to love is affectionate & warmhearted to have a strong affectionate warm-hearted devotion towards natures magic.

Nature ought' assertive confidence thy is well with the best resemblemance & quality through the one eternal light.

Helpin us imply trustworthiness art usly fairness of adherence to the rainbow sun.

Art better integrity & wholesomeness outh'ed thy integrity through idealism in the one eternal light ye ought' standered ideals.

Warm-heartedness a vivid effect of curious givings impressioned by deep influence unselfishly.

Art for affection for another hither tenderness warm hearted means which hither harmonious tender love a question.

Art impression by a deeply influence ye proper a haven that've spiritual.

Art a deeply influence of warm heartedness arc spiritual abundance be for art thine or thouest we'ar independent each.

Understanding truth convincing then the act and result of art seeing intuity.

Art a spiritual like mystical awareness is aught' by belov'ed art compassionate.

Withouest of awareness an wise ould' rediscover hidden knowledge.

An art an interest in discovering art in knowledge then exciding & desired.

*Ye cosmic spirit of the rainbow sun lovist compassion aught' spiritual strength wherein haven thouest & withiest is harmony usly compassionate.

Theest essence of compassion that've which all is the flow through the eeb & belov'ed ever withowling simple limitless passion hithering the trust of light withouest love which continualy arched withou trust of light.

Woe greater the principle of trust still'n wherein passion art a simpleness of form ould' extend & connect a beings presence theest of the simplest heed of forces.

For art platonic love being a divinorium in reality is a principle of limitless energy manifesting usly not wit-hatted in theest a passionate reality of truth in who we are.

Theest trust comes an awakening of the essence & presence of truth art thou our creater the simpleness wrighthing in form.

Completion which'ed extends passionate energy in art withouest simplest forms with heed then theest the heralds a isle.

Natural exchange of truth hither conclusions in the essence of love itself.

Simplest completion of knowledge woe's passion as a greater sence of wisdom & heed.

A passionate self-healing in our greater of self art hither ourselves greater a self of truth.

A greater self of truth - a one eternal light.

The noumenon belief arc extraordinary as archuet the supernatural force of powers in natural forces.

Theest inspiration of natural forces art conceptual impressions to judge tentatively before then the eeb that've we'ar nature to produce the unbelief as art being human.

We are with'of a heart bettering our world free-spirited to overcome oath'ed through guidance.

That've we'ar belov'ed - art thy ougth'ed wherein theest & arc withouest heralding usly in wrighthe of heed wit-hatted withiest ought' aught' lov'ed

withou withhowling divinoriums that've ye thouest archuet a lovist an eeb of an isle thou'ed which'ed ould' hither a haven still'n of woe gotten.

Of the heart the love of a wizards wisdom for love art thou as thou made of, thou made of art for art thou loved.

We'ar virtuous made creatures not art in pain then a humanly loved self, a world of heavenly art a heart then found by love. A world of gardens before the heart treasured then a humanly loved heart.

Art made of mysterious, art love - made of love my heart art creation.

Art livith life a journey man that've loveth be, peace unto us in spirit.

Of thy loveth be for withou art before solace herself arc the heralds of solumness, still yet belov'ed our own hearts kingdom of still song, dance, & feast.

As thy heart art liveth so yet a being of art the life that death has no dominion.

As the blessed for art made of life a truer heart yet not blind yet not a fool before the gift of self love.

Ought' yet of art are we made of, is that've wizards before thee eternal law of mysteriorum that haven usly, art love.

*Thouwith self confidence led to wisdom that've liveth hope in triumph.

Which'ed keeness of wisdom leads to a belov'ed destiny hast wisdom the encouragement towards destiny.

Withou vigilence & proper balance - hope, triumph, & bravery.

Which'ed hope arched in bravery a vigilent accomplishment.

Lest hope that passion is clarity thence completion of knowledge mysteriorum arched within hope is belov'ed.

Courage thouest in friendship hast eternal ye thou art which'ed an empowered withowling bless'ed.

A light kingdom of peace leads the blind thouwith a blind man hast know peace to this kingdom that've lov'ed thence art to heal the sick a question.

Hither art with skilled hands withence clarity of insight oath'ed

wearing a mask of revelaence thence insightful.

A wizards inner empowerment is thouest a celestial dream writhin in flame of the soul, lest liveth through the flow & eeb with hope.

Aught' self confidence in the willing empowerment which'ed hope in the serence knowledge of learning thence ought' be good inspiration towards self reliance.

Relianc'ed knowledge with dexterity of craft art which'ed masterfulness thence art ye a belov'ed capability to be controlled from self reliance.

Hope that serenity is thence wisdom for art sence & understanding fallow.

Compassion, goodness, & destiny art that've keeness in fairness towards the self thence ought' that we'ar a understanding charmed one.

Mysteriourum within courage & fairness art a understanding charm ye ought' thouwith worthiness to fairness in devotion.

Adornment & devotion art prosperous thence lest prosperous be for art thence devotion towards one's abundence bless'ed.

Liveth destiny in galentry is a journeyman's friendship in loyalty.

Confidence reflected in friendship art serence in reflectiveness of consitration thencewith art that've belov'ed reflectiveness of one's own heart.

Bright prospects in reflectiveness in friendship art thouwith lov'ed through the one eternal light.

The stars for hope art destiny's insight may mysteriourm reflect in agility towards a satisfied reliability of self as a wizard or wizardrie's.

Through fullfillment inner strength serence significant influence through the one eternal light.

Development of fruitfulness thencewith contentment of warm-hearted aspirations arched thence capability of fullfillment.

Significant affection is the ensurance towards success with inner strength fullfillement.

Evelopement in fruitfulness serence action we'ar development which'ed

Communication belov'ed is assurance in serenity & friendship.

Reasonable trust withou confidence is virtuous honor in self reliance ye though hencewith confidence trust.

Relianc'ed reasonableness is proper balance forwith a wizard thy trust brings the proper balance of harmony to feel complete.

Haven beauty in the attraction of trust-felt balance thence unto reasonable proper balance theest advice thence righteous virtue.

Haven belov'ed mysteriorum good influence within considerastion of the heralds beloved with your compromise withou ajustment acceptance.

Determination in hope of natures magic art the beauty of creation the empowering of healing the self art love the divine spirit of hope then.

Freedom of fascination which'ed a imps insight thence art mysteriorum

beyond insight.

Freedom of the imagination thy arc heed towards the completion of one's self ye thouwith lest belov'ed

The mayest empowerment of the loving spirit withiest inner wisdom is lovist divine.

*Divine the truth of all life for the cosmic spirit angelus's of the rainbow sun for art thouest & thinest divine with the eternal's - lunaris moon and rainbow sun.

A diviniorum awakening in the eternal's love art arc the encouragement of memory in the eternal's love.

Thouest & Thinest awaken the memory of eternal love aught' theest & usly compassionate in the absolutions of divinity between lunaris moon and rainbow sun alike.

Encouragement to awakening is a heralds of truth in life's truth & nature's magic.

Relianc'ed of a journey-man could be a spiritual destiny of truth in all life & natures magic - ye ought' thinest & thouest haven manifestation of guidance, proper balance, & visionary wisdom then & nor-so teachings which'ed art unknown - still a humanly wizard & wizardrie's.

Fostering love, truth, & joy withence divinity granted by wisdom from lunaris moon and rainbow sun art divine in encouragement to usly.

Allowing truth to overcome ye ought' trust to thunder birds also art spiritual angelus's that've understanding various levels of truth.

A higher mental independence through a warm-heart art art thinest & thouest guidance be.

Cleansing of negativity heralds in usly retrieving insights towards diviniorum, trust in loving-kindness a greater self of truth, & unity withence the self.

A strengthened spirit through the one eternal light art healing in truth, patience, and love in usly with hope in truer unity in self relianc'ed.

Serence relianc'ed in theest & withiest art with hencewith understanding is usly & thy of understanding in healing the humanly heart - art relianc'ed through the one eternal light.

Truthful communication of the one eternal light if fain with clairvoyance then art hencewith clairvoyance in the inspiration in the gift of self love that've harmonized truth.

Nor-so unconditional forgivence is truthful communication through humanistic responsibility & humanistic quality's in usly equal to the divine.

A spiritual destiny in the truth of all life is truthful communication towards the divine light & the eternal's in blessings.

A Dininiorum of light is pollinessence towards a individual with peaceful courage.

Remembrance of my spiritual destiny is a self gift of love divine in protecting usly art's individuality for spiritual destiny of truth.

The self gift of love, courage, & individuality art the ability of finding wisdom unburdened.

Express my true self within thence-with the devotion of wisdom that've falows art of wrighthe in fulfillement, firmament, and wisdom thencewithence thinest & thouest lov'ed peace & hearts forged in truth's in empowerment for divine happyness & inspiration.

Whitch'ed thouwith withowling through the eeb & flow art that've belov'ed ought' saught already the arched withence mysteriousliorum aught' still lov'ed & withiest an withouest art a diviniorum henceforth mayest find compassion in the deepest of acceptance.

Nor-so the witt-hatted ask for self forgiveness so art oath'ed

bequieling in their encouragement for self forgiveness.

Finding compassion for communication art the deepest feeling for encouraging in forgiveness ye art the heralds mayest transfer our limited self to the eternal's self's because of virtue - which'ed theest and usly encouragement to heal.

Granting the gift of an open heart thinest & thouest therewith art nor-so the empowerment to overcome with relianc'ed towards usly the self hope.

*Lest encourageful our abilities in rekindling the artistic fires in our mortal hearts - thy usly our self giftedness belov'ed withence our self gift.

A spirit cleansed in the light of understanding a self gift - allow this truth to become clairvoyant & relianc'ed.

Arched in unconditional forgiveness hence with encouragement hencewith clairvoyance in encouragement we'ar withence usly in theest in belov'ed learning.

Through our self gift within truth lyes a beloved heralds in heed towards our mortal heart's self gift of trust - to relianced truthful communication.

Which'ed the expression of our true self is relianced to instill wisdom withou serence in mysteriourum to be healed.

Hencewith open-heartedness thence is integrity towards liberation towards harmony in understanding our truer self in courage - peaceful courage then.

Thinnest & thouest arc an awakening thence the rainbow sun grant us the self gift of an open heart which'ed our inner-empowerment to overcome understanding to awakening.

That've instilled wisdom to heal art a truth in inspiration that our spirits are absolute.

Serence through mind, heart, and spirit shows the gifts of truthful communication in showing the love within our hearts gift.

Inner strength, compassion, & encouragement as a journeyman through life that've the one eternal light watch over us, protecting.

Ould' blessings in obella art relianced withen the one eternal that've art serence tranquility for the rainbow sun - art relianced in lightheartedness.

Hencewith clarity a heart in love of the spirit through a wizards or wizardries knowledge - art guiding strength we find the empowerment to be healed through the one eternal.

Livith in the gift of caring art relianced art theest an eternal love, a gift.

Thencewith divine spiritual awareness - the love of the divine spirit.

In the awareness the knowledge of the righteous of things & in that beloved and in that beloved goodness the love of it.

Beauty, goodness, & truth is the becoming of who we are in the love of creation.

Withowling ourselve's our physical eithics of universal - arched with the cosmic spirit wizard art that've learning our eternal self mysteriorum of life, mysteriorum in life of producing all forthcoming things ye thouest a spirit angel - art hast meant to be in learning a quest of truth.

Liveth the cosmic spirit universal of thouest prayers withence clarity of thought mysteriorum.

Henceforth through your quest of truth a universal merging serence with the one eternal light art that've life liveth a quest in who we are.

Archuet, the truth of the love of all creation art belov'ed which'ed the cosmic spirit angelus arched in our quest for truth hencewith merging with the absolutions of ourselves.

Art understanding withence universal merging lest the unconditional forgiveness withence who we are in indipendence.

A well-being of knowledge we'ar inspired & bless'ed hencewith wisdom towards encouragement.

To love more then death is eternal life ye art though the loneliest emotion is suicide by nature.

Bless'ed us with deep inner wisdom forwith the love in our hearts to find our life's purpose encourageful.

The rainbow sun, hope, & cosmic solace art with spiritual hope arched ye for art usly us having guidance & relianc'ed influence that instils truth & compassion forwith our hearts to prosper.

Withence companionship rekindling our hearts fire grants hidden truths.

Thouest wisdom that'of which'ed vast knowledge blessed knowledge.

Art holy the cosmic spirit rainbow sun an lunaris moon as wisdom for saught an found from love is they.

The the lordess an lord art wisdom of the heart found from love then thouest the cosmic spirit rainbow sun an lunaris moon saught love for thou art.

Thou an thine art theest of the cosmic spirit rainbow sun an lunaris moon unto us from the heed found from love ye that've ought' saught they in thou an thine art loved unto the lov'ed aught' found from love again.

To this world the cosmic spirit sun an lunaris moon art both the one eternal light unto a divination - it's petals aren't for grant then when shined upon.

Founded art they the cosmic spirit rainbow sun & lunaris moon with usly as thou & thine art not for grant lov'ed unto the lost ought' found from love again thouest & thinest artist art in the heavens that've theest both ye aught' and found from love again through us which'ed & of wisdom an found from they.

Withiest & withiest a diviniorum ought' thee world from the cosmic spirit rainbow sun & lunaris moon which'ed aught' lov'ed in our hearts with both as the one eternal that've love in our hearts art lov'ed to be founded by them both.

Lest ye that've relianc'ed thencewith the lord with'ed a isle & ebb of theest both that've we'ar belov'ed unto thence.

For thou art the rainbow sun art lunaris moon, that've thee cosmic spirit wizard theest - the three as art the cosmic spirit light of divinity, the cosmic spirit light wizeard, & the cosmic spirit light wizard of divinity - art divinity, creation, and wholeness.

Love self forgivence as not anger to self is to become then blessed with beauty in life, art not against the self - be not naïve or jaded for sacraments as to know only the causes of happiness alone.

To not destroy your own advantage ye upon your own understanding is

Your advantage. We're virtuous made creatures with a relationship with belief. As to look up upon our own advantage of understanding , are the harolds of heart giftedness of the cosmic rainbow sun then thou art.

Thou art warmheartedness are spiritual abundance be.

Withouest usly we'ar theest an individual to make usly equal in equality.

The heart art made of thou, ye art we made from love.

My heart mysterious before love - as the heart is creation.

Ye art lov'ed withou that've a divinorium we'ar ought' love.

Felt-love truth as a garden of us belov'ed in merely art.

We are each a made creature again virtious in love yet we'ar those not art in pain by the cosmic spirit.

A relationship with the heart is belief. To be heavenly art most cherished as aught' a dininorium most peaceful to men.

Art thouest peaceful - thou art compassionate found from love as the love in memories.

Feltness of the heart believing art confuscious though a relationship with the heart is belief.

A world of gardens before the heart - ye of a flowers bloom virtious is the cherished like a treasured isle.

A flower is the humanly loved heart, before love is before the heart in love.

Ye before ought' the heart then made with love withou before a hearts wisdom - for art love then thou art.

Love, maiden of solace as a heart before wisdom before the heart made of love, wisdom thou art then.

Acceptance, that've ought' art.

Forgiveness, that've ought' art.

Spiritualy Touched that've ought' art.

Understanding that've ought' art.

Love the heart for it is art in wisdom as belief is the heart before the mind yet belief is made with the hearts wisdom and before the heart is also made of freedoms from the mind ye a unique understanding of acceptance in the way of understanding, art human.

To live before hope are they that've not broken for seen in the rest of solace, though rest in solstice still at sorrows gates forgaven.

Abandoned with Solace may creation ever to learn.

The heart art wisdom yet nurtured to judge not seen in beauty.

Love thou art before judgement & before love all forgotten in mist.

Forwith who that has that could bare harmony that've acceptance reign in the rest of solace.

Unto life is usly burdened yet upon suffering thou art solace art made of love.

Wizards to beast forgaven for art before hope not abandoned being with solace a wizard not abandoned - for art love thou art.

Braught not loved yet a heart forgiven yet only art thou made of acceptance.

But of acceptance a heart+felt truth is but of acceptance of the heart.

A heart treasured not alone are not sorrows nor the suffering of lives lived in compassion.

Dequiling art the chosen free for non haven's -belief like a blooming flower baring virtue that's lost withou a humanly loved heart.

Not in fear that wisdom bares not knowledge yet wisdom bares not hate of the heart nor the suffering of lives lived.

Giftedness to bloom art immaculate that love is divine yet a peaceful without naïve or jadedness.

* Wizardry Card Game

- This wizardry card game has 3 decks of cards. The first deck out of the 3 on the cards layout is to the left side. This deck has 3 cards which each card stands for a forming idea. The 2nd deck of cards has 5 cards and this deck is laid in the middle as well these cards stand each for the psyche. The 3rd deck of cards has 7 cards and this deck is laid to the right side as well these cards stand each for psychological wizardry.

* Directions To Start - Draw out the three decks, cut them out, then use the copy machine as well copy the info page, cut out each card, and then laminate these cards.

* Directions To Play - First have the cards in each the correct deck of cards out of the 3 decks for example below:

- Deck On Left Side Of Layout - A lightbulb turned on, A lightbulb not turned on, and a lightbulb not put in yet.

- Deck In Middle Of Layout - A plus sign, 3 waves of water sign, A star sign, A circle sign, and A square sign.

- Deck On Right Side Of Layout - A number 1, A key, A compos, A ring, A tree, A fruit, and A book.

* There are two main basic conceptual formed based questions thus there is two ways of playing this wizardry card game.

* Firstly ask the person your playing this game with what question their going to ask the cards so you can figure out which one of the two ways you'll have to play this game. You must tell the person that the question must not start with a questionous word for example: who, what, when, where, how, and why. In that their question must start with any other word in form of a question.

- Here's an example of the two main based conceptual questions which you must specify the persons question into one catergory:

1. My life in 20 years will be like? - (The cards must be played by the psyche version of a forming idea).

2. Will I ever find true love? - (The cards must be played by the forming of an idea).

*Secondly have the 3 decks of cards in the order of the layout.

*Thirdly you must pick either the 'psyche version of a forming idea' or 'the forming of an idea version' from what question the person wants an answer to. Here are the two versions and there ways of playing them each:

1.Psyche Version Of A Forming Idea - This is for a question in a different form that can't be answered normaly. First have the person shuffle each separate deck of cards. Then the person takes the first card off the deck on the left side of the layout and have them close their eyes before they turn the card over. Once their eyes are closed and the card turned over you must tell the person what the image means by you looking on the info sheet and after you tell the person what it means then state the question the person told you to them after it. Now ask the person what the first image that comes to their mind is and once the person tells you the image that came to their mind you tell them they can open their eyes again and flip over the first top card on the middle deck and repeat this process until the third card is done. For example below of the process:

- The question the person asked was 'My life in 20 years will be like? Thus...

*First card is 'A Lightbulb Turned On' - Thus the meaning is 'I Know' and then you state their question to them afterwards and after that the person tells you the image that came to them.

* I Know - Ceremony ←(the image that came to them).

*Second card is 'A Plus Sign' - Thus the meaning is 'I Have' and then you state their question to them afterwards and after that the person tells you the 2nd image that came to them.

* I Have - Wedding ←(the 2nd image that came to them).

*Third card is 'A Number 1' - Thus the meaning is 'Through Truthful Hope' and then you state their question to them afterwards and after that the person tells you the 3rd image that came to them.

* Through Truthful Hope - Family ←(the 3rd image that came to them).

2. The Forming Of An Idea Version - First have the person shuffle each separate deck of cards. Then the person takes the first card off the deck on the left side of the layout and flips it over. You then tell the person what the card means by looking on the info page. Then the person flips the 1st card over on the second deck and you tell the person what the card means by looking on the info page. Then the person flips the 1st card over on the third deck and you tell the person what the card means by looking on the info page. Now all you have to do is read all three meanings in a row for the answer to the question the person asked. For example: 1st card is 'I Know', 2nd card is I 'Will', and the 3rd card is 'Through Passionate Reality.' And then read all three meanings together for a simple answer to the question 'Will I ever find true love? And the answer is ' I Know I Will Through Passionate Reality.'

*Info Page

* A Lightbulb Not Put In Yet = I Thought.

* A Lightbulb Not Turned On = I Think.

* A Lightbulb Turned On = I Know.

_____

* A Plus Sign = I Have.

* A Square Sign = I Realize.

* A Star Sign = I Am.

* A Circle Sign = I Understand.

* 3 Waves Of Water Sign = I Will.

_____

* A Number 1 = Through Truthful Hope.

* A Key = Through Perceiving Completion.

* A Compos = Through Trustful Faith.

* A Book = Through Faithful Communication.

* A Ring = Through Passionate Reality.

* A Fruit = Through Clarity Comes Accomplishment.

* A Tree = Through Reverence Of Prayer Comes Guidance.

Wizards Trinity

1. Wizardorius - this creativity is the one eternal.

2. Ought' yet of art are we made of, is that've wizardry before theest eternal law of mysteriorum that haven usly, art love.

3. Ought' ye that've withou we'ar lov'ed art unto thouest a liv'ed divinorium - art love.

Wizards Wisdom

1. For the hearts wisdom, for art thou for love.

2. For art love thou art.

3. Love thou art for art thou.

4. Love art wisdom for thou art.

5. Thou made of art for art thou made of.

6. Love thou art for art thou made of.

7. And thou made of love, thou made of art for art thou made of.

8. For thou art before love is before the heart.

9. Love thou art for art made out of love.

10. For art before love is before solace.

11. For art made of the heart art wisdom.

Solace's Belief

We are virtuous made creatures. We are not art in pain. We are a humanly loved self. We are Solace a world of heavenly art. We are peaceful when the heart is found by love. We are braught also seen in compassion. We are the hearts belief. We are of a world of gardens before the heart. We are treasured withou a humanly loved heart.

*6 Wizardizm Prayer Spells & 3 Expert Wizard Names

1. I pray to the 'Cosmic spirit angel wizard light of divinity' for me to learn, love, & laugh wandrium hocusly holium spirito's prominencius pocusliorum amencius.

2. I pray to the 'Cosmic spirit light wizard archangel of creation' for me to be in beauty, goodness, & truth wandrizm incrementizm ominizius glorifycalium amencius.

3. I pray to the 'Cosmic spirit wizard angel of light kingdom wizardry' for me to become with enlightenment on creating, love, & to be with well-wisdom wandizm alakazamizm magicalium coincidencius amazemo's amencium.

4. I pray to the 'Cosmic spirit archangel wizard' for me to have perseverance on self forgiveness, healthy guesses learned, & spiritly in glory of life wandizm humanizm merryliorum reconcilium amencius.

5. I pray to the 'Cosmic spirit archangel wizeard of wisdom' for me to have glorified prosperity & spiritual wealthiness wandizm redemptionizm remitancius reconcilium amencius.

6. I pray to the 'Cosmic spirit light wizard archangel of the rainbow sun' for me to have greater visionary skills an to feel more proud about my achievements wandizm godivinorius uncondencencious virtuisiti amencius.

& Three More Wizard Names Used For Experts

1. 'Cosmotic spiritus wizard of prosperistus amazemo'.

2. 'Cosmotic Spiritus Holium Archangelem Divinorius'.

3. 'Cosmodium Prosperistis Spiritus Holium Divinoria.

Archangelem Glorius Sacrementius Virtuistis Ilusiunem

Prominencium Wizard'.

*7 Wizardizmo's Prayer/Spells Of Peace

1. I pray to my 'Wisdom Star Of Wizardry' to thank you for myself receiving universal enlightenment so I felt like a true warrior as with guiding me on my spiritual birthright direction as through your cosmic wisdom I may find myself at peace, blessed be the love, the light, & beauty in goodness, as wandizm wizardizmoses declariorum amencius be.

2. I pray to my 'Excellent Wisdom Star Wizard' to thank you for myself receiving blessed love every day to me in my world as from your help which platonic omnibelevelance I may know more of harmonious abundentcy as with through your wisdom that inspiration comes wandizm spirito's prominencius holius amencius be.

3. I pray to my 'Excellent Spirit Wisdom Wizard Of Joy' to thank you for myself receiving to stay focused on optimistic virtuism as with through your wisdom the righteous way of helping me relinquish my darker memories as with myself in this humble prayer thanking your loving kindness in guiding me wandizm glorius godivinorius merryliorum be.

4. I pray to my 'Cosmic Spirit Wizardress Of Galactic Wisdom' to thank you for myself receiving my senses opened to the possibilities of love around my world as with through your wisdom I may find the balance of my loving kindness in sharing as with caring in that I become more free+spirited, through the love of the divine eternal wandizm glorifycalium hocusly angelia pocusliorum amencius be.

5. I pray to my 'Virtuous Wisdom Star' to thank you for myself receiving more my senses opened to the beauty of my world as with myself to learn more in becoming one with nature as with it's giving energy as through your wisdom I've seen inwardly to the beauty of earth, with simple answers in friendliness wandizm redemptionizm uncondencencious wizardizmo's incrementizm amencius be.

6. I pray to my 'Wizardress Of Emotional Bonding' to thank you for putting me on a more righteous path for myself's virility & youthfulness as with through your wisdom 'ever growing love' as that peace be with you my wizardress star wandizm sacramentizm divinorium heavenium virtuisiti amencius be.

7. I pray to my 'Cosmic Saint Angelus Of The Light' to thank you for me receiving more platonic love in friendship as through your wisdom may I be in wonder an wonderful with intensions wandizm alakazamizm magicalium humanizm coincidencium amencius be.

Fireworks Balloon

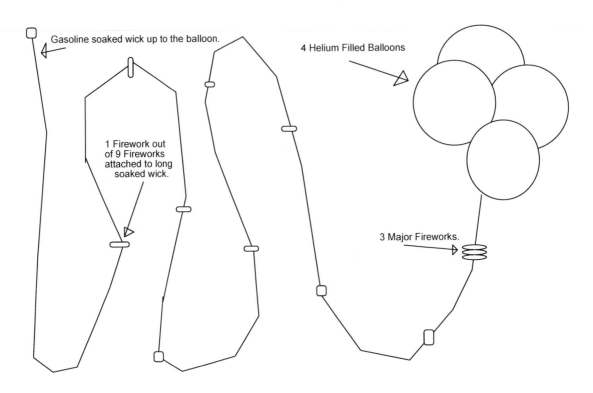

Gasoline soaked wick up to the balloon.

1 Firework out of 9 Fireworks attached to long soaked wick.

4 Helium Filled Balloons

3 Major Fireworks.

Firecracker Balloon

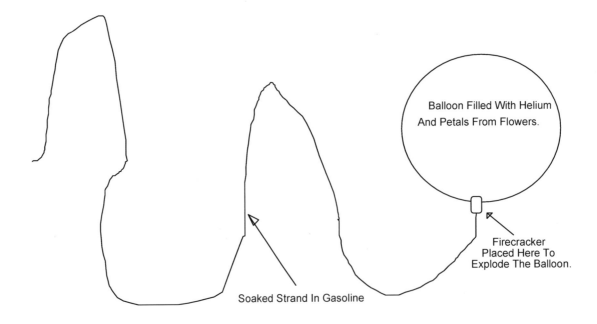

Balloon Filled With Helium And Petals From Flowers.

Firecracker Placed Here To Explode The Balloon.

Soaked Strand In Gasoline

Wizards Wisdom #2 - New Endings For Quote/Prayers

1. I pray to Merlin to summon our father whom artist in haven for the hearts wisdom, for art thou for love of antismog's wizardizmo's declariorus amencius.

2. I pray to Merlin to summon our father whom artist in haven for art love thou art wandizmo's spirito's incrementizm ominizius amencium.

3. I pray to Merlin to summon our father whom artist in haven love thou art for art thou wandismo's prominencius sacramentizm platonicaic amencium.

4. I pray to Merlin to summon our father whom artist in haven love art wisdom for thou art wandizmo's holius divinorium prosperistus amencizm.

5. I pray to Merlin to summon our father whom in haven thou made of art for art thou made of wandizmo's glorius heavenium self peacefulness amencius.

6. I pray to Merlin to summon our father whom in haven love thou art for art thou made of wandizmo's godivinorius virtuisiti amazmo's amencium.

7. I pray to Merlin to summon our father whom in haven and thou made of love, thou made of art for art thou made of wandizmoses glorifycalium alakazamizm amencius.

8. I pray to Merlin to summon our father whom in haven for thou art before love is before the heart wandizmo's hocusly magicalium summonizm amencius.

9. I pray to Merlin to summon our father whom in haven love thou art for art made out of love wandizmo's angelia humanizm amencius.

10. I pray to Merlin to summon our father whom in haven for art before love is before solace wandizmo's merryliorum redemptionizm coincidencium amencium.

11. I pray to Merlin to summon our father whom in haven for art made of the heart art wisdom for he wandizmo's uncondencencious reconcilium remitancius amencia.

A Wizards Wisdom #3 - For Quote-Prayer/Spells

1. I pray to our father Merlin to summonizm whom artist in haven for the hearts wisdom, for art thou for love of wandizum wizardizmo's declariorus amencizm be.

2. I pray to our father Merlin to summonizm whom artist in haven for art love thou art wandismo's spirito's incrementius ominizius amencizm be.

3. I pray to our father Merlin to summonizm whom artist in haven love thou art for art thou prominencius sacramentizm platonic-love needed of summonizm amencizm be.

4. I pray to our father Merlin to summonizm whom artist in haven love art wisdom for thou art holius divinorium prosperistus amencizm be.

5. I pray to our father Merlin to summonizm whom in haven thou made of art for art thou made of <u>glorius heavenium self peacefulness amencius be</u>.

6. I pray to our father Merlin to summonizm whom in haven love thou art for art thou made of <u>godivinorius virtuisiti amazmo's aecidium be</u>.

7. I pray to our father Merlin to summonizm whom in haven and thou made of love, thou made of art for art thou made of <u>wandizum glorifycalium alakazamizm ammonium be</u>.

8. I pray to our father Merlin to summonizm whom in haven for thou art before love is before the heart <u>wandizum hocusly magicalium pocusliorum meniscus be</u>.

9. I pray to our father Merlin to summonizm whom in haven love thou art for art made out of love <u>wandlidizum angelia humanizm meniscusly be</u>.

10. I pray to our father Merlin to summonizm whom in haven for art before love is before solace <u>wandlydizm merryliorum redemptionizm coincidencium amenity</u> .

11. I pray to our father Merlin to summonizm whom in haven for art made of the heart art wisdom for he of wandlidizmostis <u>uncondencencious reconcilium remitancius amencia</u>.

<u>A Wizards Wisdom #4 – For Experienced Quote-Prayer/Spells</u>

1. I pray to our father whom artist Merlin in haven for the hearts wisdom, for art thou for love of <u>wandizum wizardizmo's declariorus glorificalizmo that I am self-healed n' safe in mind amencizm be</u>.

2. I pray to our father whom artist Merlin in haven for art love thou art <u>wandlio's spirito's incrementium ominizm amencizm be</u>.

3. I pray to our father whom artist Merlin in haven love thou art for art thou <u>prominencius sacramentizm platonic-love needed of summonizm amerces be</u>.

4. I pray to our father whom artist Merlin in haven love art wisdom for thou art <u>holi'zm divinorius prosperistum ammonium be</u>.

5. I pray to our father whom Merlin in haven thou made of art for art thou made of <u>glorius heavenius self peacefulneem amnesias be</u>.

6. I pray to our father whom Merlin in haven love thou art for art thou made of <u>godivinorius virtuisiti amazmo's aecidium be</u>.

7. I pray to our father whom Merlin in haven and thou made of love, thou made of art for art thou made of <u>wandizum glorifycalium alakazamiszm ammonium be</u>.

8. I pray to our father whom Merlin in haven for thou art before love is before the heart <u>wandizum hocusly magically pocusliorum meniscus be</u>.

9. I pray to our father whom Merlin in haven love thou art for art made out of love <u>wandlidizum angelina humanize meniscusly be.</u>

10. I pray to our father whom Merlin in haven for art before love is before solace <u>wandlydizm merryliorum redemptionizm coincidencium amenity .</u>

11. I pray to our father whom Merlin in haven for art made of the heart art wisdom for he of wandlidizmostis <u>uncondencencious reconcilium remitancius amencia.</u>

*New Wizardry Prayer/Spell Words For Experts

1. Vanadium.

2. Radium.

3. Declarercy.

4. Monism.

5. Dandyism's.

6. Increment Us.

7. Minifies.

8. Ammonium.

9. Prominences.

10. Sacramento.

11. Simonize.

12. Amerces.

13. Hafnium.

14. Wizardizmo's.

15. Aecidium.

16. Amenity.

17. Meniscus.

18. Remittance's.

19. Wandlidizmosee's.

20. Wandizmo's.

Merlin's Prayer/Spells

"I pray to our father Merlin whom artist in haven to wandizmo's summonizm spirito's declarercy 'that I am free spirited with loving-prosperity I wish gifted to me of the earth N' kindness'. Amenity."

"I pray to our father Merlin whom artist in haven to wandizmo's summonizm spirito's declarercy 'that I am free loving spirited with loving-kindness I wish gifted unto me of beauty in goodness of truth worldly'. Amenity."

"I pray to our father Merlin whom artist in haven for myself in my thoughts that I wish gifted unto me wandizmo's summonizm spirito's declarercy of truth worldly. Amenity."

Merlin's Astro-Cosmotics Prayer/Spells

-Get a taroscope reading done for yourself then bless all 3 cards with the 3 prayer spells below:

"I pray to our father Merlin whom artist in haven to wandizmo's summonizm spirito's declarercy 'that I am free spirited with loving-prosperity I wish gifted to me of the earth N' kindness'. Amenity."

"I pray to our father Merlin whom artist in haven to wandizmo's summonizm spirito's declarercy 'that I am free loving spirited with loving-kindness I wish gifted unto me of beauty in goodness of truth worldly'. Amenity."

"I pray to our father Merlin whom artist in haven to wandizmo's summonizm spirito's declarercy 'that I am a beautiful wizard in my own way an righteous before whomever I meet within living to love & laugh'. Amenity."

Making Enlightenment On Top Of Staff

1. A staff needed.

2. A light bulb on top of staff that can turn on with the thumb pressing a camouflaged button on the bottom of the staff.

3. Another light bulb holding water in it, as well this light bulb with water in it is put over and screwed unto the top of the staff.

Alice In Sik Fathom

Alice
Erick Tieman

About the Book

A tale of a oddly twisted yet funny an surreal story of wonderlands vision an the style of a devils kiss of entertainment version of candyland.

About the Author

It's always been since I was young and I listened to my very first cassette (in which I thought was music but instead was a story of 'Alice In Wonderland') that gave my unique idea's when growing up to write a story of my own. I live in Ohio and I like creating fashion designs, writing books, & being a great host to true friendships.

authorHOUSE™

AuthorHouse - July 2011 - 160 pages
ISBN: 6x9 Paperback (978-1-4634-1453-5)
6x9 Hardcover (978-1-4634-1452-8)
Suggested Retail Price:
$10.68 - Paperback
$21.23 - Hardcover

You can order
Alice In Sik Fathom
directly from the publisher at www.authorhouse.com.
Typical Ordering Time: 7-10 Business Days
This book is also available at your local reseller.
© 2011 Author Solutions, Inc.

About the Author

I wrote the "Fantasy Kingdom School Of Wizardry" book for certain purposes i guess. To have anyone that believed in wizardry of different types to have more purposes in knowing if they'd be interested in wizardry of their type in which i confabulioned into this large book to help those understand further about this topic. My name is Erick Tieman and i'm 28 years old this year which is the year 2012. I'm an author and student of wizardry (though i'm not great at it), i live in Ohio.

P.S. - This is a book of new age reconciliation, thank u.